The Giant Book of Animal Jokes

ALSO BY RICHARD LEDERER

Adventures of a Verbivore

Anguished English

Basic Verbal Skills (with Phillip Burnham)

The Bride of Anguished English

The Circus of Words

Comma Sense (with John Shore)

Crazy English

The Cunning Linguist

Fractured English

Get Thee to a Punnery

Have a Punny Christmas

Literary Trivia (*with* Michael Gilleland)

A Man of My Words

The Miracle of Language

More Anguished English

The Play of Words

Pun & Games

Puns Spooken Here

Sleeping Dogs Don't Lay (with Richard Dowis)

The Word Circus

Word Play Crosswords, volumes 1 and 2 (with Gayle Dean)

The Write Way (with Richard Dowis)

ALSO BY JAMES ERTNER

Super Silly Animal Riddles

The Giant Book of Animal Jokes

Beastly Humor for Grownups

Richard Lederer and James D. Ertner

Illustrations • James McLean

Stone and Scott, *Publishers*

Sherman Oaks, CA

The Giant Book of Animal Jokes: Beastly Humor for Grownups

Contact Stone and Scott, Publishers
P.O. Box 56419, Sherman Oaks, CA 91413-1419
http://www.stoneandscott.com

Illustrations © 2006 by James McLean

First Edition

ISBN-10: 1-891135-08-2
ISBN-13: 978-1-891135-08-8

Library of Congress Cataloging-in-Publication Data

Lederer, Richard, 1938-
    The giant book of animal jokes : beastly humor for grownups / Richard Lederer and James D. Ertner ; illustrations James McLean.-- 1st ed.
        p. cm.
    Includes index.
    ISBN-13: 978-1-891135-08-8 (alk. paper) 1. Animals--Humor. I. Ertner, James D. II. Title.

PN6231.A5L44 2006
818'.60208--dc22

2005021273

Book design by Kiskis Designs

10 09 08 07 06   1 2 3 4 5

Printed in the United States of America

Dedications

To Ben and Susie and Mike

Richard Lederer

To Bryce, my nine-year-old grandson, who (with his knowledgeable knack for knock-knock jokes and other riddles) portrays a propensity and a promising potential for punning

And to my daughter, Gail, I dedicate the chapter on giraffes—her favorite animal

James Ertner

Contents

Publisher's Preface

Funny thing about jokes is that some lose their currency and seem to be dead and gone but then become new again while others never go out of fashion. Jokes go back at least as far as the classic Greeks. Scholars can trace some jokes across several centuries. And there's no knowing the first appearance of most jokes—even though a few highly paid joke writers get credit for some today. (A few decades ago, a humorist wrote a sketch about discovering the origin of all jokes: an underground factory in Kansas.)

Jokes do get around. That we know. When a joke is told, a listener is likely to begin another joke with "That reminds me of the one about such and so." Just as likely, a listener may say, "That's not the way I heard it." And that reminds us of a long-ago concert by Salli Terri, a fine folk singer. In her invitation to the audience to sing along on a chorus, Terri said, "I know that your way is the correct way, but if you'll sing it my way this time, I promise to sing it your way next time."

When you encounter a joke in this book that is not the way you heard it, the publishers can only offer a variation of Terri's pledge: We'll be tickled to read the joke the (correct) way you heard it.

And the same goes for any of your favorites not included. The omission is probably authors' choice; the files and memories of Richard Lederer and James Ertner contain more than even a giant book could carry.

The authors have captured large numbers of jokes, including classics, non-classics, variations on both, and variations on variations. (A joke that turns one way can be turned another.) They've created new ones and new twists on old ones. From their wide and deep collections, they've selected a few thousand that have to do with animals and set them up in various sections according to the way the term turns. (They can tell whether a cat-vet joke goes under *cat* or under *vet*.)

In biology class, you learned that the animal kingdom is divided into *phyla*, each of which is divided into *classes*, which are divided into *orders*, which are divided into *families*, which are divided into *genera*, which are divided into *species*. That classification works well in biology class but not in a joke book. (How many "mammal" jokes do you hear?)

Thus, in Part One of *The Giant Book*, some 317 phyla, families, species, and a few mythological or non-biological animals are presented in alphabetical order—not in any zoological arrangement—with as few as one or two jokes under some headings and hundreds under other headings. Then, in Part Two, jokes that fit better into categories such as Knock-Knocks and Tom Swifties appear in eleven other sections.

The resulting collection is a special package of 4,509 numbered jokes (as we counted them). In addition, some of the numbered items contain more than one joke (some doubles and some multiples such as 3094, 3693, 4375), and many good gags and a parade of puns are packed into the authors' introduction and some unnumbered introductory paragraphs.

The fun of bear/bare jokes is in the telling, but oral jokes are elusive. This collection holds those jokes in place in print in a book that will sit well on your joke shelf and that will give the delights that jokes of all sorts give. You'll get
laughers,
       chucklers,
           smilers,
              gigglers,
                 and groaners
that will remind you of—and re-create—the delight of your pre-teen, teen, and adult joke exchanges. Whether you
read,
       skim,
           skip,
              or dip
your way through this collection, we wish you much fun with this book.

The Publisher

Introduction

Animals run, gallop, fly, swim, and crawl through our everyday lives.

> We drive Jaguars and Mustangs and Eagles and Thunderbirds.
> We root for teams named Blue Jays and Cardinals, Marlins and Sharks, Lions
> and Rams.
> We listen to the music of The Animals, Beatles, Byrds, Monkees, and Turtles.
> We read literature such as "The Raven," *To Kill a Mockingbird, Rabbit Run*, and
> *Lord of the Flies.*
> We watch movies such as *One Flew over the Cuckoo's Nest, The Black Stallion,*
> *101 Dalmatians, The Jackal, Beauty and the Beast*, and *Animal House.*

Animals teem on our tongues,
and animals inhabit hundreds of our English expressions:
> holy cow, holy cats, and holy mackerel.

Straight from the horse's mouth, a little bird told us that the human race is filled
> with congressional hawks and doves who fight like cats and dogs till the cows
> come home,
> with Wall Street bulls and bears who make a beeline for the goose that lays the
> golden egg,
> with old buzzards and young bucks, cold fish and hotdoggers, early birds and
> night owls, lone wolves and social butterflies, lame ducks, sitting ducks,
> and dead ducks.

These animal expressions are
> no fluke, no hogwash, no humbug, no cock-and-bull story.

Our world is not only riddled with animals; it is riddled with riddles.

In the world of children's humor, the riddle is the dominant form,
and many of us grow up riddling into adult life. Most riddles involve a
a play on words. (Some would say a *prey* on words.)

"What's black and white and red [read] all over? A newspaper"
has been for several generations the first riddle that English-speakers learn.
Such question-and-answer interaction represents the child's first awareness that
two or more meanings can occupy the same verbal space at the same time.

For your enjoyment and learning, we offer some 4,500 entries in what
we think is the largest collection of animal jokes ever put on display.

These jokes are guaranteed to make you
bark,
bray,
cackle,
chirp,
crow,
honk,
howl,
meow,
ribbet,
roar,
and squeal with hysterical laughter.

James D. Ertner
Richard Lederer

Part

ONE

Animals A-Z:
From Aardvark to Zyzzyva

Aardvark

1   In the beginning was the word. And the word was *aardvar*k.

2   *Aardvark:* Aan aanimal that resembles the aanteater.

3   Aardvark and no play make Jack a dull boy.

4   Did you hear about the household appliance that eats ants and tapes
TVshows?
It's the VCRdvark.

5   What did the impatient waiter ask
the gluttonous aardvark?
"Is that your final ant, sir?"

Abalone

6   *Mr. Tuna:* "Those sea mollusks told me you swallowed an entire ship."
Mr. Whale: "That's just a bunch abalone."

7   Did you hear about the two fish named Eb and Ab?
Eb was a bully and wouldn't leave Abalone.

Adder

8   Did you hear about the snake that caught a cold?
It adder viper nose.

9   Why did the snakes on the ark disobey Noah and not go
forth and multiply?
Because they were adders.

10   Did you hear about the snakes that lived in a large cage furnished with tables
made from tree trunks?
*They had numerous offspring, for, as everyone knows, adders multiply
on log tables.*

11   What did one snake hunter say to the other?
"I thought she was a boa—until I adder in a trap."

12   How was the Year of the Snake
characterized in China?
By adder Confucian.

Albatross

13   What independent bird once ran for president?
Al Bat Ross Perot.

14   Did you hear about the large pelican-like bird that wore a supportive device?
It was an alba-truss.

15   What do you call a large, angry seabird?
An alba-cross.

16   Who wrote the book titled *Large Seabirds*?
Albert Ross.

Alligator

You get crocodilian cousins in this age-old exchange:
Kid No. 1: "See you later, alligator."
Kid No. 2: "After while, crocodile."
We've got the gator gags here and the croc jokes later.

17   What is a sick crocodilian?
An illigator.

18   *Shopper:* "I'd like some alligator shoes, please."
Shoe Clerk: "Certainly. What size does it wear?"

19   Then there was the alligator at the airport that
was asked by the Skycap, "May I carry your suitcase?"
"Okay," replied the passenger, "but be careful. That's my wife."

20   Did you hear about the guy who was as nervous as an alligator in a handbag factory?

21   That, in turn, reminds us of the woman
who is so ritzy that she has alligator
bags under her eyes.

22   Or, as we like to say, alligators never die; they just become old bags.

23   *Tourist:* "Help! An alligator bit off my leg!"
Doctor: "Which one?"
Tourist: "How should I know? All these gators look alike."

24   What kind of gators
go to church?
Congregators.

25   What do you call a creature that has huge jaws and tail and lives in dark places between buildings?
An alleygator.

26   That reminds us of the horse in Kentucky that often avoided streets and tracks. *He was neither a trotter nor a pacer. He was an alley-gaiter.*

27   What kind of gators steer ships and boats?
Navigators.

28   Did you hear about the gators that joined the FBI?
They were investigators.

29   What is an alligator's favorite book?
Swamp Animals by Al E. Gator, Ali Gator, and Crockett Dial.

30   An alligator walked into the men's department of Saks Fifth Avenue. The salesperson asked, "May I help you?"
"Yes," replied the alligator. "Do you have any shirts with the little wimp on the pocket?"

31   *Florida visitor:* "Is that a famous gangster taking his rival water skiing?"
Local resident: "No. He's trolling for alligators."

32   What do alligators put on their bathroom walls?
Rep-tiles.

33   As Confucius says, "When you're up to your hips in alligators, it's difficult to recall that your original goal was to drain the swamp."

34   A politician was heard to exclaim, "I deny the allegations, and I resent the allegators!"

35   Did you hear about the new TV show on alligators?
      It was so popular that the TV station was swamped with calls.

36   Or, as one washing machine said to another, "See you later, agitator."

Amoeba

37   Why did the amoeba cross the biology lab?
      To get to the other slide.

      38   Did you hear about the amoeba state prison?
            It's so small that it has only one cell.

39   Two female amoebas started to divide, and soon one of them accused the
      other of stealing one of her digits. She said, "That's my toe, sis."

40   Or, as one amoeba said to another, "Get serious! Don't bacilli!"

      41   Or, as another amoeba said to still another, "After they made
            you, they threw away the mold."

            42   Then there's the poor guy who
                  is reminiscent of an amoeba.
                  He's a lower form of life.

                  43   What kind of protozoa
                        likes Halloween?
                        An amoeboo.

      44   Now it's time to make like an amoeba and split.

Ant

45   Do ants have conversations?
      They just make small talk.

      46   Cheerios are hula hoops for ants.

47   Speaking of cereal reminds us of the two ants on a box of cereal. One saw the
      other racing by and asked, "Why are you running like that?" The running ant
      replied, "Because the box says, 'Tear along the dotted line.'"

48   Where do insects go when they want to eat?
To a restaurant.

49   That reminds us of the opposite of a restaurant—a worker ant.

50   What kind of insect is good at math?
An accountant.

51   Who was the first ant?
Adamant.

52   What is the largest ant?
An elephant.

53   What kind of insect is sent here from foreign countries?
Important.

54   What insects come from Italy?
Romance.

55   How many insects does it take to make a landlord?
Tenants.

56   What kind of insect plays hooky from school?
A truant.

57   What kind of insect is bossy?
A tyrant.

58   What kind of insect hangs around with witches?
A covenant.

59   What kind of insect follows his daddy
down the garden wall?
A descendant.

60   What kind of insect is a floating male?
Buoyant.

61   What kind of insect is a brave female?
Gallant.

62 What type of altered insect never talks?
A mute ant.

63 If a mute ant is a mutant, will the mutant
produce more mute ants?

64 What kind of insects are the worst?
The pollutants and the contaminants.

65 The ant basketball team made a vow
To get better but didn't know how.
    It just wasn't right
    To be lacking in height.
They needed tolerance—and now.

66 Did you hear about the anxious colony of insects?
They were always "antsy."

67 There was a young fellow from France
Whose hobby was searching for ants,
    Till he took quite a spill
    On a tiny red hill,
And wound up with ants in his pants.

68 How do sick insects arrive at the hospital?
In an ambulants.

69 What sound was heard when the Pink Panther
stepped on a line of insects?
♪*"Dead ant. Dead ant! Dead ant, dead ant, dead ant . . ."*♪

70 How many relatives went on the picnic?
Three uncles and 100,000 ants.

71 To battle the ants, the picnickers formed a swat team.

72 There was a young lady from Wheeling
Who was out in her garden a-kneeling.
    When by some mischance,
    She got ants in her pants,
And invented Virginia reeling.

73 Did you hear about the man who not only had a large ant farm
but also befriended every one of them, even giving them names?
      Unfortunately, the remnants of a hurricane blew through town and
disseminated his pet creatures hither and yon. When a neighbor saw that he
was upset and asked why, the man replied, "The ants are my friends; they're
blowing in the wind."

74 What do insects take when they're ill?
Antibiotics.

75 Two German ants were on a piece of watermelon.
One said to the other, "Well, look at us. We're floating on the Rhine."

76 The first-time airplane passenger looked out of the window and marveled to his
companion, "Look at those tiny people down there. They look just like ants."
      "They *are* ants," was the reply. "We haven't taken off yet."

77 What is the oldest type of insect?
An antique.

78 What do you call someone who buys and sells old bugs?
An antique dealer.

79 A novice golfer was desperately trying to drive a ball, but he succeeded only in
digging up turf. As divots were flying, two ants on a nearby anthill assessed the
situation. One said to the other, "If we want to save our lives, we'd better get
on the ball."

Anteater

80 What does an anteater like on its pizza?
Antchovies.

81 Why don't anteaters get sick?
Because they're full of antibodies.

82 What would a cannibal be who devoured his mother's sister?
An aunt-eater.

83 Did you hear about the new book titled *Bite-Sized Snacks*?
It's by Ann Teeter.

84 What animal is like your father's sister's electric blanket?
An ant-heater.

Antelope

85 Did you hear about the new book titled *Animals with Horns*?
It's by Ann T. Lope.

86 How can we tell that deer and antelope are hard of hearing?
They never heard a discouraging word.

87 What do lions call antelopes?
Fast food.

88 What do you call marriage on the range?
Antelopement.

Ape

89 A hairy young fellow named Bryan
Forever was cryin' and sighin',
        "Do you think that my shape
        Was derived from an ape?
Well, I think Charles Darwin was lyin'."

90 Where do monkeys get their gossip?
From the ape vine.

91 Why are most monkeys not interested in politics?
Because they're ape-olitical.

92 What does the government use when it takes a census of all the monkeys in zoos?
An ape recorder.

93 What does a monkey do when he feels sorry for something he did?
He offers an ape-ology.

94 As one monkey said to another, "Why did I go ape for that baboon?"

95 What fruit does a gorilla sleep on?
An ape-ri-cot.

96   When do monkeys fall from the sky?
During ape-ril showers.

98   Maybe man did descend from the ape: his eyes still swing from limb to limb.

99   One day, an ape escaped from the Bronx Zoo. A citywide search discovered the ape in the New York Public Library. Zoo officials and animal handlers found the creature sitting at a table in the reading room. Spread in front of him were several books, including the Bible and the works of Charles Darwin. The ape was reading with great concentration.

The zookeepers asked the ape what he was doing. The ape replied, "I'm trying to figure out whether I am my brother's keeper or my keeper's brother."

97   Said an ape as he swung by his tail,
To his children, both female and male,
"From your offspring, my dears,
In a few million years,
May evolve a professor at Yale."

100   Did you hear about the new book on King Kong? It's titled *Apes of Wrath.*

Armadillo

101   Did you hear about the new book titled *Animals with Armor Protection?* *It's by R. Madillo.*

102   What do you call the group of Spanish ships that was metal-plated?
The Spanish Armadillo.

103   What should you never do if you want to feel safe from a dillo attack?
Armadillo.

Asp

104 What song did Cleopatra sing when she clasped the asp to her breast?
"Fangs for the Mammaries."

105 What did Antony do when he saw how Cleopatra handled snakes?
He made an asp of himself.

106 Why did Cleopatra like snakes so much?
Actually, she didn't. She misread a doctor's sloppy hieroglyphics and thought she was supposed to take two asps and call him in the morning.

Ass

107 What floats in space and looks like a donkey?
An assteroid.

108 What is a donkey's favorite time at school?
Assembly.

109 Did you hear about the donkey with an IQ of 160?
He doesn't have any friends because no one likes a smart ass.

110 To assume makes an ASS out of U and ME.

111 What are the three kinds of investors on Wall Street?
Bulls, bears, and asses.

112 As one guy said to another, "Why don't you make like a donkey herder and move your ass!"

113 Did you hear about the Argentinean donkey with an inflated opinion of himself?
He's a pampas ass.

114 To err is human; to admit it, assinine.

115 The ruler of mules got donkey food without paying for it.
It was free for the ass king.

116   As the new zoo employee said while holding a
      baby donkey with the tail pointed toward the
      mother, "I've got this ass backward."

      117   There once was a girl from Madras
            Who had a most beautiful ass.
                  It was not round and pink,
                  As you might think,
            But was gray, had long ears, and ate grass.

      118   As Confucius says, "Guilt-ridden donkeys are sorry asses."

      119   How is "thank you" in Spanish like a donkey draped with sod?
            It's a grassy ass.

120   The scientists that cloned the sheep named Dolly decided to try to graft some
      skin from other farm animals. They first replaced a portion of Dolly's hide with
      the epidermis from a donkey. The headline in the newspaper the next day read,
      "Ass Skin Ewe Shall Receive."

Baboon

121 What kind of apes talk a lot?
Blabboons.

122 What kind of monkey is always exploding?
A ba-BOOM.

123 Who was the famous French monkey general?
Ape-oleon Baboon-aparte.

124 Did you hear about the rancher who took his young son to the zoo for the first time?
While standing in front of the baboon's cage, the boy asked what that animal was. The rancher replied, "It must be a cowboy judging by the way the seat of his pants is worn off."

Barracuda

125 What do naked sharks swim with?
Bare-a-cudas.

126 What fish drink too much?
Beer-a-cudas.

127 What do you call a government overthrown by a vicious fish?
Barracu d'etat.

Bass

128 *Musician No. 1:* "What is a basso profundo?"
Musician No. 2: "A deep-thinking fish."

129 How do stupid fish do everything?
Bass ackward.

130 Or, as one fish said to another,
"Don't be a basstard!"

Basset

131 Did you hear about the female basset hound that placed a classified ad in the newspaper?
It read: "Wanted. Handsome male basset. Object: Bassinet."

132 What do you call a dog that plays a guitar?
A bassist hound.

Bat

133 *Wife bat:* "Would you like to go out for a bite tonight?"
Husband: "No. I think I'll just hang around."

134 Speaking of hanging reminds us why bats hang upside down: so they can drop off to sleep.

135 Bats are fly-by-night operators.

136 What floats in the ocean but only at night?
A bat buoy.

137 *Baseball coach:* "How do you hold a bat?"
Rookie player: "By the wings."

138 Then there was the young boy whose father gave him a bat for his birthday. The first time he played with it, it flew away.

139 Did you hear about the crazy baseball player who used to hit the ball with his head?
He had bats in his belfry.

140 Did you hear about the circus performer's pet bat named Acro?

141 What do winged rodents like to laugh at?
Batroom humor.

142 What did the mother bat say to the father bat?
"We'll soon hear the batter of little feet around the cave."

143 How does a girl vampire flirt?
She bats her eyes.

144 Vampire bats are neck-rophiliacs.

145 Three vampire bats swoop into a bar.
"What'll you have?" asks the waitress.
"Blood," says the biggest one.
"Blood," says the middle-sized one.
"Plasma," says the smallest one.
The waitress calls out to the bartender,
"Two bloods and a blood light."

Beagle

146   Did you hear about the dog that was inducted into the Boy Scouts?
He was a beagle scout.

147   Beagles should be kept under lox and keys.

148   And when Snoopy has breakfast,
it's a beagle and cream cheese.

Bear

149   What do you call a naked grizzly?
A bare bear.

150   Did you hear about the grizzly that was half
buried in a pile of snow?
It was a bear mid-drift.

151   "What kind of bear is that sleeping in its cage?" asked a visitor to the zoo.
"Himalayan," replied the zookeeper.
"I see that," countered the visitor, "but when is him a-gettin' up?"

152   A cheerful old bear at the zoo
Could always find something to do.
When it bored him, you know,
To walk to and fro,
He reversed it and walked fro and to.

153   Eating bear meat is a grizzly experience.

154   Did you hear about the two dumb guys who went bear hunting?
When they saw a sign that said Bear Left, they went home.

155   All the guests at the animal fair
Had to dress up before they went there.
My friend Billy Brian
Dressed up like a lion,
But I went in the nude, as a bear.

156   What animal do you look like
when you're in the shower?
A little bear.

157   Why did the doll blush?
Because she saw the teddy bear.

158   How do grizzlies walk?
In their bear feet.

159   What does a grizzly need to hibernate?
Just the bear essentials.

160   What animal hibernates on its head?
Yoga Bear.

161   The entire population of bears
greet themselves in the spring by
saying, "Hi, bear nation."

162   What is a bear's
favorite number?
Hibern-8.

163   Support your right to arm bears.

164   What is a panda's favorite
French cheese?
Camembear.

165   The famous detective Mr. Chan collected teakwood carvings. When he
discovered that some of them were mysteriously disappearing, he investigated
and found footprints that appeared to be those of a small boy without any
shoes. You can imagine his surprise when he caught the culprit. It was a big
black bear that, instead of claws, had the feet of a young lad. The victim
shouted, "Where do you think you're going, boy-foot bear with teaks of Chan?"

166   Did you hear about the advertising executive's version of a fairy tale?
It starts this way: "Once upon a time there were three bears: the regular size,
the large size, and the giant economy size."

167 The three bears were walking through the desert and decided to sit down for a brief respite. Unfortunately, they sat on cactus. Both parents jumped up in pain, but the baby bear remained on the prickly spot. Papa Bear commented to Mama Bear, "Don't tell me we're raising one of those Dead End Kids."

168 What is the name of the fairy tale about a woman who uses her premium charge card to purchase aspirin for herself and two friends?
Gold Deluxe and the Three Bayers.

169 A child told her parents that her Sunday School class sang a song about a bear. The parents couldn't think of a song about a bear and had to ask for words or tune, so the child sang:
"Gladly, the Cross-Eyed Bear."

170 What cuddly little bear complains all the time?
Whine-y the Pooh.

171 What famous bear wrote scary stories?
Edgar Allan Pooh.

172 Christopher Robin Hood steals from the rich and gives to the Pooh.

173 What do you call two cuddly bears on a big plate in a Chinese restaurant?
A Pooh-Pooh platter.

174 When did Winnie the Pooh start dating?
When he reached Pooh-bear-ty.

175 Did you hear about the newspaper editor who wanted to cover the story about the birth of a baby bear at the zoo?
He sent a cub reporter.

176 What do you get when a little bear plays in a cornfield?
Corn on the cub.

177   What is Smokey the Bear's middle name?
The.

> **178**   Who tells the same story over and over?
> *Smokey the Bore.*

179   Have you noticed that ever since they put those Smokey the Bear signs in the New York City subways, there hasn't been a single forest fire in Manhattan?

> **180**   Did you hear about the singers in
> Yellowstone National Park?
> *They're bear-itones.*

181   As Confucius says, "Husbands, never trust a man built like a bear. He's likely to run off with your honey."

> **182**   Or, as Winnie the Pooh said to his agent,
> "Show me the honey!"

183   And Mother Bear said to Father Bear,
"This is positively my last year as den mother."

> **184**   What does a grizzly call honey and a warm cave?
> *The bear necessities of life.*

> **185**   What is the sign of a successful
> bear businessman?
> *One that claws his way to the top.*

186   When Johnny tried to ride the bear,
He found he'd made a grievous error.
As, borne toward his certain ruin,
He cried, "Get help! There's trouble bruin."

Beaver

187   What did the beaver say to the tree?
"It's been nice gnawing you."

188   Or, as one beaver said to another, "I'm in a gnawful fix."

189 Why did the misbehaving pet beaver chew the furniture?
Because it was gnawty.

190 What happened to the beaver when it ate too
much rotten wood?
It became gnawseous.

191 What is a perpetual beaver colony?
Eternal dam nation.

192 As the beaver said when he hit a concrete wall, "Dam!"

193 Beavers are the best dam builders in the world.

194 And they are the best by a dam site.

195 Except the uneager beaver that just didn't give a dam.

196 Beavers cut down any size tree.
They've never been stumped yet.

197 Where does a beaver go for diversion?
Hollywood.

198 What do you say to a sad beaver?
"Why the log face?"

199 How should you feel in the presence of a beaver ghost?
Be afraid. Beaver-y afraid.

Bee

200 How are a bee and a doorbell alike?
They're both buzzers.

201 As Confucius says, "Humbug is the
political bee that buzzes in many bonnets."

202 "How was the Queen Bee's speech?"
"Oh, the usual. Just a bunch of buzzwords."

203 Old bees never die; they just buzz off.

204 How is the letter A like a flower?
A B always comes after it.

205 Why is honey so scarce in Boston?
Because there is only one B in Boston.

206 Did you hear about the bee that visited too many flowers?
It suffered from high bud pressure.

207 When the bee said to the rose, "Hi, Bud," the rose replied, "Mind your own beeswax and bug off!"

208 Concerning the bees and the flowers
In the fields and gardens and bowers,
You will note at a glance
That their ways of romance
Haven't any resemblance to ours.

209 What is a bee's favorite music?
A pollenaise.

210 What do you call a tenor bee?
An opera stinger.

211 Show us a British apiary,
and we'll show you a bee flat.

212 Where do French bees like to eat?
At a beestro.

213 As the baby bee said to the queen bee, "Swarm in here, isn't it?"

214 What does a bee wear when it goes jogging?
A swarm-up suit.

215 What do bees do when a new hive is done?
They have a house swarming party.

216   What is the healthiest insect?
A vitamin bee one.

217   What insect can't say yes or no?
A may-bee.

218   What kind of bee drops its honey?
A spilling bee.

219   Where did Noah keep his bees?
In the ark-hives.

220   Two fellows found some hidden treasure, which one hid in his grandfather's apiary.
He then told his colleague, "Booty is in the beehives of the older."

221   When two residents of an apiary flew over a nudist camp, one
remarked to the other, "What a site to bee-hold."

222   *Customer:* "Waiter, waiter! There's a bee in my soup."
Waiter: "It's alphabet soup, sir."

223   What insect gets *A*s in English class?
A spelling bee.

224   Why is it easier to spell bees than ants?
Because it's spelled with more es.

225   Did you hear about the literary bee?
His favorite quotation was from Shakespeare's play
Humlet: *"Two bees or not two bees, that is the question."*

226   Why was the bee at the baseball game?
It was the humpire.

227   Why do bees hum?
They don't know the words.

228   Where do space bees go
after they get married?
On a honeymoon.

229 All bees know that time is honey.

230 Did you hear about the worker bees that went on strike?
They wanted more honey and shorter flowers.

231 What do bees do with their honey?
They cell it.

232 Why do bees have sticky hair?
Because they use honey combs.

233 What's the favorite song in a hive?
"Bee it ever so humble, there's no place like comb."

234 Did you hear about the beekeeper who processed honey in a
blender and whipped it into a foamy fountain of sticky sweetness?
*He videotaped the process and sent it to the TV show America's
Honeyest Foam Videos.*

235 What is black and yellow and goes "zzub, zzub"?
A bumble bee flying backward.

236 What does a lumberjack bee
use to cut down trees?
A buzz saw.

237 Did you hear about the runaway from an
apiary that went to Hollywood?
It wanted to bee in show buzzness.

238 Old beekeepers never die. They just buzz off.

239 What do you call an insect with a low buzz?
A mumble bee.

240 What do bees chew?
Bumble gum.

241 A clumsy bee became sick but continued gathering pollen, thereby infecting many
flowers with its virus. The disease was dubbed "the blight of the fumble bee."

242   What kind of weapon does an apiary owner use?
A bee-bee gun.

243   As the bee with a gun said, "Hive got you covered."

244   Why did the farmer cross his bees with fireflies?
He wanted them to work at night.

245   What makes bees good debaters?
They always carry their point.

246   A bee stings for its supper.

247   Did you hear about the killer bees that joined the undercover cops?
It was for a sting operation.

248   "I washed my tail," said the queen bee,
"and now I can't do a sting with it."

249   There was a man who loved the bees,
He always was their friend.
He liked to sit upon their hives,
But they stung him in the end.

250   What old musical show do you get when you cross a bee sting and a mosquito bite?
Sting Along with Itch.

251   What kind of musical group do bees play in?
A sting ensemble.

252   What is a bee's favorite song?
"Stinging in the Rain."

253   Bees exhibit intere-sting behavior.

254   What causes bees in England to fly around crossing and uncrossing their back legs?
They're looking for a BP station.

255 The bee's a busy little soul.
He does not practice birth control.
That's why in happy days like these
You see so many sons of bees.

256 Then there was the girl who claimed that if her parents had told
her about the birds and the bees, she wouldn't have got stung.

257 What do you call a religious drone that vacates the apiary?
A bee leaver.

258 What happens when a bee leaver doesn't recite the bee attitudes?
He ends up living with Bee L. Zebub.

259 What happens in an apiary on Halloween?
The Boo bees buzz the neighborhood.

260 What do insects take when they're ill?
Antibeeotics.

261 What's riskier than being with a fool?
Fooling with a bee.

262 Why did the bee wear a yarmulke?
So people would know he wasn't a wasp.

263 What is a jealous wasp?
A wanna-bee.

264 A farmer who raised honey-producing insects for the former Soviet spy agency
was asked if he actually worked for the Russians. "I can't answer that,"
he answered cagey-bee-ly.

265 What is the ultimate bug?
The bee all ant end all.

Beetle

266 Did you hear about the newspaper headline on the wedding of the late John
Lennon and Yoko Ono?
It said: "Lennon Turns Yoko into Japanese Beatle."

267 What is the world's most widely traveled beetle?
The VW Bug.

268 What other member of the species achieved fame in newspapers?
Beetle Bailey.

Bird

Making puns on birds is a habit that crows on you. It's possible to have a starling performance, but you can also give a terrible wrendition that others simply can't swallow. The object is not to be gulled and to avoid being aukward and full of ma-lark-ey. Merely try to have a pheasant time—even if you can't tern a pun. And by all means, don't be bittern as you warble fowl language.

Suppose you perches a cage for your bird but discover a cockatoo missing and a few other mynah things wrong with it. Unfortunately, you can't take it back because you've lost the bill. Do you know what toucan do about it? Reparrot yourself.

269 How do caged canaries communicate with each other?
By making perchin' to perchin' calls.

270 Why are birds grouchy in the morning?
Their bills are over dew.

271 What do you call a wizard that moves through the air like a bird?
A flying sorcerer.

272 What do you call a dozen red birds roosting in Harvard Yard?
A college of cardinals.

273 Once there was a mama bird that laid one egg each year, which she and papa bird hatched and nurtured and loved until the little chick was ready to leave the nest.

Then, one year, they had two eggs! Well, they were so excited they could hardly stand it. That year each would have an egg to take care of and love.

One day the two eggs hatched and out came two baby birds cheeping in unison. That goes to show that two can cheep as lively as one.

274 Did you hear about the man whose
wife entertained him by making bird calls?
He liked cheep trills.

275 What is an aviary?
It's a house of trill repute.

276 That reminds us that many migrating birds view
an empty nest along the way as a cheep hotel.

277 Bird watchers are cheep dates.

278 What do you give a sick bird?
Tweetment.

279 What did the bird lieutenant shout
during battle?
"Re-tweet!"

280 Did you hear the one about the farmer who was faced with the
predicament of having birds build nests in his favorite horse's mane?
A veterinarian told him to try putting yeast in the horse's hair.
Amazingly, it resulted in the immediate departure of the birds. Which just
goes to prove that yeast is yeast, nest is nest, and never the mane shall tweet.

281 What is a bird's favorite song?
"Home Tweet Home."

282 Did you hear about the two love
birds that got married?
They were childhood tweethearts.

283 What do birds say on Halloween?
"Twick or tweet."

284 *Patient:* "Doctor, doctor! I think I'm a bird."
Doctor: "Just perch over there. I'll tweet you in a minute."

285 Did you hear about the new disease affecting birds?
It's called chirpies, and unfortunately it's untweetable.

286   What is a bird's favorite cookie?
Chocolate chirp.

287   What did the canary get after reading some
Shakespearian sonnets?
A Bard's-eye view.

288   Why did the bird's wings hurt?
It was a soar subject.

289   Did you hear about the frenzied, flying, feathered creature?
He was called Birdserk.

290   Why do baby birds in a nest always agree?
Because they don't want to fall out.

291   Where do birds meet for coffee?
In a nest cafe.

292   Did you hear about the bird that built a
nest in the executive branch of government?

293   What is the adult version of the birds and the bees?
He calls her honey, and she starts wanting to build a nest.

294   Then there was the bird that got home very late for dinner one night
with his feathers bedraggled and his eyes bloodshot. "I was just minding
my own business," he explained to his wife, "when boom! I got caught in
a badminton game."

295   Two birds were sitting on the roof of the White House.
One bird asked, "Are you for the president?"
The other bird replied, "Well, he's for us."

296   Did you hear about the investor
whose nest egg hatched the other day?
Unfortunately, it was for the birds.

297   Why did the worm take judo lessons?
Because he wanted to flip the bird.

298   Or, as the bird said with a worm dangling from its beak,
"I'm waiting with baited breath."

> **299**   Why did the worm sleep in?
> *It didn't want to be caught by the early bird.*

>> **300**   It's noted, however, that the
>> early bird still has to eat worms.

301   Why did the bird sleep under the old car?
To catch the oily worm.

> **302**   A medical journal published the finding that
> impolite people resist intestinal diseases better than
> polite people do. Apparently, it's not the surly bird
> that catches the germ.

>> **303**   Why do some fishermen use helicopters
>> to catch their bait?
>> *Because the whirlybird gets the worm.*

304   Did you hear about the helicopter that transported the
ashes of a former head of state to a memorial site?
It was an example of the whirlybird getting the urn.

> **305**   A man eating an ice cream cone on his patio was
> pestered by two birds. When the man finished the ice cream,
> he placed the empty cone on the ground. Both birds instantly
> ceased bothering him and started eating the treat.
>   *It was merely a case of stilling two birds with one's cone.*

>> **306**   Did you hear about the clever baker who put the check
>> inside a large biscuit and then presented it to
>> the pair of customers from northern Iraq?
>> *He was merely billing two Kurds with one scone.*

>>> **307**   A woman who noticed a going-out-of-business sign in
>>> a pet shop window dashed in and asked the proprietor
>>> if he had any birds left. "You're in luck, ma'am," replied
>>> the owner. "All that twitters is not sold."

308 Two birds were watching a jet fly by. One bird says,
"I bet I could fly that fast if my tail was on fire."

309 What bird is found in space?
A starling.

310 What bird works in a bakery?
A dough-dough.

311 What birds are always unhappy?
Bluebirds.

312 If you see a bluebird in Los
Angeles, it could be a sparrow
holding its breath.

313 What bird is chocolate on the
outside and vanilla on the inside?
A Baltimore Oreo.

314 *Customer:* "I'd like to buy a bird.
Can you charge it and send
me the bill?"
Pet store owner: "No, you'll have to
take the whole bird."

315 How do scientific birds measure water?
In their beakers.

316 What does a bird wear to the beach?
A beak-ini.

317 Birds in Southeast Africa have Mozambeaks.

318 What birds spend all of their time on their knees?
Birds of pray.

319 Did you hear about the bird that flew into a taxidermist's shop?
He found it a stuffy place. And it gave him mounting apprehension.

320 Three romantic poets, arrested for crimes against the state in Stalinist
USSR, were put in a single cell with shackles on their ankles. Already in the cell
was a beautiful young woman. Attempting to reach her, the poets began to
thrash one another, thereby proving that bards of a fetter flog to get her.

321 Did you hear about the bird that fell into a can of varnish and drowned?
It was a sad way to die, but the bird did have a beautiful finish.

> **322** What do you call a bath in cold water?
> *A brrrrrd bath.*

> > **323** As the heckler said, "You sing like a bird.
> > And you have a brain to match."

324 When the mediocre mezzo-soprano sings,
her voice can charm the birds right out of the
trees—birds such as buzzards, crows, and vultures.

> **325** Did you hear about the woman who eats like a bird?
> *It's a peck at a time.*

> > **326** Did you hear about the moody umbrella bird?
> > *He had his ups and downs.*

> > > **327** What bird cannot fly, is known by many
> > > names, and annoys others when it sings?
> > > *A jailbird.*

328 A prisoner is only a bird in a guilty cage.

> > **329** As Confucius says, "A bird in a cage is like a
> > convict in prison. Leave the door open and both
> > will fly the coop."

> > > **330** How do you catch a unique bird?
> > > *Unique up on him.*

331 How do you catch a tame bird?
Tame way: unique up on him.

Bison

332 What did the buffalo say to his boy when he departed on a long journey?
"Bison."

333   What do the buffalo celebrate every two hundred years?
Their Bisontennial.

> **334**   *Woman No. 1:* "Do you like bison?"
> *Woman No. 2:* "I don't know. I've never bised."

Bloodhound

335   What's Dracula's favorite breed of dog?
Bloodhound.

> **336**   How are bloodhounds taught to track people?
> *By trail and error.*

> > **337**   How do we know bloodhounds
> > have lots of money?
> > *They're always picking up scents.*

338   Or, as one escaped convict said to another,
"I got away from the bloodhounds by
throwing a handful of pennies into the woods,
and they followed the wrong cent."

> > **339**   A policeman told a woman jogger in a park,
> > "We're looking for a grizzled man with a cat."
> > *The woman replied, "Wouldn't a bloodhound be more effective?"*

> > > **340**   How is a bloodhound like
> > > a tall basketball player?
> > > *They're both scenters.*

341   Did you hear about the neurotic bloodhound?
He thought that people were following him.

Boa

342   Did you hear about the two boa
constrictors that got married?
They had a crush on each other.

343 After the boa constrictor escaped from the zoo,
what sign was put on its empty cage?
Out to Crunch.

> **344** What snakes build houses in the jungle?
> *Boa constructors.*

345 What did the history teacher name his boa constrictor?
Julius Squeezer.

> **346** What do you call the winner of a snake
> beauty contest that is a perfect ten?
> *Boa Derek.*

> **347** What do snakes wear with a tuxedo?
> *A boa tie.*

Boar

348 Did you hear about the pig
that tells long, dull stories?
He's a real boar.

> **349** Did you hear about the man who had three pet boars?
> *He named them Boarwinkle, Boaris Karloff, and Boared Stiff.*

> **350** And then there was the squealing German tennis player: Boaris Becker.

351 A musician in Russia went hunting and shot a wild boar. That kill not
only satisfied his urge to hunt but also inspired him to compose an opera
about his experience. He titled his opera *Boar Is Good Enough.*

Buck

352 Did you hear about the fleet-footed doe that
won an animal race when she passed the buck?

> **353** Who was the first deer astronaut?
> *Buck Rogers.*

354 Or, as the doe said as she came out the woods, "That's
the last time I do that for a couple of bucks!"

Buffalo

355 Show us a home where the buffalo roam,
and we'll show you a messy house.

356 When the chips are down, the buffalo's empty.

357 What does the buffalo on old nickels stand for?
No room to sit.

358 "I'd like a ticket to New York City," the traveler said.
The agent asked, "Do you want to go by Buffalo?"
"No," replied the traveler, "I prefer the train."

359 Did you hear about the herd of bison that
Canada once sold to the United States?
America received a buffalo bill.

360 Counterfeit money is a buffaloed bill.

361 An old chief told his tribe, "I have some good news and some bad news. First
the bad news: We have nothing but buffalo dung to eat. The good news,
though, is that there's plenty of buffalo dung."

362 Or, in Buffalo Bill's last words,
"I'll see you when I'm in the chips."

Bug

363 How do we know the potato bug is musically inclined?
It plays on the tuber.

364 When are pipes like humbugs?
When they're meerschaums.

365 Did you hear about the bug in a computer?
It was looking for a byte to eat.

366 Did you hear about
the overworked entomologist?
His job drove him buggy.

367 Have you heard about the bedbug
that had a baby in the spring?

368 Then there was the exterminator
who advertised that he invented
a new spray for infested bed
sheets.
However, he still had a few
bugs to iron out.

369 Speaking of spray reminds us of the CIA
agent who sprayed his apartment with insect
repellant because he heard that it might be bugged.

370 Did you hear about the other
exterminator's slogan?
"When you call, we step on it."

371 What's the quickest way for a bug
to get from the ground to a tree trunk?
Take the shortest root.

372 *Sign in a Volkswagen showroom:*
Our Store Has Bugs.

373 *Patient:* "Doctor, doctor! I think an infected
mosquito is circling me all the time."
Doctor: "It's just a bug that's going around."

374 Did you hear the one about the man who was
accidentally bitten by the star flea in a flea circus?
The doctor ordered him to take a week for
recuperation. During his time off, he visited Hollywood
and managed to win a small part in a film. He thus
was the first person to become an actor because
he was bitten by an acting bug.

Bulldog

375 *Dad:* "Why are you making
faces at that bulldog?"
Son: "He started it."

376 Why is a bulldog like an auctioneer?
Because they both look for bidding.

Burro

377 Did you hear about the donkey that was living on burro'd time?

378 Why was it difficult making a living in the Old West?
Because people had to beg, burro, and steal.

379 What's the most important donkey
in New York City?
The burro of Manhattan.

380 How do donkeys search
for buried treasure?
They burro down after it.

381 What do you call a donkey that's cold?
A brrrr-o.

Butterfly

382 Isn't it fascinating to see a
butterfly flutter by?

383 Why did the boy throw margarine
out of the kitchen window?
He wanted to see butterfly.

384 If honey bees make honey, shouldn't
butterflies make butter?

385   As one caterpillar said to another when they
       watched a butterfly float by, "You'll never get
       me up in one of those things."

386   As the heckler told the elderly lady sitting in the front
       row, "You're so old that you probably knew Madame
       Butterfly when she was a caterpillar."

       387   Which reminds us, what kind of
              opera is *Madame Butterfly?*
              A lepidopera.

       388   "Madam Director," said a Chinese factory worker
              to his supervisor, "I am going to the opera tonight."
                     The supervisor replied, "Please don't call me
              'Madam Director.' We are all comrades. But, what opera
              are you going to see?"
                     The worker answered, "*Comrade Butterfly.*"

389   Composer Puccini in Florida wrote
       An opera based on that frustrating vote.
       He punched the wrong hole to elect the wrong guy.
       So goes *The Ballot of My Damn Butterfly.*

       390   Did you hear about the tailor who thought that
              a butterfly was a zipper on the front of a stick of margarine?

              391   What do nuts chase after with little nets?
                     Peanut butterflies.

392   Two friends were talking. The first said, "I'm so nervous about giving
       this speech that I have butterflies in my stomach."
                     "Why don't you take an aspirin?" the second man suggested.
                     "I did," replied the first, "but the butterflies are playing croquet with it."

       393   Moths swim by doing the butterfly.

              394   That reminds us of the lepidopterist
                     who went to a swimming meet when
                     he heard there was a 100-meter butterfly.

395   If you find a cocoon, how can you tell
whether it's a moth or a butterfly?
It's an emerge-and-see situation.

Buzzard

396   What is a bee's favorite bird?
A buzzard.

> **397**   Did you hear about the woman
> who can do bird imitations?
> *She has the disposition of a buzzard.*

398   Two buzzards sat in the airplane, tucked in their napkins, and stretched
their carcass dinner across their trays, ready to start their in-flight meal.
Just then—and much to the dismay of the buzzards—the flight
attendant announced: "At this time, we ask that all carrion items be stowed
under the seat in front of you."

Calamari

399   Did you hear about the squid opera singer? She sang a calam-aria.

Camel

400   Did you hear about the new book titled *Desert Crossing*?
It's by I. Rhoda Camel.

401   Show us someone who is over the hump, and we'll show you a bareback camel rider.

402   What is a camel's favorite tourist spot in New York City?
The Humpire State Building.

    403   What do you call a camel with two humps?
    A Bactrian.
    What do you call a camel with one hump?
    A dromedary.
    And what do you call a camel with no humps?
    Humphrey.

        404   What kind of camel makes the most noise?
        A drumedary.

405   Speaking of dromedaries, what do you call a camel that
has two heads, one of them where its rear end should be?
A palindromedary.

    406   Or, as one camel said to another at a tea party,
    "One hump or two?"

        407   Why did nomads use camels on
        their long treks?
        To get them over the hump.

408   What camel couldn't all the king's horses put together?
Humpy Dumpy.

    409   *Bumper sticker:* Camels Do It Humpingly.

        410   A camel is a horse designed by a committee.

411   A camel is a horse with a bucket seat.

        412   An army recruit wrote home: "As for the straw
        that broke the camel's back, I'm sleeping on it."

413   Where are used dromedaries sold in Saudi Arabia?
At a camel lot.

414   Did you hear about the Arab who named his pet camel Lot?

415 After buying a used camel, the proud new owner was told about the three basic commands: say "few" to make the camel walk, say "many" to make it run, and say "amen" to make it stop. The man mounted his camel, said, "Few," and the camel started walking. He then shouted, "Many," and the camel began to run.

As the camel trotted toward the edge of a cliff, the panic-stricken owner forgot the command to make the camel stop. In desperation, he prayed, "God save me. Amen."

As soon as it heard "amen," the camel immediately stopped at the very edge of the precipice. The man gasped a sigh of relief and exclaimed, "Phew!"

416 If a camel can go five hundred miles in the desert without water, can you imagine how far it could go *with* water?

417 If birds come in flocks and fish travel in schools, then what do camels come in?
Packs.

418 Did you know that cigarettes are mentioned in the Bible?
It's in the Book of Genesis, when Rebecca saw Isaac and "lighted off the Camel."

419 In the zoo there's an animal, Hamel,
A spitting, young ornery camel.
  He'd rather be free
  Like a bird or a bee,
And hates being classified "mammal."

420 What do Arab soldiers use to hide from their enemies in the desert?
Camelflage.

421 What is the favorite Christmas carol in the Arabian desert?
"O Camel Ye Faithful."

Canary

422 What do you call a canary run over by a lawn mower?
Shredded tweet.

423   Did you hear about the canary in Holland that paid its own way on a date?
It was Dutch tweet.

424   What does a five-hundred-pound canary
do on Halloween?
Tweet and then twick.

425   What do you call a canary that flies
into a pastry dish?
Tweetie Pie.

426   *Patient:* "Doctor, doctor! I feel like a canary."
Doctor: "Don't worry. Your condition is tweetable."

427   Did you hear the one about the man who checked
into a psychiatric hospital because he thought he
was a canary?
      His wife telephoned the doctor later to ask about
her husband's progress. "He's doing fine," replied the
psychiatrist. "For several days I haven't even heard
a peep out of him."

428   What warning did the veterinarian
give after hearing that a pet canary
swallowed a gun?
"Beware of cheep shots."

429   What do you call a canary that joins the Ice Capades?
A cheep skate.

430   What kind of canary does a bargain hunter shop for?
A cheaper cheeper.

431   Did you hear about the man who bought his canary for a song?

432   As the man said to the diva, "You sing like a canary.
And your birdcage is pretty good, too."

433   Did you hear about the artist who painted a picture of a canary?
He called it Mother's Whistler.

434   What do you call a victorious boxing canary?
A featherweight champion.

        435   Where do canaries go when they have foot trouble?
        To the chirpodist.

                436   What is the favorite vacation
                        spot for birds?
                        The Canary Islands.

Carp

437   How do fish travel to work?
In carp pools.

        438   Why do carp have trouble swimming
                through narrow spaces?
        Because they have carp tunnel syndrome.

                439   Did you hear about the fish that kept
                        getting stuck in an underwater pipeline?
                It was an example of carp-in-tunnel syndrome.

440   A man accidentally dropped his billfold overboard while sailing.
Two fish fought over this unfamiliar object, repeatedly grabbing it from
one another. The fisherman remarked, "That's the first time I've seen
carp-to-carp walleting."

        441   Did you hear about the best-selling book on fish?
        It was titled The World According to Carp.

                442   What game do young fish enjoy playing?
                Carps and robbers.

                        443   What is the fisherman's motto?
                        "Carpe carp," or "Seize the fish."

444   Did you hear about the new credit card for fish?
It's Carp Blanche.

445   A well-known chef bought several cases of carp. Endeavoring to create a new signature dish, he tried combining herbs and spices with shortening, but found that the cooking time had to be exact. So when the chef received a phone call during the dinner hour, he had to cut it short, explaining, "I left my carp in saffron Crisco."

446   What is the honorary college society for anglers?
Fly-Bait-A-Carp-A.

Cat

To show that the cat didn't get our tongues, here's a catalog of cat puns that's the cat's meow, the cat's pajamas, and the cat's whiskers. It would be a catastrophe and a cataclysm if you didn't give this category of humor a CAT scan.
To err is human; to make cat puns, feline. Please make a feline for these puns right now.

447   To my dear friend, the dog:
I'm so sorry about your being sent to the dog pound for the lamp you did not break, the fish you did not eat, and the carpet you did not wet. Things here at the house are calmer now, and just to show you that I have no hard feelings, I'm sending you a picture, so you'll always remember me.

Best regards, the cat

448   Did you hear about the guy whose cat got run over by a steamroller?
He just stood there with a long puss.

449   What happens when a boxer puts a cat in a washing machine?
He gets a sock in the puss.

450   How do you keep your cat from sleeping in bed with you?
You do what you have to if puss comes to shove.

451   Then there was the mathematician who added numbers and always concluded by saying "plus a cat." For example, he might say, "The total amount is 1,500 plus a cat." Apparently he had an add-a-puss complex.

452   Did you hear about the dog that
compulsively devoured cats?
It had an eat-a-puss complex.

>   **453**   Where might you find a psychic cat?
>   *At the E.S.P.C.A.*

>   >   **454**   What is a frightened feline?
>   >   *A scaredy cat.*

455   The musical *Cats* was great. But after three hours, it gave you pause.

>   **456**   What do cats call their mother's father?
>   *Grandpaw.*

>   >   **457**   What is the worst weather
>   >   for mice?
>   >   *When it's raining cats and dogs.*

458   What's even worse than raining cats and dogs?
Hailing taxicabs.

>   **459**   When it rains cats and dogs in England, what do the
>   British call it?
>   *Beastly weather.*

460   Did you hear the one about the Japanese automobile manufacturer who
had to send for an emergency shipment of cogs for some engines?
    The parts were being transported on a small private airplane, but the
pilot reported turbulence and ordered all excess weight to be jettisoned. A
couple was sitting on the patio when the husband glanced up and exclaimed,
"Look! It's raining Datsun cogs."

>   **461**   Did you hear about the pet cat named Mandu?

>   >   **462**   Did you hear about the unemployed cat
>   >   from Nepal that became a burglar?
>   >   *What else can a Katmandu?*

463   What do you call felines that rob McDonald's restaurants?
Cat burger-lars.

464   Why did the cat give birth on the side of the road?
Because the sign said Fine for Littering.

> **465**   Why did the mother cat put stamps on her kittens?
> *Because she wanted to mail a litter.*

466   "Have you heard from your boyfriend?" one cat asked another.
"Yes," was the reply. "I had a litter from him yesterday."

> **467**   *Cat-erbury Tails* is litter-ature.

>> **468**   Why was the lady so upset with her pet cat?
>> *Because when the cat littered up the place, she
>> did it litter-ally.*

469   Or, as the Martian said to the cat, "Take me to your litter."

> **470**   What did the fast cat put in his litter box?
> *Quicksand.*

>> **471**   Why does a cat like inclement weather?
>> *Because when it rains, it purrs.*

>>> **472**   How is cat food priced?
>>> *So much purr can.*

473   Did you hear about the cat burglar?
He was a purr-snatcher.

> **474**   The leather workers say there is more than one way to
> skin a cat, but we've never been purr-sueded it's true.

475   What is the color of a happy cat?
Purrple.

> **476**   Where do cats go when they die?
> *To purrgatory.*

>> **477**   What is the favorite college for cats?
>> *Purrdue University.*

478   Haiku about cats:
              There is nothing worse
              Than poems about cute cats.
              It is all purrverse.

    479   How do cats control a family's finances?
              They hold the purr strings.

        480   Where do many Arabic cats vacation?
                   In the Purrsian Gulf.

            481   What government agency finds
                        lost cats?
                        The Bureau of Missing Persians.

482   Did you hear about the old cat that became forgetful
           and stopped making any sounds?
           It developed a purr-senility disorder.

    483   What symptom does an attractive, aging, transgressing feline
                have after losing her voice upon drinking quinine water?
                A cute cat-a-tonic purr-senility sin-drome.

        484   *Man:* "Doctor, doctor! I'm worried. My
                       cat is always looking over his shoulder."
                       Vet: "Don't worry. It's only purranoia."

485   Did you hear about the guy who was afraid of cats?
           He had clawstrophobia.

    486   What can you say about the cat that was
                walking along the beach on Christmas Eve?
                Sandy claws.

        487   Why did the cat climb the drapes?
                       He had good claws to.

488   A woman walked into the pet store. "I haven't got much money," she told the
           clerk, "so I'd like to know if you've any kittens you'll let go cheap."
           "I'd let them, ma'am," said the clerk, "but they prefer to go meow."

489   What do cats read for current events?
The daily mewspaper.

491   What did the cat say when it got hurt?
"Me ow."

492   Who was a famous former feline
leader in China?
Meow Tse-tung.

493   *Sign by a cat cage in a pet store:*
Get Meowt of Here!

494   There was a kind curate of Kew
Who kept a large cat in a pew.
        There he taught it each week
        A new letter of Greek,
But it never got further than mu.

495   How do mother cats locate their
lost kittens?
Just like poets, they learn to follow their mews.

490   What was the name of
Shakespeare's cat?
Romeow.

496   Did you hear about the new cell
phone commercial that uses cats?
"Can you hear me meow?"

497   What's the name of a special art gallery that displays only old
sculptures, photos, and drawings of cats?
A mew-see-em.

498   Hotel owner's ad for cat to catch mice:
"Must be inn-experienced."

499   Or, as the cat said after eating some cheese and
then sitting by a mouse hole, "I wait with baited breath."

500   Burma Shave signs once carried this verse:
        He asked his kitten to pet and purr.
        She eyed his puss and screamed, "What fur!"

501 Did you hear about the cat that played all night under the Christmas tree?
It got a fir coat.

502 That reminds us of why cats eat furballs.
Like punsters, they love a good gag.

503 What kind of formal dances do cats have?
Hairballs.

504 *Boy No. 1:* "Why is your cat so small?"
Boy No. 2: "I feed him condensed milk."

505 A cat is one animal that never cries over spilled milk.

506 Why is a cat drinking milk like a track star?
Because they both enjoy taking a few laps.

507 A New England antiques dealer noticed a mangy cat lapping milk from a rare porcelain saucer in front of a general store. He went inside and offered ten dollars for the cat, but the owner said the cat wasn't for sale. The savvy dealer explained that he enjoyed rescuing wayward cats and raised his offer to fifty dollars.
"It's a deal," said the proprietor as he pocketed the money.
"For that sum," said the connoisseur, "I'm sure you won't mind if I take his saucer."
"Oh, I can't part with the saucer," replied the owner. It's helped me sell twenty-seven cats this week."

508 Then there were the two cats that were racing to the milk bowl. The winner beat the loser by a lap.

509 Or, as one cat said to another,
"He that laps last, laps best."

510 *Customer:* "How did you get the Maltese Cross?"
Jeweler: "By stepping on its tail."

511 Did you hear about the man who saw a sign at a pet store that said Free Cats?
He went in, and he did.

512   What happened when the Frenchman tried to teach his
three young kittens how to swim by throwing them in a lake?
Un, deux, trois *cats sank.*

> **513**   Four French kittens were playing with several balls of yarn.
> How many did they tear apart?
> Quatre *cats shredded* huit.

> **514**   A cat was courting his favorite feline. "I would die for
> you," he proclaimed. She replied, "How many times?"

515   The young cat pleaded with his parents, "Why don't you let me
lead one of my own lives?"

> **516**   A cat in the town of St. Ives
> Stole honey from several large hives.
> Once stung by eight bees,
> He said, "Stop it, please.
> You know I have only nine lives."

> **517**   What are palindromic, old, and confused cats?
> *Senile felines.*

518   *Man:* "I just ran over your cat, and I'd like to replace it."
Boy: "Well, get busy. There's a mouse in the basement."

> **519**   What do you call a kitty with chutzpah?
> *A pushy cat.*

> **520**   What goes, "zzzz, meow, zzzz, meow"?
> *Someone taking a catnap.*

521   What is the feline end-of-year greeting?
Have yourself Furry Catnaps and a Happy Mew Year.

> **522**   What is a feline's favorite sailboat?
> *A catamaran.*

> **523**   What is a pirate's favorite pet?
> *A cat-o'-nine-tails.*

524 What do you call a German cat that was run over by a lawn mower?
A cat-o'-nein-tails.

> **525** As the cat said when its tail got caught in a lawn mower, "It won't be long now."

> > **526** What did the private eye do to the Manx cat?
> > *He put a tail on it.*

527 Did you hear about the old tomcat that stopped marking his territory when he ran out of "perfume"?
Hoping to get a refill, he scent for a male cat odor-log.

> > **528** What did the country bumpkin say to the veterinarian?
> > *"Our dog got fleas, but our catgut kittens."*

529 Have you heard about the feline that impeded the iceman's work?
The cat got his tong.

> **530** *Patient:* "Every time I stroke a cat, I get an upset stomach."
> *Doctor:* "Don't worry, it's just a gut reaction."

> > **531** Or, as one cat said to another while watching a tennis match, "My father's in that racket."

532 Then there was the cat that took a family tennis racket to a psychiatrist.
The diagnosis: "Your sister is too high-strung."

> > **533** What did the cat say as she rescued her daughter from the violin factory?
> > *"I didn't raise my daughter to be fiddled with."*

534 *Man No. 1:* "How do you like my violin playing?"
Man No. 2: "Sounds as if the strings are still in the cat."

> **535** A cat jumped out and surprised a family of mice. The mother mouse shouted, "Bow-wow," and the cat ran away. "See, children," said the mother mouse, "how important it is to speak another language?"

536   *Father:* "I can't wake Junior up."
Mother: "I just throw the cat on the bed."
Father: "How does that help?"
Mother: "Junior sleeps with the dog."

537   When do cats and dogs get along together?
When you have hot dogs with catsup.

538   Did you hear about the cat that liked to
lounge around the stereo?
*He hoped to catch the tweeter for
lunch—unless the woofer got him first.*

539   That reminds us of the cat that took first prize at the bird show.
He ate the prize canary.

540   Cranky cats have *pfssst* fights.

541   There oncet was two cats of Kilkenny;
Each thought there was one cat too many.
So they quarreled and they fit,
They scratched and they bit,
Till 'stead of two cats, there wasn't any.

542   Why can't some animals keep secrets?
Because pigs squeal, yaks yak, and someone always lets the cat out of the bag.

543   Did you hear about the cat that let the gossip out of the bag?

544   What happened to the cat that swallowed a ball of wool?
She had mittens.
And all her kittens were born wearing sweaters.
That's some yarn.
And you're no knit-wit.

545   Did you hear about the cat that entertained himself with a piece of yarn?
With a little effort, he had a ball.

546   *Mother:* "Did you put the cat out?"
Father: "Oh, dear! Is he on fire again?"

547   Did you hear about the tailor who let his cat out?

548   A couple left town suddenly and unannounced, but they stuck
this note on a neighbor's door: "Would you please feed our cat?
But don't put yourselves out."

549   A female feline invited a tomcat to go home with her.
"Will your paw be there?" he asked.
"No," she replied. "I have my own pad."

550   *Cat No. 1:* "How are you feline today?"
Cat No. 2: "Not up to scratch."

551   What is a feline's favorite magazine?
The Saturday Evening Scratching Post.

552   Cowboy star Roy Rogers went bathing in a creek. Along came a mountain
lion and began nibbling one of Roy's brand-new boots, which his wife, Dale
Evans, gave him as a birthday gift.
    Dale entered the scene, pulled out her trusty six-shooter, and fired
some shots in the air, which chased the varmint away. She turned to her
husband and asked, "Pardon me, Roy, is that the cat that chewed
your new shoe?"

553   What do you call a fat cat?
A flabby tabby.

554   Did you hear about the
advice column that advertising
legend Morris the Cat is going to
write in his retirement?
It'll be called "Dear Tabby."

555   What did Hamlet say when trying
to decide what kind of cat to have?
"Tabby or not tabby."

556   What do you call the DNA genome for felines?
Helix the cat.

557   Said a cat as he playfully threw
His wife down a well in Peru,
          "Relax, dearest Dora,
          Please don't be angora.
I was only artesian you."

558   What did the owner do when his cat fell down a well?
He bought a book on how to raise cats.

559   Did you hear about the cat named Ben Hur?
*It was no longer called Ben after it had kittens—
only Her.*

560   What kind of feline likes bowling?
An alley cat.

561   Did you hear about the generous guy who gave his
wife an anniversary present that keeps on giving?
It was a pregnant cat.

562   That reminds us of the one about the genie who granted a wish to a spinster.
The woman requested that her faithful cat be transformed into a handsome
prince. After the miracle was performed, the prince romantically whispered
in her ear, "Now aren't you sorry you had me fixed?"

563   Some people call it "getting fixed," but we
prefer to call a spayed a spayed.

564   Or, as one altered cat said to another,
"The pain in spaying is mostly in the brain."

565   A woman took her cat to the veterinarian for its annual checkup. The
doctor concluded his routine examination by slowly walking around the table
while repeatedly looking back and forth. When he finished, he gave the woman
some medication and presented her with the bill.
          "Two hundred dollars for a couple of pills?" she exclaimed.
          "Not merely the pills," replied the vet. "I also gave him a cat scan."

566   Why is a cat's tail like the end of the world?
Because it's so fur to the end. (And this is the end of the cat jokes!)

Caterpillar

567   Did you hear about the caterpillar's New Year's resolution?
It promised to turn over a new leaf.

> **568**   What is a high-strung cocoon?
> *A wound-up caterpillar.*

> > **569**   A caterpillar is an upholstered worm.

570   A worm was basking in the sunlight one afternoon when a hoity-toity caterpillar crawled by. "Hmph," muttered the worm. "I'd like to know how she got that fur coat!"

> **571**   What is a caterpillar's main enemy?
> *A dog-erpillar.*

> > **572**   Why is hot bread like a caterpillar?
> > *Because it's the grub that makes the butter fly.*

573   *Tractor salesman No. 1:* "How's business?"
Tractor salesman No. 2: "Caterpillar stock is inching up. In midseason the stock may appear dormant, but it retains the potential for a lofty flight and colorful crowds of investors."

> **574**   Did you hear about the new book titled
> From *Caterpillar to Butterfly?*
> *It's by Chris A. Liss.*

> > **575**   What pillar is never used to hold up a building?
> > *A caterpillar.*

576   Speaking of caterpillars reminds us that many public officials consider themselves the pillars of society. However, they are more properly the caterpillars, having reached their high positions by crawling.

> **577**   Or, as one caterpillar said to another,
> "Look before you creep."

Catfish

578   Why did the boy bait his hook with a mouse?
He was fishing for catfish.

579   "Have you ever seen a catfish?"
"No. How would it hold the rod?"

580   Why did the dog jump into the river?
He wanted to chase a catfish.

Cattle

Wholly Cow! We found the cattle-list—and that's no bull!

Ruminate on this: To err is human; to make cattle puns, bovine.

Now is a good time to stop beefing and stewing and to shoot the bull and run some bull and cow jokes pasture eyes.

The favorite moospapers of cows are *The Daily Moos* and *The Moo York Times*, with its motto "All the Moos That's Fit to Print."

The most popular tune for cattle themselves is "My Whey."

The game the cows most enjoy playing is moosical chairs.

Their favorite magazines? *Breeder's Digest* and *Mad.*

Their favorite book? *Dairy of a Mad Housewife.*

Their most popular television show? *Maverick*, of course.

Cowabunga! You'll be amazed at how many times the cattle get your tongue till the cows come home. Here follows a cattle-list that is bound to cattle-ize you into action, which is a lot better than being cattle-leptic. We're sure that you haven't herd them all—and that's no bum steer. Even the bulls and cows laugh at these. They've become the laughing stock of the ranch.

Sharpen your pun cells, everybody. It's time for déjà moo—the feeling that you've heard this bull before. And remember that a good pun is like a good steak—a rare medium well done.

581   What did the British bull say after visiting the china shop?
"I had a smashing good time."

582   The only bull in most china shops is the sales pitch.

583   Did you hear about the politician who reminds audiences of Moses?
Every time he opens his mouth, the bull rushes.

584 Why did the cowslip?
Because it saw the bulrush.

585 Or, as the orator began his speech, "It's a privilege speaking in this auditorium. It's a word, by the way, that comes from two Latin words: *audio*, meaning 'I hear,' and *taurus*, 'the bull.'"

586 Unlike in Spain, there are no bullrings in the United States. Unless, of course, you count the one political candidates throw their hats into.

587 That reminds us that some political speeches are like the horns on a healthy steer: a point here and there with a lot of bull between.

588 Did you hear about the politician who took judo lessons?
He wanted to learn how to throw the bull.

589 Why was the Taurus new-car salesman so successful?
He convinced everyone to buy his bull.

590 *Woman No. 1:* "Can you see the bull behind the tapestry?"
Woman No. 2: "No, I can't see the Taurus for the frieze."

591 Did you hear about the new book titled *The Bull?*
It's by Matt T. Door.

592 How does the bullfighter get into his house?
Through the mata-door.

593 Did you hear about the matador who became a baseball player?
He could always be found in the bullpen.

594 That reminds us of the Spanish golfer named Juan, who became a matador. One day the bull made a hole in Juan.

595 Golf is the game that has turned the cows out of the pasture and let the bull in.

596   Then there was the intelligent bull that gored the matador according to his place of residence. For example, if a bullfighter was from New Jersey, the bull stuck him in the shirt. If he was from North Dakota, the bull gored him in the coat. Upon hearing this, one matador exclaimed, "I'm not going to face that bull. I'm from Pantsylvania."

597   At a dinner party, a bullfighter was being lectured endlessly by the hostess on the alleged cruelty of his sport. She continued to drone on despite all of his polite counterarguments. Finally, in desperation, the guest said, "Madam, I may have killed many bulls, but I have always spared them the ultimate cruelty. Not one did I ever bore to death."

    598   A matador was at another dinner party when he commented, "In South America, our most popular sport is bullfighting."
        The hostess gasped, "Bullfighting! I think it's revolting!"
        "No," replied the matador. "Revolting used to be our favorite sport."

599   Among the spectators watching a famed Mexican matador perform in the bullring was an outspoken Texan. The matador deftly avoided the animal's sharp horns only by inches and flipped the cape aside as the bull roared past. He repeated this until the Texan could stand it no longer. He got to his feet and shouted, "Bud, he ain't never going to run into that sack unless you hold it still."

    600   What do matadors use to write with?
    Bull-point pens.

601   Recently, the government of Spain has found that bulls are winning fewer and fewer bullfights. To make the contests more nearly even, the government has constructed an exercise area in each major arena, equipped with treadmills, weights, and pulleys. Each area is known as the pulley bull-pit.

    602   Some talk shows remind us of a famous Native American: Sitting Bull.

    603   A hunter was confronted by both a bull and a lion. He shot the lion first because he could always shoot the bull.

604 A mountain lion ate an entire bull and, feeling good, started roaring and roaring. Finally a hunter came along and plugged the critter, proving that you should keep your mouth shut when you're full of bull.

605 How did the bullfight end?
It was a toss-up.

606 An anarchist was sneaking along a rural road with a bomb hidden in his trench coat. He saw another man in a trench coat approaching, and, fearing that he was facing a government agent, the anarchist rolled the bomb into a nearby pasture.
A bull walked up to the rolling object, sniffed it, and swallowed it whole. What is the resulting situation in a single word?
Abominable.

607 And what single word describes the situation five seconds later?
Noble.

608 If an escaped prisoner murdered your male bovine with a large knife, whom should you call?
The con-stab-bull.

609 How do male cattle proceed down a steep slope?
They tum-bull.

610 What international city is named for a sunbathing animal?
Istanbul.

611 Why do people like brass bands on platforms at political rallies?
So they can take the bull by the horns.

612 Why did members of the brass band store their instruments in the barn?
So they could take the horns by the bull.

613   Have you heard about the five young bulls that were standing in the
pasture discussing what they wanted to be when they grew up?
> The first said he wanted to go to Rome and become a papal bull.
> The second said he wanted to go to New York and become a bull
> on Wall Street.
> The third wanted to go to the Windy City to become a Chicago Bull.
> The fourth said he wanted to go to Beijing and be a bull in a
> China shop.
> The fifth said he was just going to stay in the pasture for heifer and
> heifer and heifer.

614   Then there was the time that three bulls escaped from a ranch.
The largest bull was so slow that he was caught in no time flat. The
medium-sized bull was captured some time later. The smallest bull,
however, eluded the rancher for several hours. Which just goes to
show that a little bull goes a long way.

> **615**   Why is it impossible to knock down baby bulls?
> *Because wee bulls wobble, but they don't fall down.*

> **616**   Did you hear about the woman who shops like a bull?
> *She charges everything.*

> **617**   Why did the banker want to become a farmer?
> *So he could trade in T-bulls.*

618   Did you hear about the stockbroker's son who hadn't finished learning
about the birds and the bees before his father wanted him to learn about
the bulls and the bears?

> **619**   Where is the favorite vacation spot for European cows?
> *Bulgaria.*

> **620**   Did you hear about the farmer who bred bulls
> and transported them all over the globe?
> *Today he's the biggest bull shipper in the world.*

621   It's a little-known fact that the world's most beloved
and best-selling book is also what the cow said when her gentleman
friend left the pasture: "Bye, bull."

622   Bible: Purchasing a male bovine creature.

623   *Bumper sticker on Texas rancher's car:* For Whom the Bulls Toil.

624   What do you call four bullfighters in quicksand?
Quatro sinko.

625   Cattle in outer space taste better because they are meteor.

626   Have you heard about the man who bequeathed his boys a cattle ranch named Focus?
It was the place where the sun's rays meet—and the sons raise meat!

627   On what charge was the woman wearing a silk dress on a cattle ranch arrested?
Rustling.

628   What kind of cowboy steals teapots?
A kettle rustler.

629   What kind of eggs do cattle rustlers like?
Poached.

630   What do you call explosive cow vomit?
A cud missile.

631   What do you call a cow with two legs?
Lean beef.

632   What do you call a cow with no legs?
Ground beef.

633   What else do you call a cow with no legs?
It doesn't matter what you call her; she still won't come.

634   What do you call a cow with no feet?
It behooves you to call her lack-toes deficient.

635   Do butcher shops have medicow programs?

636 What key do cattle sing in?
Beef-flat.

637 That reminds us of the song that was composed to commemorate the cow that was run over by a train.
It was written in beef-flat.

638 Show us a herd of cattle with a sense of humor, and we'll show you the laughing stock.

639 How did Noah become the world's first financial investor?
He floated his stock while everyone else was being liquidated.

640 Why doesn't Sweden export cattle?
It wants to keep its Stockholm.

641 A city slicker was helping a rancher drive his cattle. When he was asked to hold the bull for a minute, the city dweller replied, "I don't mind being a director in this company, but I object to being a stockholder."

642 How did cattle feel when the branding iron was invented?
They were very impressed.

643 Did you hear about the new book for ranchers titled *How to Identify Cattle*?
It's by Brandon Iron.

644 What happens during branding on a ranch?
Cowboys get sore calves.

645 What happens to heretical cattle?
They're burned at the steak.

646 Did you hear about the detective who was spying on a herd of cattle?
He was on a steak-out.

647 Did you hear about the cowboy who heard voices during cattle drives?
He was deranged.

648   Did you hear about the cows that were shipped by
raft down the Mississippi River?
It was the first cattle-log business.

> **649**   *Visitor:* "How many head of cattle do you have over there?"
> *Rancher:* "I can't tell. They're facing the wrong way."

> > **650**   How can you tell a milkmaid?
> > *She's the one with the prominent dairy air.*

> > **651**   Isn't it easy to milk a cow?
> > *Yes, any little jerk can do it. (But if the
> > little jerk gets too enthusiastic, the result
> > could turn out to be beyond the pail.)*

652   Forgetful cows give milk of amnesia. Pampered cows give spoiled milk.
Nervous cows give milk shakes. Cows that read *Reader's Digest* give
condensed milk. Invisible cows give evaporated milk.

> **653**   As Confucius says, "Instead of buying milk at a store,
> why not purchase a cow and take matters into your own hands?"

> > **654**   Why did the gentleman farmer tip his
> > hat every time he milked a cow?
> > *Because he didn't have a pail.*

> > **655**   Did you hear about the Scottish farmer
> > who, on a very foggy day, milked three
> > cows before he realized he wasn't playing
> > the bagpipes?

656   Here's a great opening line for a public speaker: "I appreciate your
welcome. Or, as the cow said to the farmer on a cold morning,
'Thank you for the warm hand.'"

> **657**   That reminds us of the farmer who said it was so cold
> one morning that he milked for ten minutes before he
> realized he was shaking hands with himself.

658   Cow comedians always milk their laughs.

659 How are lawyers similar to dairy farmers?
They milk you for all you've got.

660 Did you hear about the dairy farmer who paid his legal fees in a quart of law?

661 What gives milk and has a horn?
A milk truck.

662 Where did the cow land when it jumped over the moon?
On the Milky Way.

663 Why did the farmer put his cow on the scales?
He wanted to see how much the milky weighed.

664 A city slicker asked a farmer how long cows should be milked. The farmer replied, "Same as short ones."

665 Why shouldn't you be upset when a cow falls over?
Because it's no use crying over spilt milk.

666 Then there was the woman who called the dairy farm to order enough milk for a bath.
"Pasteurized?" asked the farmer.
"No," replied the woman, "just up to my neck."

667 After seeing a milk truck with a sign that read Pasteurized, Homogenized, Vitamin D Added, one cow said to another, "Makes you feel sort of inadequate, doesn't it?"

668 Why is milk the quickest drink?
Because it's past your eyes before you can drink it.

669 Why don't cows have any money?
Because the farmers milk them dry.

670 Did you hear about the slick salesman?
He sold two milking machines to a farmer with only one cow.
And then took the cow as a down payment.

671   One day a discontented cow complained to her farmer,
"Go ahead and milk me. See if I give a dram!"

672   Did you hear about the cow with hiccups?
It made its own butter.

673   Why did the farmer put whiskey in the cow's food?
He wanted to raise stewed beef.

674   Did you hear about the farmer that used a tooth
brush on his cow's teeth?
Now the cow's giving dental cream.

675   What do you get from an Arctic cow?
Cold cream.

676   What do Alaskans call their cows?
Eskimoos.

677   Whose cow speaks Russian?
Ma's cow.

678   Where do Russian cattle breeders live?
In Mooscow.

679   What do cows wear while
vacationing in Hawaii?
Moo moos.

680   Two women met on a street corner. "How do I look in my muumuu?"
asked one. The other replied, "Like a cow-cow."

681   What state has the most cows?
Moossouri.

682   Cattle tastes are lowbrow in that they love
Moozak. It's their favorite grain elevator music.

683   What are the favorite moosicals of cows and bulls?
A Chorus Loin, Fiddler on the Hoof, and West Hide Story.

684 What musical is about a diseased cow?
The Sound of Moo Sick.

685 What happened to the cow that ate too many blueberries?
It mooed indigo.

686 The sound that cows make is moo,
And that's what they usually doo,
Except when grass grows
Way up to their nose,
And then they sneeze achoo.

687 Why did the farmer take his cow to the vet?
Because the cow was moody.

688 What goes "oom, oom, oom"?
A cow walking backward.

689 Where do cows go for entertainment?
To the moovies. (And to amoosment parks.)

690 What movie do cows enjoy watching?
Mootiny on the Bounty.

691 Why is raising cows a lucrative business?
Because you make a lot of moola. (Of course, there are many expenses in curd.)

692 Three thieves were being chased by a policeman, so they climbed some trees in hopes of hiding.
The cop heard a noise and yelled up into a tree, "Who's there?"
The first thief said, "Hoot-hoot," so the cop, thinking it was an owl, went to the next tree and shouted, "Who's there?"
The second thief replied, "Cheep-cheep," like a bird, so the lawman went to the next tree and repeated, "Who's there?"
The third thief said, "Moo-moo."

693 What is a cow's favorite syrup?
Moolasses.

694 Why do cows use telephones?
So they can commoonicate.

696 Why was the calf afraid?
Because he was a cow-herd.

697 Two men were arguing. The first said firmly, "I disagree with you, and I will not be bullied."
The second man retorted, "And I will not be cowed."

698 What do cattle order in Italian restaurants?
Cow-zones.

699 Where do smart cattle go to college and what do they study?
They study cowculus at Cowlumbia University.

700 A Mr. Michael Howe went to the post office and asked, "Is there any mail for Mike Howe?"
The clerk replied, "There's no mail for your cow—and none for your horse, either."

695 What did Leonardo da Vinci's cow paint?
The Moona Lisa.

701 Did you hear about the cattle that worked together harmoniously?
It was real cowoperation.

702 As the steer said when he jumped off a bridge, "Cowabungee!"

703 A man was being interrogated by the police after his car accidentally hit a cow. "Was it a Jersey cow?" one officer asked.
"I don't know," replied the man. "I didn't see its license plate."

704 What do you call a group of Australians in line for grilled steak?
A barbie queue.

705 Did you hear about the snobby cow?
She thought she was a cutlet above the rest.

706   A couple was looking at the menu in a fancy restaurant, and the wife
mused, "I wonder what that veal entree is."
       Her husband replied, "Let's call the waitress and veal Oscar."

   707   As the chef told the newspaperman, "I never re-veal my sauces."

      708   Why did the cow cross the road?
             To get to the udder side.

         709   Or, as the cow said upon waking
                  early one morning, "It's the start
                  of an udder day."

710   That somehow reminds us that India is going to remake a classic
Hollywood movie and call it *Gandhi with the Wind.*
       In this version, Rhett has left Scarlett to take care of his sacred cow.
The film concludes with Scarlett ruminating, "Here today; Gandhi tomorrow.
But tomorrow is an udder day."

   711   A city slicker was watching a cow being milked when a fly flew
          into the cow's ear. Then the man noticed a fly in the milk pail.
          He asked the farmer how that could have happened.
             "It's simple," said the farmer. "In one ear and out the udder."

      712   What results when cows refuse to be milked?
             Udder chaos.

         713   Which reminds us of the cross-eyed milkmaid
                  who found herself in a state of udder confusion.

714   Why did the cow go to the doctor?
Because she was udderly exhausted.

   715   What happened when the cow tried to jump
          over the barbed-wire fence?
          It was udder disaster.

      716   What is it that a cow has four of and a
             woman has two of?
             Feet.

717   What is the Golden Rule for cows?
Do unto udders as you would have udders do unto you.

718   What is some other good advice for cows?
Turn the udder cheek and mooove on.

719   Why was a special pail invented for electric milking machines?
Because one good urn deserves an udder.

720   Did you hear the one about the department store that had cows
as employees?
One cow was in charge of household goods, a second one had
responsibility for hardware items, and the third cow ran the clothing section.
When a customer inquired about a new suit, the manager replied,
"There are clothes in counters of the third kine."

721   What two members of the cow family go everywhere with you?
Your calves.

722   What happens to a cow when it gives birth?
It gets de-calf-inated.

723   Did you hear about the bowlegged cowboy?
He couldn't keep his calves together.

724   As one woman insulted another,
"You have calves that only a cow would like."

725   Or, as the opera critic said after a performance,
"The only signs of a biblical source were the fatted calves."

726   Where do baby cows eat?
In calfeterias.

727   What is a calf after it is six months old?
Seven months old.

728   Did you hear about the member of a women's liberation
organization who favors freedom for cows?
She's a calves libber.

729   Why did the crazy chef watch the lazy cow?
He wanted to see the meat loaf.

> **730**   There once was an African Mau-Mau
> Who got into a rather bad row-row.
>> The cause of the friction
>> Was his practicing diction,
> Saying, "How-how now-now brown-brown cow-cow."

731   Did you hear the one about the guy whose wife went on a chopped-meat binge one week?

On Monday she served meat loaf, on Tuesday hamburger, on Wednesday sloppy Joes, and on Thursday meatballs. On Friday morning the man stopped his wife in the kitchen and asked resignedly, "How now, ground cow?"

> **732**   Did you hear about the guy who eats like a horse?
> *He'd eat like a cow, but he doesn't have the stomach for it.*

> **733**   *Sign in a church kitchen:*
> Food Served Here Is Sacred Chow.

734   As a man told his wife, "I don't want to say anything about my mother-in-law. However, if she lived in India, she'd be sacred."

735   A farmer was approached by a stranger who asked him, "How much is that prize Jersey cow of yours worth?"

The farmer mulled this over and then replied, "That depends. Are you the tax assessor or have you run over her?"

> **736**   Did you hear about the dairy farm slogan that was adopted by a competitive corporation?
> *"Our cows are not contented. They're always striving to do better."*

737   Some cows that were to be auctioned off at a state fair broke free and mingled among the musicians from the local high school marching band. They obviously became the center of attraction, which had the unexpected benefit of eventually bringing twice the anticipated price at the auction.

The moral of this little story is that a herd in the band is worth two in the bush.

738   Did you hear about the Greek cows that saved their money in special vases?
Their money was herd-urned.

> **739**   *Visitor:* "Look at that bunch of cows."
> *Farmer:* "Not bunch. Herd."
> *Visitor:* "Heard what?"
> *Farmer:* "Herd of cows."
> *Visitor:* "Sure I've heard of cows."
> *Farmer:* "No. A cow herd."
> *Visitor:* "She can listen. I've got no secrets from a cow."

> > **740**   As the bovine mom and pop said to their
> > offspring, "Calves should be seen and not herd."

741   What is a cow's favorite sport?
Jumping the hurdles.

> **742**   Have you heard about the bunch of cattle put into a satellite?
> *It was called the herd shot round the world.*

> > **743**   What animal is a cannibal?
> > *The cow. She eats her fodder.*

744   A young boy asked the shoemaker what he used to repair shoes.
"Hide," replied the man.
"Why should I hide?" asked the boy.
"No," countered the cobbler, "hide! The cow's outside."
Said the boy, "Who's afraid of a cow?"

> **745**   What's a metaphor?
> *For cows to eat grass in.*

746   Did you hear about the farmer who lost control of his tractor in the cow pasture?
It didn't hurt the cows. It just grazed them.

> **747**   How did the farmer find his missing cow?
> *He tractor down.*

> > **748**   Then there was the farmer who was a magician.
> > *He turned his cows in to pasture.*

749   And then there was the rancher who let his cows roam anywhere they wished, letting the chips fall where they may.

750   *Farmer No. 1:* "I have 200 cows on my farm."
Farmer No. 2: "Yesterday, you told me that you had 199 cows."
Farmer No. 1: "That was before I rounded them up."

751   A woman complained to her friend, "He told me that he'd love me until the cows came home. How was I to know that he was a cattle rancher?"

752   Why do cows have bells around their necks?
Because their horns don't work.

753   Have you heard the story about the cow bell?
It has never been tolled.

754   What is brown and sounds like a cow bell?
Dung.

755   A cow-pie contest is a dung deal.

756   What do you get if you lie under a cow?
A pat on the head.

757   Little birdie flying high,
Dropped a message from the sky.
"Oh," said the farmer, wiping his eye,
"Isn't it lucky cows don't fly?"

758   What would happen if cows could fly?
Apart from having to carry a strong umbrella, we'd see beef go up.

759   When was beef the highest?
When the cow jumped over the moon.

760   Did you hear about the baseball game that was played in a cow pasture?
It ended when a runner slid into what he thought was third base.

761   A male fly was cruising around looking for female companionship, and he spotted one sunning herself on a pile of cow manure. He flew up to her and asked, "Pardon me, but is this stool taken?"

762   An Italian bull named Caesar was scheduled to be shipped across a river to its buyer. The barge's deckhands found the bull munching grass in a pasture instead of being ready at the dock, whereupon one the deckhands said, "We've come to ferry Caesar, not to graze him."

763   Then there was the woman who spoke with her late husband through a spiritualist. "Are you happy?" she asked.

He replied, "It's just heavenly. The pastures are lush, and the females are beautiful."

The wife told him, "I look forward to joining you in heaven."

"What do you mean, heaven?" the man exclaimed. "I'm a bull in Texas."

764   Two colleagues were chatting. One said, "While I was walking across a barnyard, a bull tossed me over the fence."

"What a terrible accident."

"It was no accident. The bull did it on purpose."

765   Old bulls never die. They just breed their last.

Centaur

766   Centaurs were half hoarse because they lived in damp caves.

767   Did you hear about the mythology exhibit that was featured in a circus?
It got centaur ring.

768   Why did the centaur lose the marathon?
He ran a half-assed race.

769   What's the difference between a centaur and a senator?
One is half man and half horse's ass—and the other is a creature in mythology.

Centipede

770   What lies on the ground 100 feet in the air?
A centipede on its back.

771   As one centipede said to another, "I just hate it when I start the day off on the wrong foot."

772   How do you drive a centipede crazy?
Ask him to put his best foot forward.

773   What's worse than a giraffe with a sore throat?
A centipede with fallen arches.

774   I'm as unhappy as a tender-footed centipede on a hot pavement.

775   Why was the centipede uncomfortable?
Because he had athlete's foot.

776   What goes 99-thump, 99-thump, 99-thump?
A centipede with a wooden leg.

777   Did you hear about the speedy centipede
that won a race by a hundred feet?

778   Did you hear about the two centipedes walking down lovers' lane
hand-in-hand, hand-in-hand, hand-in-hand . . . ?

779   Why did the father centipede wear earmuffs?
*He was tired of hearing the pitter-patter, pitter-patter,
pitter-patter of little feet.*

780   Then there was the exasperated centipede who told her husband that she was
sick and tired of waiting on him hand and foot, hand and foot, hand and foot . . .

781   *Centipede teacher:* "Why are you late to school?"
Centipede student: "My mother was playing This
Little Piggy Went to Market with me."

782   Did you hear about the centipede that went home late one night
and was afraid of waking his wife?
He wanted to sneak upstairs, but he spent the whole night taking off his shoes.

783   What has lots of legs and wears perfume?
A scentipede.

784   Did you hear about the new book titled *Insects with Many Legs?*
It's by Millie Pede.

785 Then there was the new book titled *Everything You Ever Wanted To Know About Centipedes.* About 75% of the book is footnotes.

786 Why do centipedes taste like chewing gum?
Because they're wrigglies.

787 What has a hundred legs and goes in one ear and out the other?
A centipede in a cornfield.

Chameleon

788 Did you hear about the lizard that tells jokes and changes colors?
It's a stand-up chameleon.

789 What has two humps and changes colors?
A camel-eon.

790 Why is a chameleon good in the kitchen?
It's a good blender.

791 Did you hear about Benedict Arnold's pet chameleon?
It turned its coat from Colonial blue to British red.

Cheetah

792 Why is it dangerous to play poker in the jungle?
Because of all the cheetahs.

793 Did you hear about the two lions that got into a fight?
It all began when one called the other a cheetah.
(But he was lion.)

794 Why are cheetahs an endangered species?
Because cheetahs never prosper.

Chicken

And now, we proudly present Poultry in Motion, a show in which we hatch chicken jokes by the dozen. Whether you like chicks from a setter, an incubator, or a brooder, you'll cackle till you fall off the roost. You'll get more cluck for the buck in this henhouse than in a coop full of Cornish, White Leghorns, and Rhode Island Reds.

795   Uncle John was in the fertilized-egg business. He had several hundred young layers, called pullets, and eight or ten roosters. The roosters were there for one purpose: to fertilize the eggs.

Uncle John kept records, and any rooster or pullet that didn't perform well went into the pot to be cooked for supper. The unfortunate victims were then replaced by other, more productive candidates. Now, that took all of Uncle John's time, so he bought a set of eight tiny bells, each of which rang a different tone.

He glued a piece of foam rubber to each clapper shaft so the bell wouldn't ring except when violently shaken. He hung a bell on each rooster's neck, which allowed him simply to listen to the different tones of the bells and mark down each encounter. Then, he could sit on the porch and sip a mint julep while filling out efficiency reports.

His favorite rooster was old Brewster. A very fine specimen he was, and yet as Uncle John sat listening, he did not hear Brewster's bell all morning. He went to investigate. Several roosters were chasing pullets, bells a-ringing.

But Brewster had his bell in his beak so it couldn't ring. He'd sneak up on a pullet, do his job, and slip on to the next one. Uncle John was so proud of Brewster that he entered him in the county fair.

Brewster was an overnight sensation. Judges not only awarded him the No Bell Prize but also the Pullet Surprise.

796   Did you hear about the farmer chasing after a chicken?
He was faster than a speeding pullet.

797   What kind of vest do fighting chickens wear?
Pullet-proof.

798   Did you hear about the husband who complained about having chicken dinners too often?
He got tired of biting the pullet.

799 That reminds us of the man whose wife asked him to buy a chicken at the grocery store on the way home from work.
"Do you want a pullet?" asked the butcher.
"No," replied the man. "I'd prefer to carry it."

800 What do you call a hen that gets sunburned in Florida?
Southern fried chicken.

801 Did you hear about the industrious two-hundred-pound chicken that opened a fast-food restaurant in Georgia?
It's called Southern Fried Colonel.

802 What did the hen do when it saw a large order of Kentucky Fried Chicken?
It kicked the bucket.

803 Did you hear about the new cookbook titled *How to Fry Chicken?*
It's by Ken Tucky.

804 What do you call a facelift on a chicken?
Fryer Tuck.

805 Why did the chicken cross the road?
To get away from Colonel Sanders.

806 Why did the chicken cross the road?
The rooster egged her on.

807 Why did the chicken cross the road?
To see a man lay a sidewalk.

808 Why did the chicken take so long to cross the road?
It was a for-layin' highway.

809 Why did the apple farmer's chicken cross the road?
To get to the other cider.

810 If a chicken crosses the road, rolls in the mud, and then crosses back, what is it?
A dirty double-crosser.

811   Why did Charles Dickens's chicken cross the road?
To get to the author's side.

812   Why did Dr. Jekyll's chicken cross the road?
To get to the other Hyde.

813   Why did the chicken go only halfway across the road?
To lay it on the line.

814   Why did the chicken cross Harvard Square?
To get to the Coop.

815   Did you hear about the former airline pilot who bought
a chicken farm and then air-transported everything to a new site?
He flew the coop.

816   Why does a chicken coop have two doors?
Because if it had four it would be a chicken sedan.

817   What do you call a serious blow for chickens?
A coop de grace.

818   Did you hear about the chicken
that ran away from home?
It was tired of being cooped up.

819   That reminds us of the minister who offered to give away some
of his chickens free—because his coop runneth over.

820   What do you call a government
overthrown by timid radicals?
Chicken coop d'etat.

821   What happened when the farmer lost
all his chickens through a hole in his fence?
He had to recoop his losses.

822   Why did the chicken movie fan
cross the road?
To see Gregory Peck.

823   Show us a rooster dressed in a full suit of armor,
and we'll show you an impeccable chicken.

> **824**   What did the little chick say to the big chick?
> *"Peck on someone your own size."*

>> **825**   How can you tell when chickens are in love?
>> *They give each other a peck on the cheek.*

826   What game do baby chickens like to play?
Peck-a-boo. (Which is also the sound a poultrygeist makes!)

> **827**   Why didn't Beethoven like his pet chicken?
> *Because it kept saying, "Bach, Bach, Bach."*

>> **828**   Why did the rooster refuse to cross the road?
>> *To show he wasn't chicken.*

829   A medieval king sentenced one of his counts to be executed for not confessing to a certain crime. Just as the executioner's ax severed the poor chap's head, a confessional message was belatedly handed to the king.
The moral of the story is: Don't hatchet your count before he chickens.

> **830**   Old Kentucky colonels never die. They just chicken out.

>> **831**   Did you hear about the chicken doll?
>> *You wind it up and it turns yellow.*

>>> **832**   What is a frightened skin diver?
>>> *Chicken of the Sea.*

833   Show us a cowardly congressman, and we'll show you chicken of D.C.

> **834**   Identify Chicken Teriyaki.
> *The world's only surviving kamikaze pilot.*

>> **835**   Why did the Roman chicken cross
>> into Switzerland?
>> *She was afraid that someone would Caesar.*

836   Did you hear about the woman who, when she serves chicken,
takes it in on a wing and a prayer?

> **837**   Did you hear about the Revolutionary War patriot
> who trained a chicken to find British loyalists?
> *It was the first example of chicken catch a Tory.*

> > **838**   *Mother:* "My daughter got food poisoning from chicken."
> > *Doctor:* "Croquette?"
> > *Mother:* "Not yet, but she's very sick."

839   Why did the man always order Chicken Napoleon?
So he could pull the bone apart.

> **840**   What is coq au vin?
> *Chicken on a truck.*

> > **841**   What is a rotisserie?
> > *A Ferris wheel for chickens.*

842   The star in *Gone with the Wind* once took the last chicken leg at a meal.
His costar pleaded with him to share it, but he replied,
"Frankly, Scarlett, I don't div a gam."

> **843**   Did you hear about the timid feminist hen?
> *She was a chicken libber.*

> > **844**   As the teacher said to encourage her students,
> > "Make like a chicken and suck seed."

> > > **845**   As the commentator said about the
> > > loudmouthed boxer, "He couldn't lick
> > > his fingers after a chicken dinner."

846   *Customer:* "That chicken I bought here yesterday didn't have a wishbone."
Butcher: "The chickens we sell here are so happy that they have nothing
to wish for."

> **847**   *Customer:* "This chicken is nothing but skin and bones."
> *Waiter:* "Just a minute and I'll get you some feathers."

848 *Customer:* "Is it okay to eat fried chicken with my fingers?"
Waiter: "No, you should eat your fingers separately."

849 *Waiter:* "Would you like a hero sandwich?"
Customer: "No, thanks. I'm the chicken type."

850 *Customer:* "How old was that chicken you served me?"
Waiter: "We don't furnish dates with the chicken—just soup and salad."

851 *Customer:* "It looks like rain."
Waiter: "It sure does. But it's really chicken soup."

852 Did you hear about the Jewish woman who had two chickens as pets?
One chicken got sick, so she killed the other one to make chicken soup
for the sick one.

853 *Customer:* "I've changed my mind. I don't want chicken soup.
I want pea soup."
Waiter (shouting to cook): "Hold the chicken! Make it pea!"

854 *Customer:* "This chicken is as tough as a paving stone."
Waiter: "That's because it's a Plymouth Rock."

855 Did you hear about the Rhode Island farmer
whose chicken laid a square egg?
It was an act of Providence.

856 Did you hear about the chicken that eats grass, leaves, and flowers?
It lays eggplants.

857 What is a chicken's favorite dessert?
Layer cake.

858 The chickens on a farm weren't performing up to their usual standards
of egg laying. When a neighbor's football was accidentally kicked into the
barnyard, the rooster eyed the football for a minute and then said to the hens,
"I'm not complaining. But look at the work they're turning out next door."

859 Did you hear about the chickens that found a stash of torn-up
racing forms and ate them?
The next morning they were laying odds.

860   Why couldn't the chicken find her eggs?
Because she mislaid them.

> **861**   What are the laziest animals on the farm?
> *Chickens—because they are always laying around.*

> **862**   What does an evil chicken lay?
> *Deviled eggs.*

> **863**   What did the Spanish farmer
> say to his chickens?
> *"Olé!"*

> **864**   Why do French chickens lay one
> egg at a time?
> *Because one egg is un oeuf.*

865   What did one little chicken say to another
when it found citrus fruit in their nest?
"Look at the orange Mama laid."

> **866**   Or, as the proud farmer said while boasting about his eggs,
> "Better laid than never."

> **867**   *Farmer:* "These are the best eggs we've had in years."
> *Customer:* "I'd prefer some you haven't had so long."

868   A famous English author once raised chickens. On a certain morning,
his wife sent their daughter out to check on the eggs and hens.
The girl returned and announced, "Some are set, Mom."

869   What drink do you get when you
cross a chicken and a skull?
Egg noggin'.

> **870**   Where do tough chickens come from?
> *Hard-boiled eggs.*

> **871**   Why did the chicken farmer become a schoolteacher?
> *He wanted to grade his eggs.*

872   A woman visited a farm to buy a chicken. When the farmer presented her with one, she asked if he had one a bit larger. Its being his only chicken, the farmer took it into the back room and tried to plump it up. He then returned and showed it to the lady. "That's much better," she said. "I'll take both of them."

873   Have you heard about the new book on farm animals?
It's called Great Eggspectations, *by Charles Chickens.*

874   Or, as the chicken said when she came out of the shell, "What an eggsperience."

875   Where did the chicken go on her vacation?
San Di-egg-o.

876   *Patient:* "Doctor, doctor! My wife thinks she's been a chicken for the past year."
Doctor: "Why didn't you bring her to see me sooner?"
Patient: "We needed the eggs."

877   An employee complained to his boss, "Why do you give me such a poultry paycheck?"
"You mean *paltry*," corrected the boss.
"No," countered the worker. "I mean *poultry*. It's chicken feed."

878   Why didn't the chicken enter the prizefight?
Because she heard that the winner got only a poultry sum.

879   Why is a running chicken a beautiful sight?
Because it's poultry in motion.

880   A chicken in love is poultry emotion.

881   Did you hear about the razor that can shave the fuzz off a baby chick?
It's called Chicken Schick.

882   What did people think when chicken broth was first canned?
Everyone thought it was souper.

883   As Confucius says, "If the chicken had used his noodle,
he wouldn't be in the soup."

884   Speaking of soup reminds us: Why did the chef raise
the egg carton high above his head?
He wanted to make egg drop soup.

885   Where are chickens put on board a ship?
In the hatchway.

886   Why did the chicken sit on the ax?
So she could hatchet.

887   Did you hear about the sick chicken?
It had people pox.

888   Did you hear about the farmer whose ducks and chickens were
mysteriously disappearing from his barn without a trace?
It was the work of a poultryheist.

889   How do chickens start a race?
From scratch.

890   Did you hear about the chickens that danced at the fowl ball?

891   How can you tell whether a chicken is angry?
It's in a fowl mood.

892   Obscene chickens speak fowl language.

893   What is a personal foul?
A chicken you can call your own.

894   Why did the basketball player sit on the
sideline and sketch pictures of chickens?
He was learning how to draw fowls.

895   What Shakespearean character killed the most chickens?
Claudius (in Hamlet) did murder most foul.

896 What did Barbie, the play director, do when the actor playing Chicken Little forgot his lines?
Barbie cued the chicken.

897 Why did the stingy farmer get married in his own barnyard?
So his chickens could have the rice.

898 Or, as the baby chicken said to the miserly farmer, "Cheap, cheap."

899 What did the sign next to the chicken incubator say?
Cheepers by the Dozen.

900 What do baby chickens like to read?
Peeple magazine.

901 What noise does Rice Chickies cereal make?
"Snap, cackle, peep."

902 What do chickens have on their front doors?
Peepholes.

903 On which side does a chicken have the most feathers?
The outside.

904 Did you hear about the hen in a grocery store?
She worked in the chick-out line.

905 How do chickens dance?
Chick to chick.

906 Where are baby chickens born?
In Chick-cago.

907 Did you hear about the romantic movie on young hens?
It was a chick flick.

908   What did the Martian chicken say to the farmer?
"Take me to your feeder."

909   A farmer and his wife were planning their thirtieth
wedding anniversary, and the wife suggested, "Why don't you
go out and kill a chicken?"
    The farmer replied, "Why kill a chicken for what
happened thirty years ago?"

910   *Sign on a chicken farm:* May They Roost in Peace.

911   *Farmer:* "I like to go to bed and wake up with the chickens."
Visitor: "I prefer my own bed."

912   What do you call a chicken boxer?
A bantamweight.

913   How long did the authors work on these chicken puns?
Around the cluck.

Chihuahua

914   What is the funniest kind of dog?
A Chihua-ha.

915   What did the Chihuahua say when the lights went out?
"Yo quiero Taco Bulb."

916   A man was out walking his little dog and decided
that he wanted to eat in a fancy restaurant. So he
put on dark glasses and entered the restaurant
with his dog. The maître d' explained to the man
that he could not enter the place with his dog.
    "I'm blind, and this animal is my seeing-eye dog,"
the man explained.
    "But you're walking with a Chihuahua," explained
the maître d'.
    "A Chihuahua!" exclaimed the man. "They gave
me a Chihuahua?"

Chimpanzee

917   What do you say about a baby primate?
He's a chimp off the old block.

918   Why was Tarzan so hard to get along with?
He had a chimp on his shoulder.

919   What are astronauts noted for?
Taking over when the chimps are down.

920   Did you hear about the foolish monkey?
He was a chumpanzee.

921   What is a monkey's favorite dessert?
Chocolate chimp cookies.

922   What ocean will make you go ape?
The Chimpan-Sea.

Chinchilla

923   If you catch a chinchilla in Chile,
And cut off its beard willy-nilly
With a small razor blade,
You can say that you've made
A Chilean chinchilla's chin chilly.

924   Why do razor users like chinchillas?
Because they cool the razor burn.

925   *Man No. 1:* "I gave my wife a chin-chinchilla coat."
Man No. 2: "Chin-chinchilla coat? Why the double chin?"
Man No. 1: "Because she eats too much."

Chipmunk

926   What do you call a computer expert in the monastery?
A chip monk.

927	What can you say about a true friend to chipmunks?
He's there for the munks when the chips are down.

Chow

928	A woman, showing off her recently purchased pet
to a neighbor, said, "This is my new dog."
The neighbor asked, "A chow?"
And the woman replied, "*Gesundheit.*"

Clam

929	What is stranger than
seeing a shrimp roll?
Seeing a clam bake.

930	What is biased, hates other fish, wears white sheets,
and lives at the bottom of the ocean?
The Ku Klux Clam.

931	Where do shellfish stealers end up?
In small clams court.

932	Who is a home-run hitter in the
shellfish baseball league?
Clammy Sosa.

933	How do shellfish take photos of each other?
With a clamera.

934	What was the closing line of the version of
Gone with the Wind for sea creatures?
"Frankly, Scallop, I don't give a clam."

935	A clever clam named Sam owned a nightclub in San Francisco. He hired
a forgetful harpist, who played so well his first night that he bounced out the
door and began singing as he walked home. When he got to his door, he
looked at his empty hands and changed his tune to "I left my harp in Sam
Clam's disco."

936   What do you call weeping and wailing by mollusks?
Clamentations.

Cobra

937   What is Indian roulette?
You sit down next to a snake charmer with six cobras, one of which is deaf.

Cockatoo

938   Did you hear about the arrogant parrot?
It was a cocky-too.

939   What do you call a dancing parrot's ballet skirt?
A cocka-tutu.

940   What is a cockatoo called after it's two years old?
A cockathree.

941   What bird charms bar patrons for a certain period of time?
Cockatoo till two.

Cockroach

942   Show us an arrogant insect, and we'll show you a cocky roach.

943   How do beetles tell time?
With a clock-roach.

944   Or, as the grasshopper said to the cockroach,
"Bug, you man me!"

945   Did you hear about the cockroach doll?
You wind it up and it runs under the kitchen sink.

946   As one insect said to another, "Why haven't you written?
After all, I roach you a letter."

947   Two cockroaches were chatting, and one asked: "Have you been to
that new restaurant down the street? What a place! The shelves are spotless,
the refrigerator and sink are clean, and—"
"Stop!" interrupted the other roach. "Not while I'm eating!"

948 *Customer:* "Waiter, there's a dead cockroach in my wine."
Waiter: "You asked for something with a little body."

Cod

949 Did you hear about the pregnant mermaid?
She said it was an act of cod.

950 Two cod were swimming in the English Channel when they noticed a huge shadow overhead. "There must be quite a storm up there," one fish cod-gitated.

The other fish corrected him, "That's no storm cloud. That's the Queen Mary 2's bottom."

The first fish replied in amazement, "God save the king!"

951 That reminds us of the Englishman who has a pet cod named Save the King!

952 What is a favorite song of fish?
"Nearer, My Cod, to Thee."

953 *Sign in fish factory:* Many Are Cod, but Few Are Frozen.

954 Did you hear about the new book of seafood recipes?
It's called What Hath Cod Wrought.

955 What lives at the bottom of the ocean
and makes you an offer you can't refuse?
The Codfather.

956 A delivery man announced at a woman's front door, "I have a package of fish for you and it's marked C.O.D."

"Take it back," the lady retorted. "I ordered halibut."

957 How do you fix a fish that squeaks?
Give it some cod liver oil.

958 Did you hear about the fight at the seafood restaurant?
Two cod got battered.

959 What fish wears spurs and a cowboy hat?
Billy the Cod.

960 What is the fiercest fish in the ocean?
Codzilla.

961 What lives in the ocean and goes "dot-dot-dash-dot"?
A Morse cod.

962 *Woman No. 1:* "Do you like codfish balls?"
Woman No. 2: "I don't know. I've never been to any."

963 Two chefs in Boston were competing for the title of finest fish fryer. Their talents were about equal, their dishes equally excellent. However, at the last moment one of the chefs glazed his entry and won the title.
"Alas!" lamented the other. "There but for the glaze of cod go I!"

964 What lives in the ocean and is sent to you in December?
A Christmas cod.

965 As the fisherman said to the magician,
"Go ahead. Pick a cod. Any cod."

966 Or, as the firefighting fisherman said, "Keep those cods and ladders coming!"

Collie

967 What happened when the man put his dog in the bathtub?
He got ring around the collie.

968

Did you hear about the dog that ate a cantaloupe?
He felt rather melon collie.

Conch

969 What do you call a bunch of half-alert shellfish?
Semi-conches.

970 What do you call the ramblings of a gastropod?
Stream of conchesness.

Condor

971 As Confucius says, "A large vulture with sincerity is a condor with candor."

Crab

972 Why does the ocean roar?
*You'd roar, too, if you had
crabs on your bottom.*

973 How much do crabs eat?
Just a pinch.

974 Why was the crab arrested?
He pinched one thing too many.

975 What is a fisherman's favorite fruit?
Crab apples.

976 What sea animal gives people rides?
A taxi crab.

977 *Customer:* "Waiter, do you serve crabs here?"
Waiter: "Yes, sir. We serve everyone."

978 Did you hear about the crab that played the violin?
He was a fiddler on the reef.

979   Then there was the one about a male crab that was observed walking straight instead of sideways.
        A female crab was so impressed with his unique prowess that she immediately accepted his marriage proposal.
        After the honeymoon, she noticed her new husband walking sideways like all the other crabs, and she became upset. "What happened?" she asked. "You used to walk straight before we were married."
        "My dear," he replied, "I can't drink that much every day."

Crane

980   What bird can lift more than any other?
A crane.

981   What bird flies faster than seventy-four miles per hour?
A hurricrane.

982   The trustees of the Madrid Zoo heard that there were only twenty-seven whooping cranes left in the United States, and they determined that they must have one before the breed became extinct. A whooping crane was soon dispatched via air freight. However, when the American bird arrived at Madrid's airport, it refused to debark. Thus the trustees had to return empty-handed to their zoo.
  The moral of this story is that cranes in Spain stick mainly to the plane.

Cricket

983   Who wore a coonskin cap and played a British game?
Davy Cricket.

984   Why don't grasshoppers go to baseball games?
Because they prefer cricket.

985   What is the Jiminy Cricket computer virus?
It changes your zip disk into a zip-a-dee doo-dah disk.

986   Two men were discussing the national sports in various European countries, notably cricket in Great Britain and bullfighting in Spain. When one man indicated that he'd rather play in England, the other fellow asked why.
  "Because," explained the former, "it's easier to fight crickets."

Crocodile

987   The customer said to the waiter, "I'd like some crocodile soup. And make it snappy!"

988   *Boy No. 1:* "I've got a crocodile named Ginger."
Boy No. 2: "Does Ginger bite?"
Boy No. 1: "No, but Ginger snaps."

989 Why did the crocodile want to get rid of his wife?
She'd turned into an old bag.

990 While on a safari in Africa, a man decided to take a refreshing swim in a river. He asked the guide if there were any sharks in the water and was assured that there were none.

The man dived in, surfaced, and shouted again to the guide, "Are you absolutely sure there are no sharks in here?"
"No sharks," came the reply. "Sharks afraid of crocodiles."

991 You will find by the banks of the Nile
The haunts of the great crocodile.
He will welcome you in
With an innocent grin,
Which gives way to a satisfied smile.

992 The prosecutor confronted the criminal crocodile and asked if he killed the man in cold blood.

To which the crocodile replied, "Of course I did it in cold blood. I'm a reptile."

993 What does a crocodilian have in common with a jar of soap?
Each is a crocodile.

994 Two crocodilians were asked to name a favorite song.
The younger one said, "Rock Around the Croc."
The older one said, "Egrets, I've had quite a few."

995 *Patient*: "Doctor, doctor! I keep seeing pink striped crocodiles."
Doctor: "Have you seen a psychiatrist?"
Patient: "No, only pink striped crocodiles."

996 Then there was the man who did go see a psychiatrist and recounted a horrible nightmare. "My mother-in-law was chasing me with a bloodthirsty crocodile on a leash. It was terrifying. I saw the yellow eyes, the dry scaly skin, and the decaying razor-sharp teeth, and I smelled the foul breath."
"Sounds disgusting," agreed the shrink.
"Yes," replied the man, "but wait till I tell you about the crocodile."

997 What reptiles prefer old-fashioned telephones?
Croco-dials.

Crow

998   Why was the crow arrested?
For making crank caws.

999   Why are lawyers like crows?
They like to have their caws heard.

1000   What's a legal term for chewing gum for blackbirds?
Quid pro crow.

1001   Did you hear about the pet crow named Magnon?

1002   Sign in pet store:
Caw Us and We'll Tweet You Right.

1003   Distressed crows complain with caws.

1004   Why did the crow cross the road?
Just be-caws.

1005   What do political crows like doing?
Holding a caw-cuss.

1006   What would grow if you planted an angry crow?
Crow-cusses.

1007   Why is a royal blackbird like a frog?
Because it's crowking.

1008   Just how scary was the super scarecrow?
The crows not only stopped stealing corn; they also returned the corn they stole the week before.

1009   As the mother bird said to her baby, "If you've got to crow, you've got to crow."

1010   Why did the baby blackbird cry?
Because it had crowing pains.

1011   Pointing to the top of a ship's mast on a naval base,
the lady tourist asked a sailor, "What's that way up there?"
      "That's the crow's nest, ma'am," replied the tar.
      "Oh, really?" exclaimed the woman.
"May I just peek at the little darlings?"

1012   *Tourist:* "How far is it to the next town?"
      Native: "Two miles as the crow flies."
      Tourist: "How far is it if the crow has to walk and roll a flat tire?"

1013   What is a crow's
favorite game?
Croquet.

1014   What kind of birds
stick together?
Vel-crows.

1015   What TV anchorman reported the story about
a male cat that damaged a crow's voice box?
Tom Brokecaw.

1016   Did you hear about the veterinarian who performs
autopsies on ravens to determine the caws of death?
He's an end o' crow knowledgist.

1017   What sort of instrument would be used
to measure the age of a black bird?
A crow-nometer.

1018   Did you hear about the crow that liked to sit on
telephone wires and vocalize robustly?
He was making long-distance caws.

1019   What advice did the stockbroker give the dark avian?
Buy! Buy! Blackbird.

1020   If a dark-winged being could pack up all his woe and purchase a
new lease on life, we'd sing, "Good buy by blackbird."

Cuckoo

1021 What do you call a government overthrown by Swiss clockmakers?
Cuckoo d'etat.

1022 What bird works in a kitchen?
A cookoo.

1023 Sign in a repair shop:
Cuckoo Clocks Psychoanalyzed.

1024 What do you call a crazy chicken?
A cuckoo cluck.

1025 Two operatic prima donnas were exchanging insults, during which one said, "You sing like a bird. A cuckoo."

Dachshund

1026 What is taller sitting down than standing up?
A dachshund.

1027 Why are dachshunds mean?
Because they're low-down dogs.

1028 Why did the cowboy buy a dachshund?
Because his favorite song was "Get A Long Little Doggie."

1029 What advice should be given to small canines
that can't find a fire hydrant or a tree?
Get a lawn, little doggie.

1030 What is a mathematician's definition of a dachshund?
Half a dog high by a dog and a half long.

1031 Why is the dachshund a good family dog?
Because all the members of the family can pet it at the same time.

1032 Did you hear about the mascot for the yacht club?
It was a dockshund.

Dalmatian

1033 What is black and white and red all over?
An embarrassed Dalmatian.

1034 Why do Dalmatians have a hard time hiding?
Because they're always spotted.

1035 *Man:* "My Dalmatian has a rash."
Vet: "I'd better do a spot check."

1036 Why did the Dalmatian become an actor?
He wanted to be in the spotlight.

1037 *Boy No. 1:* "Why do you call your dog Spot? He's not a Dalmatian."
Boy No. 2: "Because it's what he does to the carpet."

Deer

1038 Why was the doe playing in the storm?
Because it was a rain-deer.

1039 How does Rudolph know when it's Christmas?
He looks at his calen-deers. (And he eats at the Deery Queen.)

1040 Did you hear about the pet deer named Abby?

> **1041** Why is venison so expensive?
> *Because it's dear.*

>> **1042** *Boy:* "Dad, where is the best place in the whole world to hunt deer?"
>> *Boy's father:* "In Venice, son."

>>> **1043** What is some good stock market advice for animals?
>>> *Buy sheep and sell deer.*

1044 What made the doe so athletic?
She had to run for her deer life.

> **1045** Where can you see deer born?
> *In Michigan.*

>> **1046** What do you call a deer with no eyes?
>> *No idea.*

>>> **1047** What do you call a deer with no eyes and no legs?
>>> *Still no idea.*

1048 What do you call a deer with no eyes, no legs, and a hole in his sock?
Still no darn idea.

> **1049** Why shouldn't a hunter shoot a deer that has an infection in one eye?
> *Because it's a bad eye deer.*

>> **1050** What do you call a deer that can kick a ball with his left and right feet?
>> *Bambidextrous.*

>>> **1051** Why wouldn't the mother take her kids to see Bambi?
>>> *Because she thought it was a stag movie.*

1052 What did Bambi get when his girlfriend
ran off with another buck?
A Deer John letter.

1053 (That reminds us of the guy whose wife ran off with a tractor
salesman. He didn't find out until he received a John Deere letter.)

1054 Did you hear about the deer that was
almost shot by an archer?
It had an arrow escape.

1055 A deer hunter needs good hindsight.

1056 *One husband to another:* "I don't think my wife loves me anymore. She
bought me a deerskin coat to wear when I go hunting."

1057 Then there was the experienced hunter who, to protect himself from
novices, wore a coat with glaring stripes of black and white. Unfortunately, he
was wounded by a novice, who was questioned by the police. "With all those
stripes," asked an officer, "how could you possibly mistake that hapless hunter
for a deer?"
    "I didn't," replied the novice. "I mistook him for a zebra."

1058 If a female deer has antlers, does a male deer have unclers?

1059 Did you hear about the movie that explores the mystery
of a caribou burial ground?
It's called Deers of Interment.

1060 Hunters are always saddened by "the deer departed."

1061 Did you hear about the distraught Texan down home on the range?
He discovered his dear and the interloper playing.

Dinosaur

1062 What did the cavewoman say to her husband while
they were surrounded by a herd of dinosaurs?
"Don't just stand there. Slay something."

1063 How many people assist an archeologist in
digging up dinosaur bones?
Not many. He works with a skeleton crew.

1064 What did one dinosaur say to another after seeing a xylophone?
"She's cute. But she's all skin and bones."

1065 Dinosaur remains become a colossal fossil.

1066 A coprolite (fossil feces) was recently discovered which was 17 inches
long by 5 inches wide, 65,000,000 years old, and had chopped-up dinosaur
bone in it. Paleontologists announced that it was probably from
a Tyrannosaurus Rex. They determined it was from a T. Rex by a process
of elimination.

1067 How do we know that dinosaurs raced?
Because archeologists found dinosaur tracks.

1068 What do you call a dinosaur that limps?
A stagger-saurus.

1069 What famous dinosaur always said
the same thing in many different ways?
Roget, the Saurus.

1070 What dinosaur likes walking in mud?
The brown-toe-saurus.

1071 What kind of dinosaurs did prehistoric cowboys ride in rodeos?
A bucking bronco-saurus.

1072 What dinosaur was named after the wounds
of Victorian-era female sibling authors?
Bronte-sores.

1073 Where did prehistoric animals go on vacation?
To the dino-shore. (And they shopped in dino-stores.)

1074 That reminds us of the sleeping prehistoric animal:
It was a dino-snore. (Or a bronto-snoreus.)

1075 Who is the head of a college for prehistoric animals?
The dean-osaur.

1076 How would you move a thousand-ton dinosaur?
With dino-mite.

1077 What did stone-age men call the dinosaur from which they were hiding?
D'you-think-he-saurus.

1078 Did you hear about the prehistoric animal that exercised too much?
It was a dino-sore.

1079 Did you hear about the researcher who discovered a cure for a virus that is found in restaurants and causes tiny sores?
He was commended for his role in the extinction of the diner sores.

1080 How did the student dinosaur pass his exams?
With extinction.

1081 There once was a Tyrannosaurus
Who lived when the earth was all porous.
But it fainted with shame
When it first heard its name,
And departed the earth long before us.

1082 What do you call a dinosaur that loves his mother?
Oedipus Rex.

1083 What do you call an anxious dinosaur?
A nervous rex.

1084 What were ship disasters at sea called in prehistoric days?
Tyrannosaurus wrecks.

1085 What dinosaurs ate burritos and enchiladas?
Tyrannosaurus Mex.

1086 What is a brontosaurus?
A salamander designed to military specifications.

1087 Why did some dinosaurs opt to live on land and others in the water?
It was either slink or swim.

Doe

1088 What kind of deer is transparent?
A win-doe.

1089 What do you call a deer that howls at a full moon?
A weirdoe.

1090 What is a favorite food of deer?
Doe-nuts.

1091 What happens when two deer meet at a square dance?
Doe-see-doe.

1092 How do you take a deer census?
By going doe to doe.

1093 How did the doe win the race?
By passing the buck.

1094 Two elderly deer were chatting in the woods, and one observed, "Look at that deer making a fool of herself for two bucks."
"Yes," sighed the other, "I could use a little doe myself."

Dog

We hope we don't sound doggone dogmatic when we say, "Hot dog! It's time that you make these pages dog-eared. To err is human; to make dog puns, canine." (Or, to err is human; two curs, canine.)

1095 Show us a dog whose bark is worse than his bite, and we'll show you a dog with dentures.

1096 That reminds us of the orthodontist's dog.
His bark was worse than his overbite.

> **1097** Then there was the man who fed his dog garlic.
> *Now, his bark is definitely worse than his bite.*

>> **1098** Did you hear about the dog with a minor case of mange?
>> *His bark is worse than his blight.*

1099 Incidentally, a computer made out of a tree has a bark much worse than its byte.

> **1100** A man ran up to his neighbor and said, "I thought you told me your dog's bark is worse than his bite."
> "That's correct," replied the neighbor.
> "Then for heaven's sake," grimaced the man, "don't let him bark at me."

>> **1101** As Confucius says, "A barking dog never bites— while he's barking."

>>> **1102** Why should you never buy a watchdog that's on sale?
>>> *Because a bargain dog never bites.*

1103 What happened when the cross-eyed dog chased a squirrel in the woods?
It barked up the wrong tree.

> **1104** How can you distinguish a dogwood tree from the others?
> *By its bark.*

>> **1105** Why is a dog's tail like the inside of a tree?
>> *Because it's farthest from the bark.*

>>> **1106** What's the best way to keep a dog off the street?
>>> *Put it in a barking lot.*

1107 Why was the dog summoned to appear in court?
Because it got a barking ticket.

1108   That reminds us of the sign above a veterinarian's office: Apartment for Rent. Indoor Barking. Long Leash.

1109   As Confucius says, "Man begins to bark at others when he realizes he is going to the dogs."

1110   A sportsman had a successful weekend at a hunting lodge, thanks to a bird dog named Salesman. When he returned the following year, the hunter asked for the same dog. He was informed that the dog was no good anymore. It seems that some other hunter called the dog Sales Manager for a week, and now all the dog does is sit on his tail and bark.

1111   A French poodle met a visiting Russian wolfhound in Paris and asked how things were in Russia. "Everything's absolutely wonderful," the Russian replied.

"Then why did you come to France if things are so wonderful?" asked the petite Parisian poodle.

The Russian wolfhound replied, "Sometimes I like to bark."

1112   Did you hear about the dog that graduated from obedience school?
He received a barkalaureate degree.

1113   What's a dog's favorite breakfast?
Woofles.

1114   Where are homeless dogs sent?
To an arf-anage.

1115   Did you hear about the prize-winning dog?
It was a show-arf.

1116   When do an old dog's bones ache?
When he has arf-ritis.

1117   What organization do old, retired dogs join?
AARF.

1118   Who was a famous dog general?
Dogless MacArffur.

1119 *Man:* "Please call your dog off."
Boy: "But I always call him Rover."

1120 Did you hear about the dogcatcher with a wooden leg?
He didn't have to catch the dogs. They went to him.

1121 Did you hear about the dumb guy
who was elected dogcatcher?
He knew he was supposed to catch dogs—but at what?

1122 The city councilor told the mayor, "I've got some good news and
some bad news. The good news is that you won the election. The bad
news is that you're the new dogcatcher."

1123 *Mom:* "Has anyone seen the dog bowl?"
Son: "No, but I've seen him make some good catches."

1124 Did you hear about the baseball dog?
*He wears a muzzle, catches flies, chases fowls,
and beats it for home.*

1125 A father listened to his young daughter scratch away on her violin
as the family dog howled. In desperation, he finally asked, "Can't you play
something the dog doesn't know?"

1126 Did you hear about the two dogs that went out on a date?
They had a howling good time.

1127 Did you hear about the dog whose tail was
cut off in a meat grinder?
The owner had to wholesale it, since he couldn't retail it.

1128 Every dog must have its day. But
a dog with a broken tail has a weak end.

1129 How is a good manager like a dog pointing?
They both exhibit attention to detail.

1130 Why is a dog biting its own tail like a good manager?
Because he makes both ends meet.

1131 Did you hear about the wit who complained that he was always being told one of his own stories?
It was a plain case of the tale dogging the wag.

1132 "Which dog would you like?" the pet store owner asked the boy. Seeing a puppy with a wagging tail, the young customer replied, "I'd like the one with the happy ending."

1133 What do you call dogs migrating in the Old West?
A waggin' train.

1134 An ordinance was proposed to prohibit all dogs in the community from expressing affection or pleasure in a certain way. Surprisingly, it passed unanimously without any debate. You might say that the members of the town council were just jumping on the banned waggin'.

1135 Did you hear about the movie star who was given a dog as a gift?
It was an example of hitching a waggin' to a star.

1136 A hot dog feeds the hand that bites it.

1137 *Man No. 1:* "I took my dog to the vet because it bit my mother-in-law."
Man No. 2: "Did you have it put to sleep?"
Man No. 1: "No," replied the former, "I had its teeth sharpened."

1138 *Man No. 1:* "I had to take my dog to the vet to get a rabies shot."
Man No. 2: "Was it mad?"
Man No. 1: "It sure wasn't happy about it."

1139 What do mad dogs like to do on vacation?
Go rafting down a river on whitewater rabids.

1140 A rabid dog bit an elderly gent, who was told to make out a will just in case he developed rabies. After watching his client write for an hour, the lawyer asked, "Why are you making such a long will?"
The grouchy old man replied, "I haven't started the will yet. This is a list of the people I intend to bite."

1141   Did you hear about the dog named Photographer?
He was always snapping at people.

1142   *Patient:* "Doctor, doctor! A dog bit my leg."
Doctor: "Did you put anything on it?"
Patient: "No, he liked it just the way it was."

1143   A man refused to visit his friend's home again after being bitten by
their huge dog. The man eventually agreed to visit, being reassured that the
dog had died. When he arrived at the friend's home, however, a huge dog bit
him on the leg.
"I thought you told me your dog died!" he exclaimed.
"That one did die," replied the owner. "This one is the heir of the
dog that bit you."

1144   That reminds us of the man we once knew who
was as nervous as a letter carrier at a dog show.

1145   Did you hear about the playboy whose car always
seems to run out of gas during dates in the summer?
*In the winter, he takes girls for dog sled rides and runs
out of dog food.*

1146   That reminds us of the guy who said, "I've got some good news and
some bad news. The good news is that a gorgeous girl invited me for dinner
and asked me to pick up some dog food on the way over. The bad news is
that she doesn't have a dog."

1147   Speaking of good news and bad news,
a Hollywood agent told a writer, "The good news is that
Paramount just loved your novel and ate it up. The bad
news is that Paramount is my dog."

1148   What did the author do when he caught his
dog chewing up the notes for his new novel?
He took the words right out of his mouth.

1149   *Owner:* "Don't worry. This dog will eat off your hand."
Guest: "That's what I'm afraid of."

1150 What happened to the dog when he ate table scraps?
He got splinters in his tongue.

1151 There was a young man from Bengal
Who was invited to a costume ball.
He said he would risk it
And went as a biscuit;
But a dog ate him crust and all.

1152 Why did the dog keep barking after it was fed?
He wanted a second yelping.

1153 That reminds us of the defenseless puppy. He felt totally yelpless.

1154 Did you hear the one about the man who took his dog
an Italian dish made with flour, tomatoes, and cheese?
*The man propped it against the dog's food bowl and then
called it the "leaning pizza of Towser."*

1155 Or, as the owner said to his dog after giving him a
special treat, "Bone appétit."

1156 Why did the dog go aboard Star Trek's spaceship?
Because he heard that it had Bones on board.

1157 Why did the man call his dog Russian Winter?
Because the dog knew how to take a Bonaparte.

1158 Did you hear about the two arguing dogs
that had a bone of contention?

1159 Did you hear about the company that
once a year threw its dogs a bonus?

1160 Why did the dog go to the vet?
He wanted to get a new leash on life.

1161 That reminds us of the dog that was
allowed to run free.
His leash expired.

1162 Where do you buy metal leashes for dogs?
In a chain store.

1163 Did you hear about the new Oriental cookbook?
It's called 101 Ways to Wok Your Dog.

1164 *Doctor:* "Walking your dog is good for weight loss."
Patient: "Yes, but who wants a skinny dog?"

1165 *Man No 1:* "My dog and I go for a tramp in the woods every day."
Man No. 2: "Does your dog enjoy it?"
Man No. 1: "Of course. But the tramp is getting a bit fed up."

1166 Did you hear about the dog that chased cars?
He ended up exhausted.

1167 What gave the dog a flat nose?
Chasing parked cars.

1168 How can you tell whether a dog has a sweet tooth?
He chases only bakery trucks.

1169 What did one woman say to another when she saw her elderly husband flirting with the younger women at a party?
"He's like a dog chasing cars. He wouldn't know what to do if he caught one."

1170 Why did the man name his dog Timex?
Because it's a watchdog.

1171 *Patient:* "Doctor, doctor! My dog has ticks."
Doctor: "Well, don't over-wind him."

1172 Why did the dog keep running around in circles?
He was a watchdog, winding himself up.

1173 *Boy No. 1:* "Is your new pet a watchdog?"
Boy No. 2: "Yes, he watches TV."

1174 What does a dog use for playing golf?
A kennel club.

1175 Speaking of kennels reminds us of the guy who was looking for a place to board his dog while he went on vacation. He found one kennel that offered air-conditioning, gourmet food, and lots of affection. He was so impressed that he sent his dog on vacation, and he stayed at the kennel.

1176 Did you hear about the new play about Pavlov's experiments with dogs?
It's called *Bell, Bark, and Kennel.*

1177 What made the dogcatcher wealthy?
He was paid by the pound.

1178 What is unique about a canine scale?
It weighs only in dog pounds.

1179 What's the favorite song at animal shelters?
You Ain't Nothin' but a Pound Dog.

1180 That reminds us of the song that is reminiscent of a boy using his lunch money to buy a mutt named Elvis.
He Ate Nothin'; Bought a Hound Dog.

1181 What do you call a fox being chased by dogs?
Hounded.

1182 Speaking of hounds reminds us of the German who bought some former clothing mills and converted them into dog kennels. This prompted a local musician to write a song that began, "The mills are alive with the hounds of Munich."

1183 Did you hear about the Conservative member of the British Parliament who took everyone involved in a court case on a fox hunt?
Unfortunately, the car broke down, and a tow truck was needed. The imbecilic driver had difficulties but, at last, towed the car, which still contained the Conservative MP, his dogs, and the courtroom personnel. It was a Tory, towed by an idiot, full of hounds and jury, dignifying nothing.

1184 An elegant frankfurter is a haute dog.

1185 What's the opposite of a cool cat?
A hot dog.

1187 *Customer:* "Does that dog have a good pedigree?"
Store owner: "If he could talk, he wouldn't speak to us."

1188 Why does a thoroughbred dog get hotter in the summer than a mongrel?
Because the thoroughbred dog has more pedigrees.

1189 What kind of dog biscuit is popular around Christmas?
A muttcracker's sweet.

1186 What do you call a cold canine?
A chili dog.

1190 Who is a dog's best friend?
His mutter.

1191 A cranky old man died and bequeathed his dog to a neighbor. The dog, however, was even more foul-tempered than his late owner. This is an example of the cur being worse than the deceased.

1192 Why is a tin can tied to a dog's tail like an accident waiting to happen?
Because it's something bound to a cur.

1193 *Poodle:* "My name is Fifi. What's your name?"
Mongrel: "Phydeaux."

1194 What did the veterinarian have on his vanity license plate?
K-9.

1195 How do you call a police dog?
By dialing K-911.

1196 Why was the dog operated on by the veterinarian?
Because a stitch in time saves canine.

1197   A dog was being treated by a veterinarian for a skin irritation and somehow managed to escape from the doctor's grip and run outside into the parking lot. As the vet was walking around the cars, the parking lot attendant sauntered over. The doc said, "I'm looking for an itchy poochie."

The attendant replied, "I can never tell one foreign car from another."

1198   What trousers have no pockets?
A dog's pants.

1199   A dog's tongue is the seat of its pants.

1200   What does a young boy in summer have in common with a tired dog?
They both have short pants.

1201   Why does a dog get so hot in the summer?
Because he wears a coat and pants.

1202   As one dog said to another, "The pest things in life are flea."

1203   A dog opened his computer and got this message: "You've got flea-mail."

1204   Why is a dog cheaper than a wife?
The license costs less, and it already has a fur coat.

1205   Or, from an opposing vantage point: A wife complained so much that her husband said, "You'd think I treat you like a dog."

"No," replied the woman, "a dog has a fur coat."

1206   Did you hear about the TV evangelist who taught his dog to heal?

1207   Why did the doctor name his dog Physician?
So he could command the dog, "Physician, heel thyself."

1208   *Mom:* "Why is our puppy like a positive creed, Pa?"
Dad: "Because he's a dog, Ma."

1209   Did you hear about the guy who's leading a dog's life?
Creditors are dogging his footsteps.

1210   Or, as the lost puppy said, "Well, I'll be doggone."

1211   An untalented writer persisted in sending his manuscripts to a publisher. The publisher eventually wrote the man, "Please curb your doggerel."

1212   Why did the financial planner name her dog Broker?
Because it did all its business on the street.

1213   In theory, housebreaking your dog may seem like a fine idea, but it doesn't look good on paper.

1214   What do you say to a bad puppy at Christmas?
"Felix naughty dog."

1215   Did you hear about the city in Alaska that expelled every puppy?
It's now called Dogless Fairbanks.

1216   Did you hear about the vet whose books had dog-eared pages?

1217   When Daniel Boone gave up pioneering and became a congressman, he insisted on taking his hunting dog with him into government buildings.
The special dispensation granted him resulted in the term "government boondoggling."

1218   What is the famous dog star called?
Rin Tin Tin.

1219   As a couple was gazing into the sky one night, the wife observed, "There's the dog star."
Replied her husband, "Are you Sirius?"

1220   Two guys were talking about a dog with no nose.
"How does he smell?" asked one.
The other replied, "Awful."

1221   Why wouldn't the dog go into a yard?
Because it had four feet.

1222 What are most of a dog's mistakes caused by?
Its faux pas.

1223 Did you hear about the dog detective
who took prints of all his suspects?
He was an artist with paw traits.

1224 What do dogs do when they see a VCR?
They push the pause button.

1225 What has forty feet and says
"Beware of the dog"?
A picket fence with a sign on it.

1226 That reminds us of the sign in front of a house with a dog.
It read: "Electric Company Man: Beware of Meter Reader Eater."

1227 How is a cowardly dog like a leaky faucet?
They both run.

1228 Why did Fido need a psychiatrist?
He'd lost all desire to fetch.

1229 Did you hear about the dog that was a
cross between a Labrador retriever and a
golden retriever?
It was quite a fetching combination.

1230 And did you hear the story about the dog that ran three miles after a stick?
Okay, we admit that it's too far-fetched.

1231 What did the dog say to the policeman after being apprehended
for giving birth to puppies on the roadside?
"But, Officer, the sign reads Fine for Littering."

1232 What happened after the dog swallowed a spoon?
Nothing. He was unable to stir.

1233 Why is the dog named Locksmith?
Whenever you throw anything at him, he makes a bolt for the door.

1234   *Mom:* "Oh, no! The dog's on the sofa again."
Dad: "Quick, get the Spot remover!"

1235   Did you hear about the dry-cleaning store owner
who refused to name his dog Spot?

1236   Do you remember the children's book about
Dick, Jane, and Spot?
*Spot was a dog, and Jane was nothing to brag
about either.*

1237   Did you hear about the house that was Spotless because the dog died?

1238   Two guys were talking, and one said, "My dog died,
but I can't understand it. He was the picture of health."
The other replied, "You must've been looking at the negative."

1239   A man went to a minister and asked to have a funeral for a dog.
The clergyman said that dogs don't have souls; therefore, he wouldn't
perform the ceremony.
The man replied, "Can you recommend a church that would perform
a funeral for the dog? The owner left ten thousand dollars in his will just for
that purpose."
The preacher quickly responded, "Why didn't you tell me that old
Fido was a Baptist?"

1240   What are ministers called at churches for dogs in Berlin?
German shepherds.

1241   Did you hear about the dog that accidentally
drank a gallon of kerosene and then ran around
in circles until he collapsed?
He didn't die. He ran out of gas.

1242   An insurance salesman was trying to convince a woman to take
out a life insurance policy on her husband. "Suppose your husband died,"
he argued. "What would you get?"
She replied, "Probably a collie. They always make good company."

1243   What did the dog take when he was run down?
The license number of the car that hit him.

1244 What do you call a mutt that's
been run over by a truck?
Dog tired.

1245   Did you hear about the nearsighted man who was knocked
off the curb by a large dog?
          As he was getting up, a subcompact car hit him and sent him
sprawling. A concerned citizen rushed over and asked if he was hurt.
"The dog didn't hurt me at all," replied the myopic man. "But that tin
can tied to his tail nearly finished me off."

1246 Two guys were talking, and one commented,
"I got a cute dog for my sister."
"Where," asked the other, "did you make
a great trade like that?"

1247   "What would you say," asked the Eskimo man on a date, "if I told you
that I pushed my dog team for a week through a blizzard just to tell you that
I love you?"
          "I'd say," replied the lady, "that was a lot of mush."

1248 When do Eskimo workers travel by dogsled?
During mush hour.

1249 "Are these dogs Alaskan?" he asked huskily.
"Oh, yes," she replied mushily.

1250 Did you hear about the Eskimo who was arrested for bigamy?
When the judge heard that the man had wives in Juneau, Fairbanks,
and Nome, he asked, "How could you do such a thing?"
          The man replied, "Fast dog team."

1251   Two guys were duck hunting with their dogs, but they
weren't having any success. One of them finally blurted out,
"I know what we're doing wrong. We're not throwing
the dogs high enough."

1252 Why won't England relax regulations on the
quarantine of dogs entering the country?
Because Britannia will not waive the rules.

1253 *Patient:* "Doctor, doctor! I feel like a dog."
Doctor: "Sit!"

1254 *Patient:* "Doctor, doctor! I think I'm a dog."
Doctor: "Lie down on the couch."
Patient: "I'm not allowed on the furniture."

1255 Did you hear about the talking dogs?
They were having a bow-wow powwow.

1256 What did the dark horse candidate do when his momentum went to the dogs?
He decided to bow-wowt of the race.

1257 What is a dog's favorite color?
Grrrreen.

1258 A woman held a bone over her dog's head and shouted, "Speak! Speak!" The dog replied, "I hardly know what to say."

1259 Did you hear about the dog that talks in his sleep?
He's not content, however, merely to talk. He persists in telling fibs and untruths. His owner says, "I just let sleeping dogs lie."

1260 That reminds us of the domesticated Great Dane that got fired from his job as a janitor because he claimed he had swept a floor when he hadn't.
The owners wouldn't let a sweeping dog lie.

1261 A dog acrobat, precariously balanced in the middle of a high-wire act, couldn't shake one nagging thought: He was old, and this was a new trick.

1262 A man and his two dogs went to a Hollywood talent agency for an audition. The first dog started telling jokes, but he was interrupted by the excited agent, who exclaimed, "That dog is amazing!"
The owner replied, "That dog is nothing. The other dog is a ventriloquist."

1263　　　Another man and a dog went to a talent scout. "What's the opposite of smooth?" asked the owner, and the dog said, "Rough." The agent saw right through the sham and said, "That's an old trick. The dog's just barking."

　　　The owner replied, "No, he can really talk. Fido, what's on top of a house?"

　　　And the dog said, "Roof."

　　　"Get out!" shouted the agent.

　　　"No, wait," pleaded the owner. "He really does talk. Fido, who was the greatest baseball player of all time?"

　　　The dog said, "Ruth."

　　　The agent was furious and threw both man and dog out of his office. As they were leaving the building, the dog turned to his owner and asked, "Should I have said DiMaggio?"

1264　　　A couple went to a movie and noticed a man and his dog watching the film together. They were especially amazed when they saw the dog laughing during the funny parts. After the movie ended, the couple approached the unlikely pair.

　　　The husband said, "I'm absolutely astonished. It seems as if your dog actually enjoyed the movie."

　　　"I was a bit surprised myself," replied the dog's owner, "because he didn't like the book."

1265　Did you hear about the man who lost his dog
　　　but wouldn't put an ad in the paper?
　　　He said it would be of no use because his dog couldn't read.

1266　　　Two guys were talking, and one of them
　　　said, "Your dog must be very smart if he can play
　　　the trumpet."
　　　　　"Not really," was the reply. "He can't read music."

1267　One neighbor complained to another,
　　　"Your dog keeps chasing me on a bicycle."
　　　"That's not true," came the reply. "My dog can't ride a bicycle."

1268　Did you hear about the dog who was trained to beg?
　　　Last week he came back with five hundred dollars.

1269　What did Elvis teach his dog?
　　　To rock 'n' roll over.

1270 *Patient:* "This hospital is terrible. They treat us like dogs."
Doctor: "You know that's not true. Now, roll over."

1271 What do you call an operation that is a cure
for dogs that won't stop barking?
A yappin'-dectomy.

1272 That reminds us of the vet who
was so sick of treating dogs that
he threw a distemper tantrum.

1273 Did you hear about the dog that
barked only at ministers?
He was a cross-breed.

1274 In the original shaggy dog
story, a woman placed an ad in
a newspaper, offering a reward
for the return of her very shaggy
dog. In an alley, a man found the
shaggiest dog he had ever seen,
so he picked it up and went to the
woman's home. When she opened
the door, the man held up the
pooch and asked, "Is this your lost
shaggy dog?"

"No," she exclaimed, "it
wasn't that shaggy!"

1275 What do you get when you add up all the dogs that went to Oz?
The grand Toto.

1276 During a raging storm in the Dark Ages, a knight got
off his weary horse at a stable and asked the owner if he could
borrow a replacement. When he was informed that there were
no more horses available, the knight gallantly stated, "In that
case, I will ride that huge dog sitting over there in the corner."

"Oh, no," countered the owner. "I wouldn't send a knight
out on a dog like this."

1277 With the high cost of living, you have to work like
a dog to live like a dog.

1278 Why do many pets prefer to stay at home?
Because it's a dog-eat-dog world out there.

1279 Why did the police dog like to stay at home in bed?
He was an undercover agent.

1280 An imposing structure for a dog is an edifice Rex.

1281 What did Sophocles ask his suspiciously fat dog?
"Et a puss, Rex?"

1282 What is a puppy's favorite game?
Dog tag.

1283 *Epitaph in a dog cemetery:*
"He never met a man he didn't lick."

1284 Why does the dog walk around in two circles before lying down?
Because one good turn deserves another.

1285 Did you hear about the boss who
treats his secretary like a dog?
Like a lap dog.

1286 What is the similarity between two fighting dogs
and a man who puts his socks on inside out?
You have to turn the hose on each of them.

1287 What is a dog's favorite classical composer?
Poochini.

1288 How are bathrooms labeled at dog shows?
Pointers and Setters.

1289 A man was fidgeting in a train station during Prohibition, trying to hide from the crowd. A federal agent noticed something in the man's pocket from which drops of fluid were falling. The fed held his hand under the drops and tasted it.
"Scotch?" he asked with a gleam in his eye.
"No," replied the man. "Airedale pup."

1290 *Sign on a front lawn:* Everyone on the Premises Is a Vegetarian Except the Dog.

> **1291** A man had dogs named Rover, Fido, and Liberace.
> Rover was the largest, Fido was medium-sized, and Liberace
> was the peeinest.

> **1292** That reminds us of the lazy dog. Whenever his
> owner waters the garden, the dog never lifts a leg to help.

> **1293** Did you hear about the guy who bought a cheap
> toupee made out of dog hair?
> *Every time he passes a fire hydrant, one end of it lifts up.*

1294 Or, as the dog said when he lifted his leg in a bar,
"Let's have one on the house."

> **1295** What does a dog do that a person steps in?
> *Pants.*

> **1296** What is it that men do standing up, women do sitting
> down, and dogs do on three legs?
> *Shake hands.*

> **1297** *Texan:* "We have the fastest-running dogs in the country."
> *Tourist:* "That's because the trees are so far apart."

1298 Did you hear about the family that visited the giant
redwood trees on their California vacation?
It didn't particularly excite the kids, but it gave the dog a heart attack.

> **1299** Why did the adventurer name his dog Arctic Explorer?
> *Because it went from pole to pole.*

1300 That reminds us of the army dog that requested a transfer to a new post.

1301 A man from the country was visiting a friend in the city and told him,
"My town is so small that the fire department consists of a hose cart
and four dogs."
> "What do the dogs do, pull the cart?" asked the friend.
> "No," replied the visitor, "they find the hydrant."

Donkey

1302 Why can't donkeys be used to steer a ship?
Because all they do is helm and haw.

1303 Donkey meat is a feast of burden.

1304 Did you hear about the German fellow
who named his pet donkey Shane?

1305 As Confucius says, "If one man calls you a donkey, ignore him.
If more than one man calls you a donkey, get a saddle."

1306 What keys won't open doors?
Donkeys. (Monkeys and turkeys won't either.)

1307 What happens if you tickle a donkey?
You get a big kick out of it.

1308 A man named Mills told his neighbor about his burro, named Hotey,
that was so frail the gentlest of breezes would have him leaning.
The neighbor replied, "So would you say that's a case of donkey Hotey
tilting at wind, Mills?"

Dove

1309 When was paper money first mentioned in the Bible?
When the dove took green back to Noah.

1310 Why didn't the last dove return to the ark?
It had sufficient grounds to stay away.

1311 What has a shell and flies?
A turtledove.

Dragon

1312 How do dragons vent their frustrations?
They let off steam.

1313 So what's the best way to calm a fire-breathing dragon?
Throw water on it.

1314 Speaking of fire-breathing dragons reminds us of the brave knight who carefully planned how he would kill the beast and then marry the king's daughter. Unfortunately, when he confronted the dragon, all his plans went up in smoke—and he smote no more.

1315 Why did the mother dragon complain about her twins?
She couldn't extinguish them apart.

1316 A dragon came home from work and asked, "Am I late for dinner?" "Yes," was the reply. "Everyone's eaten."

1317 Why do dragons sleep during the day?
So they can hunt knights.

1318 Why don't baby dragons like knights?
They can't stand canned food.

1319 Or, as the exasperated dragon sighed, "Mother said there would be knights like this."

1320 Why didn't the cowardly dragon observe the Sabbath?
He only preyed on weak knights.

1321 Did you hear about the sorcerer who changed a man's donkey into a dragon?
Now the man's ass is dragon.

1322 (That reminds us of another one we can drag in. It's about the chap who felt like a snapdragon.
No snap and everything draggin'.)

Dragonfly

1323 Have you heard about the alcoholic dragonfly?
He always drank his flagon dry.

1324 If you ever see a dragonfly, get out of sight.

Duck

1325 As an introducktion, why did the man use a
duck as an alarm clock?
So it would wake him up at the quack of dawn.

1326 What bird is useful in boxing matches?
Duck.

1327 What do you call a mallard that plays basketball?
A slam duck.

1328 What indicated that the duck was smart?
It always made wise quacks.

1329 A smart duck is a wise quacker.

1330 *Waiter:* "How is your duck dinner, sir?"
Patron: "It isn't all it was quacked up to be."

1331 What are a duck's favorite hors d'oeuvres?
Cheese and quackers.

1332 Did you hear about the new
cookbook titled *Duck Recipes?*
It's by Betty Quacker.

1333 As Confucius says, "Duck that fly upside down have quack up."

1334 What do you call an unemployed duck?
A fired quacker.

1335 A duck on the farm was a slacker,
The farmer knew he had to sack 'er.
      The duck she did sob
      About losing her job,
But on July 4th was a fired quacker.

1336 What has webbed feet and fangs?
Count Quackula.

1338 What do ducks enjoy for breakfast?
Quacker Oats.

1339 What do ducks use in their car engines?
Quacker State Motor Oil.

1340 *Patient:* "Doctor, doctor! I feel like a duckdoo."
Doctor: "What's a duckdoo?"
Patient: "It goes, 'quack, quack.'"

1341 You can call a doctor a quack, but you can't duck the bill.

1342 A job hunter received a call from an employment agency: "We've got some good news and some bad news. The good news is that we've found a job for you that fills the bill. The bad news is that it's feeding ducks at a petting zoo."

1337 What is a duck's favorite ballet?
The Nutquacker.

1343 Why are duck actors so annoying?
Because they always want top billing.

1344 Haiku on ducks:
Noah's ark had a till,
So the frog took a green back;
The duck took a bill.

1345 *Visitor:* "How's your duck farm doing? Business picking up?"
Farmer: "No, picking down."

1346 *Visitor:* "Has the price of feathers increased?"
Farmer: "Yes. Now even down is up."

1347 *Patron:* "Waiter, this soup is weak."
Waiter: "But it's our best duck soup."
Patron: "No, it's watered down."

1348 Why do ducks often look so sad?
Because when they preen their feathers, they get down in the mouth.

1349 What do young ducks wear?
Hand-me-downs.

1350 Did you hear about the biologist who knew so much about ducks that he tended to talk down to people?

1351 Why did the man go canoeing on the Swanee River with a set of scales?
So that when a duck went by, he could weigh down on the Swanee River.

1352 That reminds us of the Hindu religious leader who got sick after eating raw duck mixed with cheese curds. The doctor found whey down upon the swami's liver.

1353 A man asked a butcher for a large duck.
"I'm sorry," apologized the butcher, "but we have no ducks today. How about a nice leg of lamb?"
"Don't be daft," grumbled the customer.
"How can I tell my wife I shot a leg of lamb?"

1354 A sportsman returned from a hunting vacation in England and was recounting his experiences to a friend. "I went duck hunting with a duke, and the next day we had a lovely duke dinner."
"You mean duck dinner," corrected his friend.
"No," replied the hunter. "Duke dinner. The duke forgot to duck."

1355 Did you hear about the excited tourist in England who said he saw the home of a duck and doochess?

1356 Who's the most famous duck explorer?
Sir Francis Drake.

1357 And who's the most famous duck president?
Mallard Fillmore.

1358 Who stole the soap from the bathroom?
The robber duckie.

1359   Have you heard of the Canard Lines?
They're for when you want to duck out for a cruise.

    1360   Did you hear about the two ducks in a race?
    It resulted in the thrill of victory and the agony of webbed feet.

1361   Show us a fowl with an artificial leg, and we'll show you a lame duck.

    1362   What has feathers and crosses valleys?
    A via-duck.

      1363   What has feathers and carries water?
      An aqua-duck.

    1364   Or, as one woman said to the other, "It must be about to rain. I saw a duck with a capon."

1365   There was a fowl special on TV that was a duckumentary. It had an excellent introducktion in which it was noted that ducks enjoy vacationing in both North and South Duckota.

  1366   As one fowl said to another, "What's up, duck?"

    1367   Did you hear about the farmer who named his pet duck Hickory Dickory?

  1368   *Patron:* "Waiter, do you serve wild duck?"
  Waiter: "No, but we can take a tame one and irritate it for you."

    1369   *Patron:* "How is your Peking duck?"
    Waiter: "All left wings."

    1370   What's the favorite fairy tale of Chinese jewelers?
    "The Ugly Duck Ring."

1371   What do you call formal attire for waterfowl?
A ducksedo.

    1372   Then there was a musical starring dancing ducks.
    Waddle they think of next?

1373   Behave like a duck. Keep calm and unruffled on the surface,
but paddle like crazy underneath.

1374   Or, as one duck said to another, "What are you wading for?"

1375   Why do ducks go under water?
For divers reasons.

1376   And why do ducks come out of the water?
For sun-dry purposes.

1377   A visitor on horseback approached a stream and asked a young boy if
the water was deep. "No," replied the lad. The rider started to cross the stream
but soon found himself submerged. Upon reaching the other side, the traveler
shouted at the boy, "I thought you said it wasn't deep!"
   "It isn't," the young whippersnapper replied. "It only comes up to the
middle of ducks."

1378   Two men were playing golf when a bird flew overhead. "Look at the
duck," one man observed.
   "Goose," corrected his colleague.
   "Duck!" said the first.
   "Goose!" shouted the second.
   This argument continued for several minutes. About an hour later,
a man playing behind them yelled, "Fore!" and hit the ball. The first man saw
the ball coming and warned his cohort by yelling, "Duck!"
   "Goose!" countered the other.
   Boing!

1379   Two men were painting a barn, one of them on a ladder and the other
on the ground directly below.
   The man on the ladder spilled a can of paint and immediately yelled,
"Quack, quack, gobble, gobble!"
   "What in the world did that mean?" asked the gent on the ground,
who was drenched with paint.
   The one on the ladder replied, "Duck, turkey."

1380   As one duck said to another on a sunny day, "It's nice weather for people."

1381   Did you hear about the inept farmer who was trying to protect his
house from possible attacks by terrorists?
He got his duck taped but didn't know what to do next.

Eagle

1382 Why do eagles go to church?
Because they're birds of pray.

1383 Nature reserves are an eagle-opportunity employer.

1384 That reminds us of the lobbyists for a safe environment for our national bird.
They have proposed an Eagle Rights Amendment.

1385 Did you hear about the epileptic veterinarian who was arrested for operating on a sick bird?
The judge threw out the case because it was an ill eagle surgeon seizure.

1386 Did you hear about the eagle in a large Navy town?
It had a sailor tattooed on its chest.

1387 Did you hear about the man whose wife is like a bird?
She watches him with eagle eyes.

1388 Have you ever seen a bald eagle that wears a hairpiece?

1389 A legal eagle has his writs about him.

1390 Did you hear about the lawyer who once played football for Philadelphia?
He was a legal Eagle.

1391 Two guys were walking along the beach when one pointed overhead and exclaimed, "Look at the eagle!"
The other guy replied, "That doesn't look like an eagle."
"That's not surprising," added the former, "for eagles are masters of de skies."

Earwig

1392 As the insect said while falling off the bush, "Earwig go again."

Eel

1393 Did you hear about the electric eel that was arrested?
It was brought up on charges.

1394 What was the verdict at the eel's trial?
It was found guilty of shocking and revolting behavior.

1395   What do electric eels do after earthquakes?
Generate aftershocks.

1396   What is an eel's favorite sport?
Ice shockey.

1397   Did you hear the story about the slippery eel?
Never mind. You wouldn't be able to grasp it.

1398   What happened when the two morays met?
They fell head over eels in love, and each started singing, "That's a moray!"

1399   Why do shoe manufacturers like fish?
Because they use soles and eels.

1400   What makes fishermen industrious workers?
They put their shoulders to the eel.

1401   How do you catch an eel?
With a lightning rod.

1402   Did you hear about the sad electric eel in the aquarium?
He was AC and found out that his partner was DC.

1403   What kind of musical instrument do some fish play?
The eel-ectric guitar.

1404   How do morays enter politics?
By winning eel-ections.

1405   Where do young fish study?
At eel-ementary schools.

1406   What is the rubbery material made from snakelike fish?
Eel-lastic.

1407   Why did Franklin Roosevelt like the unclothed moray?
Because it was a nude eel.

1408 Why can't snakelike fish play the trumpet?
Because an eel wind blows no good.

1409 How did the unscrupulous snakelike fish make his fortune?
By accumulating eel-gotten gains.

1410 What is long, slippery, and whistles "Dixie" backward?
Robert E. Eel.

1411 Why was the seafood restaurant forced to close?
It was a house of eel repute.

Egret

1412 *Bird No. 1:* "Are you sorry that you waded in over your head?"
Bird No. 2: "No, I have no egrets."

Elephant

1413 Why do most people prefer elephant eggs to giraffe eggs?
Because everyone likes elephant yolks.

1414 Why are there so many elephant jokes?
Because it's never hard to find a new wrinkle.

1415 Why are elephants wrinkled?
Have you ever tried to iron one?

1416 As one elephant said to another, "Do me a favor. No more people jokes."

1417 Two boys were bragging about their fathers' jobs.
"My dad has a leading position in the circus," said one.
"What does he do?" asked the other lad.
Replied the former, "He leads the elephants in."

1418 How do you make an elephant stew?
Keep it waiting for two hours.

1419 What should you do if a herd of elephants rushes toward you while you're in a telephone booth?
Make a collect call and reverse the charge.

1420   Why do elephants have trunks?
Suitcases wouldn't work.

> **1421**   Why aren't elephants allowed on some beaches?
> *Because they can't keep their trunks up.*

>> **1422**   Why can't two elephants go swimming
>> at the same time?
>> *Because they have only one pair of trunks.*

>>> **1423**   Two elephants, Harry and Fay,
>>> Couldn't kiss with their trunks in the way.
>>> So they boarded a plane,
>>> And are now kissing in Maine
>>> 'Cause their trunks got sent to L.A.

1424   How do veterinarians calm down nervous elephants?
By giving them a trunkuilizer.

> **1425**   What did Hannibal get when he crossed
> the Alps with elephants?
> *Mountains that never forget.*

>> **1426**   Did you hear about the politician who made
>> an unforgettable speech?
>> *He was talking to the elephants at the zoo.*

1427   Or, as one impatient elephant said to another, "Oh, forget it!"

> **1428**   *Inscription on an elephant's tombstone:* "We will never forget."

>> **1429**   Why do elephants trumpet?
>> *Because they can't play the piano.*

>>> **1430**   *Patient:* "Doctor, doctor! I feel like
>>> an elephant."
>>> *Doctor:* "Tusk, tusk."

> **1431**   Where do Italian elephants live?
> *In Tuskany.*

1432   Who was the most famous elephant orchestra conductor?
Tuskanini.

1433   Why did the baby elephant put its tooth under its pillow?
For the tusk fairy.

1434   What does an elephant use to wash his tusks?
Ivory Soap.

1435   How do you make an elephant laugh?
Tickle its ivories.

1436   A woman was shopping for a piano and asked the salesman why one instrument's keys were slightly yellow. "Because," the man replied, "the elephant was a heavy smoker."

1437   *Hunter No. 1:* "Did you shoot an elephant on your safari?"
Hunter No. 2: "No. Hunting elephants is illegal, as ivory well know."

1438   A zoo employee was downcast after the death of an elephant. A colleague who tried to console him said, "Don't worry, the zoo will buy another elephant."

"That's not the point," was the reply. "I'm the one who has to dig the grave." (That will be a huge undertaking.)

1439   Why was the elephant fired from the circus?
Because he kept throwing his weight around.

1440   How do you make an elephant fly?
First you get a huge zipper . . .

1441   What did one male elephant say to another when a lovely female elephant walked by?
"Look at that perfect 236-324-336."

1442   Did you hear about the guy who gave up hunting elephants?
The decoys were too heavy.

1443   What would you get if Batman and Robin were trampled by a herd of elephants?
Flatman and Ribbon.

1444   Did you hear about the guy who likes bragging that he has a really big job?
He washes elephants at the zoo.

1445   A woman asked her pediatrician, "What's the best way to raise a baby elephant?"
The doctor replied, "Use a crane."

1446   Or, as the river said when an elephant sat in it, "Well, I'll be dammed."

1447   How much does a psychiatrist charge an elephant?
Fifty dollars for each visit and five hundred dollars for the couch.

1448   Two friends were talking when one commented, "I wish I had
enough money to buy an elephant."
"Why do you want an elephant?" inquired the other.
"I don't," replied the former. "I just want the money."

1449   Or, as one elephant said after bumping into another,
"Small world, isn't it?"

1450   A new deli restaurant tried to lure new customers with the promise that
they'd pay fifteen dollars to anyone who ordered a sandwich the chefs couldn't
make. A smart aleck ordered an elephant-ear sandwich. After several minutes,
the waitress returned from the kitchen and gave the customer fifteen dollars,
saying they couldn't make that sandwich.
The customer said, "I didn't think you could find elephant ears."
"Oh, it's not the ears," replied the waitress.
"We're out of those big buns."

1451   What did the elephant do when he broke his toe?
He called a tow truck.

1452   England's King George was having trouble collecting his taxes because
the peasants weren't paying their fair share. To remedy the situation, King
George had a huge portable torture rack built to send around the country to
intimidate the peasants. But the unit was so bulky that horses couldn't pull it.
Thus, the king imported two elephants and their trainer from India.
The result became known as the rambling rack for George's tax and an
elephant engineer.

1453 What did the grape say after an elephant stepped on it?
It didn't say anything. It just let out a little whine.

1454 What is a pink elephant?
A beast of bourbon.

1455 Did you hear about the new cocktail made with gin, grenadine, and Slim-Fast?
You still see pink elephants, but they're thinner.

1456 That reminds us of the elephant who got so drunk that he saw pink people.

1457 What do you do with a blue elephant?
Cheer him up.

1458 Three boys were in juvenile court for their delinquent behavior at the zoo. The judge asked each of them to give his name and state what he did wrong.

The first said, "My name is Tom, and I just threw peanuts into the elephant cage."

The second said, "My name is Dick, and I just threw peanuts into the elephant cage."

The third said, "My name is Peanuts."

1459 Why did the elephants at the circus go on strike?
They were tired of working for peanuts.

1460 Did you hear the one about the guy who quit a well-paying job and joined the circus?

It was more than a year before he saw his former neighbor, who was curious how things were going in the new career. After hearing that his friend's job was cleaning out the elephants' cages and the pay was merely fifty dollars a week, the neighbor asked, "Why don't you come back to your old job?"

"What!" exclaimed the man. "And give up show business?"

1461 What's big, gray, and goes "choo-choo-choo"?
An elephant with hay fever.

1462 What do you give a seasick elephant?
Plenty of room.

1463 As the elephant said to the maharajah, "Get off my back."

1464 Did you hear about the nearsighted man with insomnia?
He counts elephants instead of sheep.

1465 What's gray on the inside and clear on the outside?
An elephant in a plastic sandwich bag.

1466 If there were two elephants in the kitchen, which one would be the cowboy?
The one on the range.

1467 How does an elephant get down from a tree?
He sits on a leaf and waits for the fall.

1468 How do you get down from an elephant?
You don't get down from an elephant. You get down from a goose.

1469 What weighs four tons and sings?
Harry Elefonte and Elephant Gerald.

1470 Did you hear about the new book titled *Pachyderms?*
It's by L. E. Fant.

1471 How do elephants communicate?
They talk on the elephone.

1472 What's the biggest ghost in the world?
An elephantom.

1473 Who weighs six thousand pounds and wears glass slippers?
Cinderelephant.

1474 An elephant's opinion carries a lot of weight.

1475 What's big and gray and can fly straight up?
An elecopter.

1476 What do elephants do for entertainment?
Watch elevision.

1477 Why do elephants wear suspenders?
To hold up their elepants.

> **1478** From a Marx Brothers movie:
> "What has four legs and a trunk?"
> "That's irrelevant."
> "That's-a right."

> **1479** Speaking of the Marx Brothers reminds us of one of Groucho's most famous lines (from the movie *Animal Crackers*): "I shot an elephant in my pajamas. How he got in my pajamas I'll never know." Groucho also explained that it's easier to extract tusks in Alabama because that's where "the Tuscaloosa."

> **1480** Did you hear about the elephant comedian?
> *He was a mastodon of ceremonies.*

1481 What do you call a toothless elephant?
Gumbo.

> **1482** Where can you buy an elephant?
> *At a jumbo sale.*

> **1483** What is an elephant that can talk?
> *Mumbo jumbo.*

> **1484** How powerful is the squirt from an elephant's trunk?
> *A jumbo jet can keep four hundred people in the air.*

> **1485** An elephant from hilly Tibet
> In his cage one day wouldn't get.
>   So his keeper quite near
>   Put a hose in his rear,
> And invented the first jumbo jet.

1486 An elephant escaped from the circus and wound up grazing in an elderly, nearsighted lady's garden. She called the police and exclaimed, "There's a huge, strange-looking gray animal in my garden pulling up heads of lettuce with its tail." The unbelieving cop asked, "And just what is he doing with them?"
The lady replied, "If I told you, you would not believe me."

1487   If you're swallowed by an elephant, how do you get out of its stomach?
You run around in circles until you're pooped out.

> **1488**   What do you do to an elephant with three balls?
> *You walk him and pitch to the giraffe.*

> > **1489**   What do you call a skin doctor who treats elephants?
> > *A pachydermatologist.*

> > **1490**   Why did the elephant cross the road?
> > *It was the chicken's day off.*

Elk

1491   What did the deer do about his indigestion?
He took some Elk-a-Seltzer.

> **1492**   A hunter returned from an outing and proudly announced that he shot an elk.
> "How do you know it was an elk?" his wife asked.
> The husband replied, "By his membership card."

> > **1493**   *Student:* "How do lions find partners?"
> > *Teacher:* "I don't know. Most of my friends are Elks."

1494   After enduring excruciating pain with no relief, a man gave up on his physician and went to a witch doctor. He was given a strip of elk hide and told to bite off and eat a piece of it every day for a month. Having accomplished that, with no subsiding of the pain, the man returned to the witch doctor and said, "The thong is ended, but the malady lingers on."

Emu

1495   Did you hear about the ostrich-like bird that became a comedian?
He was rather emusing.

> **1496**   What do ostriches use in their guns?
> *Emu-nition. (But they strive to emu-late good safety practices.)*

Ermine

1497   Quoth an erudite, envious ermine,
"There's one thing I cannot determine:
 Why, when a woman wears my coat,
 She's a person of note.
But when I wear it, I'm called vermin."

Ewe

1498   What happened to the shepherd when he drove his sheep through a town?
He was given a ticket for making a ewe turn.

1499   What are the favorite love songs of sheep?
"My Sweet Embraceable Ewe," "Only Ewe," "I Only Have Eyes
for Ewe," and "There Will Never be Another Ewe."

1500   Or, as the ram said to his mate when he presented
her with freshly frozen snow carefully collected from
crags, "I only have ice for ewe."

1501   What is the beginning of the favorite patriotic song of sheep?
"Oh, Say, Can Ewe See?"

1502   What did the sheep farmer have on the
license plate of his truck?
EWE HAUL.

1503   The sheep farmer thanked the veterinarian for some quite
good advice and added, "I'll certainly put it to good ewes."

1504   *Found in farmer newspaper:*
"Used ewes are cheap sheep."

1505   Did you hear about the book of
famous sheep?
It's called Ewe's Who.

1506   What resides underwater and goes "baaa" at ships?
A ewe-boat.

1507   What do sheep sailors wear?
Ewe-niforms.

1508   The old man looked at his devastated flock and sighed as he parceled out the few remaining sheep to his sons. "Jake can have the ram, and Al can have the yearlings." Then, petting his favorite, he said, "And this ewe's for Bud."

1509   Where do sheep like to shop?
At the Ewenique Boutique.

1510   What is a promissory note from a sheep?
An I.O.Ewe.

1511   A monk began peddling flowers in front of an office building, irritating the tenants with incessant and annoying sales tactics. Some tenants finally took a lamb to the roof and dropped it, killing the flower-selling monk below. Which just goes to show that only ewes can prevent florist friars.

Fawn

1512   What did the buck say to the doe?
"Let's have a little fawn, baby."

1513   As one doe said to another, "Time flies when you're having fawn."

1514   What does a doe do to get attention from a buck?
Fawns over him.

1515 How do deer communicate?
By tell-a-fawn.

> **1516** Who is the favorite composer among deer?
> *Ralph Fawn Williams.*

Ferret

1517 Did you hear about the philosophical weasel?
He wanted to ferret out the truth.

> **1518** What is a popular pet in New York City?
> *The Staten Island ferret.*

Finch

1519 What bird lives in a refrigerator?
A coldfinch.

> **1520** What do you call a close race
> between two canaries?
> *A photo finch.*

> > **1521** How can a dozen birds look like a foot?
> > *When they're twelve finches.*

Firefly

1522 Did you hear about the two fireflies that met at sunrise?
It was love at first light.

> **1523** What did the frog have for a light meal?
> *A firefly.*

> > **1524** Why did the firefly cross the road?
> > *Because the light was with her.*

1525 What did the mother firefly say to her husband while looking at their son?
"He's bright for his age, isn't he?"

1526 How do races for fireflies begin?
The official shouts, "Ready, set, glow!"

1527 Or, as the boy firefly said to his girlfriend, "I really glow for you."

1528 What did one female firefly say to another?
"You glow, girl."

1529 What did one male firefly say to another?
"What time are you going out tonight?"

1530 As the theatrical firefly often proclaims, "When ya gotta glow, ya gotta glow."

1531 What did the firefly say after it flew into a screen door?
"Delighted, no end."

Fish

We were talking recently over a guppy coffee at Salmon's Bar and Krill with a friend named Moray about day trading. Once upon a time Moray was going to become a brain sturgeon but had to give it up when he became hard of herring.

He said, "I don't trade just for the halibut. I'm one of a large number of soles trying to mako living, so I can put fugu on the table. But I'm floundering."

So we said, "Abalone! We know you're just fishing for investment tips. Oh my cod, did we just say that? What we r-eel-y manta say was 'Squid while you're a shad.' Well, it's time for us to stop carping. See you aground!"

Moray said, "Don't be a pain in the bass!" then sniffed for a moment, took a puffer his cigarette, and responded, "Do you smelt something? I think it's coming from under the tarpon the back of my pickup truck. Maybe if I ignore it, it'll just go aweigh. I'll just sing a happy tuna: 'Don't worry, be crappie!'"

We peeked in the truck seabed, and everywhere we looked we sawfish. That was about all we could hake. We were tired of being a goby-tween, so we told him, "Clam up, you pike-r."

We guess he decided to mullet over, for he got down off his perch, swallowed the last of his jellyfish doughnut, got in his gar, waved, and said, "Seal later!" as he drove off.

Jest for the halibut, here are some more finny lines.

1532 Did you hear about the fisherwoman named Annette?
She really got caught up in her work.

1533 Why are fish poor tennis players?
They don't like to play close to the net.

1534 Inept fishermen have no net income.

1535 Why don't fish go near computers?
Because they are afraid to be caught Internet.

1536 Two members of a monastery decided to open a fish-and-chips eatery to make a little extra spending money. On opening day, the first customer complained to one of the owners about his overcooked filet of sole. (Soul food, of course, was the specialty of these men of the cloth.)

"I'm very sorry," said the co-owner, "but you'll have to speak with the fish friar. I'm just the chip monk."

1537 What's the difference between a newspaper and a television set?
You can't wrap fish and chips in a television set.

1538 The Department of Fish and Game is merging with the Bureau of Gambling Casinos.
It'll be called The Department of Fish and Chips.

1539 It's a little known fact that high tariffs placed on unfair competition in sales of flounder and integrated circuits protect our fish and chips.

1540 What is a sea monster's favorite meal?
Fish and ships.

1541 Did you hear about the pet store that sells animals that can both swim and fly?
It's a fish-and-cheep shop.

1542 Did you hear about the two fish that went into business together?
They started on a small scale.

1543 Another fish became a waiter.
He liked customers to tip the scales.

1544 As one fish said to another, "Where there's a gill, there's a way."

1545 What did the Cinderella fish wear to the ball?
Glass flippers.

1546 How did the fish's tail get caught in the boat's anchor?
It was just a fluke.

1547 Where do fish find jobs?
In the kelp wanted ads.

1548 Where do fish keep their money?
In riverbanks.

1549 Where do fish wash themselves?
In river basins.

1550 Where do fish sleep?
In riverbeds.

1551 What's the favorite furniture of fish?
A waterbed.

1552 When the fish restaurant offered free meals, diners asked, "What's the catch?"

1553 Did you hear about the fight in the seafood restaurant?
Two fish got battered.

1554 *Sign at a fish market:* If Our Fish Were Any Fresher, They'd Be Insulting.

1555 *Sign at another seafood market:*
Our Fish Come from the Best Schools.

1556 What makes most fish well-educated?
They travel in schools.

1557 Why do some fish swim on the bottom of the ocean?
Because they dropped out of school.

1558 What do you call a religion that worships fish as gods?
Ichtheology. Members include Southern Basstists, Anglercans, Une-Aquarians, and Assemblies of Cod.

1559   Two flounders were dining in a seafood restaurant when one of them started frantically waving his empty glass in the air. One waiter said to another, "I think there's a fish out of water over there."

In the hen section, you'll read about eggasperating and eggscruciating puns on eggs. Fish have eggs, too, and we have to lay a few on you here, but we'll reel back to fish before you miss a scale, and you can get the full eggsotic eggsperience later.

1560   What is a line of fish eggs?
A roe row.

1561   What is a fertile fish's working song?
"Roe, Roe, Roe Your Boat."

1562   *Baby salmon: "Are we fish or egg?"*
Mother salmon: "Roe, Roe, Roe, you're both."

1563   Did you hear about the degenerate fish?
It ended up on squid roe.

1564   Then there was the teacher's pet in a school of fish.
He always sat in the front roe.

1565   A mermaid is a deep-she fish.

1566   How do you communicate with a fish?
By dropping it a line.

1567   Did you hear about the gullible fish?
It always falls for pranks, hook, line, and sinker.

1568   Why are fish more intelligent than human beings?
Have you ever seen a fish spend a lot of money trying to hook a human?

1569   For a fish, the end of a barbed hook is the "point" of no return.

1570   *Sign on a nuclear physicist's door:* Gone Fission.

1571   Old fishermen never die; they just get reel tired.

1572   Why did the optometrist go ice fishing?
She had perfect ice site.

1573   Why are witches good at fishing?
Because they know how to cast a spell.

1574   The play on fishing had quite a cast.

1575   How did the fisherman prepare his reels for the big fishing trip?
With caster oil.

1576   *A fisherman in a boat calls out:* "Hey, fish, have I got a lure or have I got a lure!?"
One fish says to another: "Don't answer. He's just fishing for a compliment."

1577   Or, as the Irish-Spanish fisherman said when his casting fly ripped, "Tore a lure, *olé.*"

1578   What is the most popular fishing weight in Germany?
Der Meister Sinker.

1579   Argumentative fishermen often debait the subject.

1580   *Fisherman No. 1:* "What is that you're using for bait?"
Fisherman No. 2: "Crack cocaine!"
Fisherman No. 1: "Dare I ask why you're using drugs to catch fish?"
Fisherman No. 2: "Everyone knows it's easy to get hooked on this stuff."

1581   What is a French fisherman's motto?
"One man's meat is another man's poisson."

1582   How do French seafood lovers telephone each other?
Poisson to poisson.

1583   Why is a lunatic like a Parisian fish?
They're both in Seine.

1584 What sea creature is a bargain to buy?
A sailfish.

1585 Bargain-hunting sea creatures have sailfish motives.

1586 *Fish No. 1:* "How's life treating you?"
Fish No. 2: "I'm managing to keep my head below water."

1587 Or, as one fish said to another while watching a fishing boat above them, "Many are trawled, but few are frozen."

1588 What are frothen fith fingerth?
Items on a shopping lithp.

1589 Where do fish go to see a film?
At a dive-in movie.

1590 Did you hear about the aristocratic fish?
His ancestors swam under the Mayflower.

1591 Why did the fish cross the road?
To get to the other tide.

1592 What is a popular summer vacation spot for fish?
Martha's Finyard.

1593 What is another vacation spot for fish?
Finland.

1594 What did Tom Sawyer name his pet fish?
Huckleberry Fin.

1595 What part of a fish is like the end of this chapter?
The fin-is.

Flamingo

1596 Why do flamingos stand on one leg?
Because if they picked up the other leg, they'd fall over.

1597   Did you hear about the family of flamingos?
They decorated their front lawn with plastic humans.

Flea

1598   Did you hear about the dog
that went to a flea circus?
He stole the whole show.

    1599   "That's an amazing flea you have trained," said a tourist
to the owner of a flea circus. "Did you educate it yourself?"
"Yes," replied the owner, "I raised him from a pup."

        1600   As one flea said to another,
"Shall we walk or take the dog?"

            1601   *Customer:* "What do you have that'll cure fleas
on my dog?"
Druggist: "It depends on what's ailing the fleas."

1602   Why were the flea's parents so discouraged?
They realized that even the best of fleas will eventually go to the dogs.

    1603   What did the canine comedian say to the audience?
"Take my wife's fleas."

        1604   Why did the dog go to the Asian psychoanalyst?
For flea association.

            1605   *Sign on a pet store:* Buy One Puppy, Get One Flea.

1606   Did you hear about the flea's
house-warming party?
It was a flea-fur-all.

    1607   Why did the dog hire a lawyer?
To flea-bargain.

        1608   What do Mexican insects do in the afternoon?
Take a flea-esta.

1609 If a fish market sells fish, then what do you buy at a flea market?

1610 How can you discern where a flea bit you?
Start from scratch.

1611 Why did the dog take a flea with him to the audition at the theater?
Because he was itching to get a part.

1612 Or, as the male flea said to the female, "Come up to my place and see my itchings."

1613 How do fleas travel?
They itch-hike.

1614 Why did the flea live on the dog's chin?
He wanted a woof over his head.

1615 As the female flea said to her husband, "Let's go out for a bite."

1616 Did you hear about the mathematical flea?
It adds to your misery, subtracts from your pleasure, divides your attention, and multiplies like crazy.

1617

The World's Shortest Poem
Sometimes prosaically titled "Fleas" and which we title
Entomological Observation on the Origin of Siphonaptera
Adam
Had 'em.

1618 How do you start a flea race?
By shouting, "One, two, flea, go!"

1619 Why is a flea like a long winter?
Because it makes a backward spring.

1620 Some say that fleas are black,
But I know that is not so,
'Cause Mary had a little lamb
With fleas as white as snow.

1621   A grandfather, narrating Bible stories to his grandson, spoke of a man named Lot who was warned to take his wife and flee from the city. The grandfather explained that they were commanded not to look back as they went but that the wife did so and was turned into a pillar of salt.

The lad listened, then asked, "What happened to the flea?"

1622   *Man in bar:* "I can do impersonations."
Woman: "Then act like a dog and flea."

1623   Why did Sir Lancelot need a can opener?
Because he had a flea in his knight clothes.

1624   What did the father dog tell his adolescent puppy?
He told him about the birds and the fleas.

Flounder

1625   Did you hear about the new ocean organization called
The Royal School of Flatfish?
The flounding members named it The Royal College of Flounders.

1626   Or, as the first-time speaker nervously said,
"This is my fish market speech, so I may flounder a bit."

1627   *Fisherman No. 1:* "How's business?"
Fisherman No. 2: "Sales are floundering."

1628   A man with a highly contagious disease was confined to a hospital room. A specialist was called in and told the man, "We're going to feed you all the flounder, pancakes, and pizza you can eat."

"That's great," exclaimed the man. "Will that cure me?"

"Cure you?" replied the doctor. "Heavens, no! That's all we can slide under the door."

Fly

1629   What kind of paper is best for making kites?
Flypaper.

1630   As the fly said to the flypaper, "I'm stuck on you."

1631 Did you hear about the scientist who tried to invent flypaper but couldn't find the right formula?
He didn't give up, however; he exhibited stick-to-it-iveness.

1632 Or, as one British fly said to another after being caught in some flypaper, "This is a sticky wicket."

1633 The hand is quicker than the eye is,
But somewhat slower than the fly is.

1634 *Customer:* "Do you have anything snappy in rubber bands?"
Salesman: "No, but we have something catchy in flypaper."

1635 A couple was arguing, and the wife said, "You can catch more flies with honey than with vinegar."
"True," agreed her husband. "But who wants more flies?"

1636 Who can help if terrorist flies attack?
The SWAT team.

1637 *Hotel guest:* "Do you have a fly swatter?"
Desk clerk: "No, but we could send you a bellhop."

1638 Nothing makes one hotter
Than wielding a fly swatter.
However, it's all we've got
To teach those flies what's swat.

1639 What did the fly say after being swatted when he landed on a calculator?
"I guess my number was up."

1640 What happened when the fly blundered into a two-year-old's birthday party?
He burned his end at both candles.

1641 *Tourist:* "Don't you ever shoo all these flies?"
Native: "No, we just let them go barefoot."

1642 A mother fly complained after a sleepless night, "Junior was sick, and I had to walk the ceiling with him all night."

1643   Or, as the fly said while walking up a mirror,
"That's another way of looking at it."

> **1644**   A mother fly and her daughter were walking across the
> head of a bald man, and the mother observed, "How quickly
> times change. When I was your age, this was just a footpath."

>> **1645**   What has eighteen legs and catches flies?
>> *A baseball team.*

1646   Why did the meek baseball player have such a low batting average?
Because he wouldn't hit a fly.

> **1647**   Did you hear about the street bum who signed up for art classes?
> *All he could draw was flies.*

>> **1648**   What has four wheels and flies?
>> *A garbage truck.*

1649   That old joke from childhood days reminds us of the two flies that were in a
great mood. They were feeling good because they were down in the dumps.

> **1650**   Have you ever seen a horsefly across the river?

>> **1651**   If time flies like an arrow, fruit flies like what?
>> *A banana.*

>>> **1652**   Did you hear about the fly
>>> that didn't realize his man was open?

> **1653**   A fly and a flea in a flue
> Were trapped, so what could they do?
> Said the fly, "Let us flee!"
> Said the flea, "Let us fly!"
> So they flew through a flaw in the flue.

1654   Or, as one frog said to another, "Time sure is fun when you're having flies."

>> **1655**   How do some insects know when a picnic starts?
>> *Flies time when you're having fun.*

1656   Sunbathing is a fry in the ointment.

> **1657**   *Patron:* "Waiter, what's this fly doing in my soup?"
> *Waiter:* "It looks like the breaststroke."

That old joke conjures up a number of variations:

1658   *Patron:* "Waiter, what's this fly doing in my soup?"
Waiter: "It looks like the butterfly stroke."

> **1659**   *Patron:* "Waiter, what's this fly doing in my alphabet soup?"
> *Waiter:* "Learning to read."

>> **1660**   *Patron:* "Waiter, there's a fly in my soup."
>> *Waiter:* "It's not a fly. It's an essential bee vitamin."

>>> **1661**   *Patron:* "Waiter, there's a fly in my soup."
>>> *Waiter:* "It's not a fly. It's dirt."

1662   *Patron:* "Waiter, I don't like all the flies in my soup."
Waiter: "Tell me which ones you don't like, and I'll
chase them out for you."

> **1663**   *Patron:* "Waiter, there's a dead fly in my soup."
> *Waiter:* "It must have committed insecticide."

>> **1664**   *Patron:* "Waiter, there's a dead fly in my soup."
>> *Waiter:* "The chef's out of bug spray, so he drowned it."

>>> **1665**   *Patron:* "Waiter, there's a dead fly in my soup."
>>> *Waiter:* "What do you want? A funeral?"

1666   *Patron:* "Waiter, there's a dead fly in my soup."
Waiter: "It's the heat that kills them."

> **1667**   *Patron:* "What's this fly doing in my soup?"
> *Waiter:* "About five miles per hour."

>> **1668**   *Patron:* "Waiter, there's a fly in my soup."
>> *Waiter:* "What did you expect for two dollars? Clams?"

1669 *Patron:* "Waiter, there's a fly in my soup."
Waiter: "So? How much can it eat?"

    1670 *Patron:* "Waiter, there's a fly in my soup."
    Waiter: "Shhh! All the other customers will want one."

        1671 *Patron:* "Waiter, there's a fly in my soup."
        Waiter: "You didn't tell me you wanted to dine alone."

            1672 *Patron:* "Waiter, what's this fly doing in my soup?"
            Waiter: "Trying to get out."

1673 *Patron:* "Waiter, there's a fly in my soup."
Waiter: "I told the chef not to strain the soup through the fly swatter."

    1674 *Patron:* "Waiter, there's a fly in my soup."
    Waiter: "I didn't know you were a vegetarian."

        1675 *Patron:* "Waiter, there's a fly in my soup."
        Waiter: "How can that be? It's still daytime,
        and this place is fly-by-night."

            1676 *Patron:* "Waiter, there's a fly in my soup."
            Waiter: "No, that's the chef. The last customer
            was a witch doctor."

1677 *Patron:* "There's a fly in my soup."
Waiter: "Don't worry. The frog will get it."

    1678 That reminds us of the frog that complained,
    "Waiter, there's no fly in my soup."

        1679 *Patron:* "Waiter, there's a fly in my soup."
        Waiter: "It's possible. The chef used to be a tailor."

            1680 Or, as the waiter said after spilling the first course
            in the customer's lap, "There's soup on your fly."

1681 Or, as the cannibal said after a pilot parachuted from a plane and landed
in the cannibal's boiling pot, "There's a flier in my soup."

1682   An American was having dinner at a French restaurant in Montreal and noticed a fly in his soup. He called for the waiter, pointed at the fly, and (trying out his high school French) said, *"Le mouche."*

"*Non, monsieur,*" corrected the waiter, *"la mouche."*

The impressed Yankee said, "You've certainly got amazing eyesight!"

1683   *Patron:* "Waiter, there's a fly in my chop suey."
Waiter: "That's nothing. Wait'll you see what's in your fortune cookie."

1684   *Patron:* "Waiter, what's this fly doing in my wine?"
Waiter: "You asked for something with a little body in it."

1685   *Patron:* "Waiter, what's this fly doing in my wine?"
Waiter: "Having a very good time."

1686   *Patron:* "Waiter, there's a fly in my applesauce."
Waiter: "It's a fruit fly."

1687   *Patron:* "What's this fly doing in my ice cream?"
Waiter: "Downhill skiing."

1688   Or, as the football player complained,
"Waiter, there's a fly in my souper bowl."

1689   A Scotsman in his favorite pub found a fly in his drink.
He picked up the fly by the wings and demanded,
"Spit it out! Spit it all out!"

1690   Did you hear about the guy who went fly-fishing?
He caught a two-pound fly.

1691   Did you hear about the socializing entomologist?
He liked to hang out with a bunch of barflies.

Foal

1692   Did you hear about the horse that was born on the first day of the fourth month?
It was an April foal.

1693   Why did the farmer bottle feed his newborn horses?
Because a foal and his mommy are soon parted.

1694   A zoo held its first annual picnic for the animals, complete with a spiked punch bowl. The first to pass out were a chimp and a pony, which just goes to show that a foal and his monkey are soon potted.

1695   A pregnant horse was playing poker. On one deal, the mare was dealt a very good hoof of cards and showed a long face to avoid tipping anyone off. Unfortunately, the stress was too much. She had to foal.

Tough luck, too, because she had a foal house.

1696   Did you hear about the new horse-breeding magazine?
It has a monthly center-foal.

Fox

1697   What made the chicken run?
It saw the fox trot.

1698   A fox is a chick who gets a mink from a wolf.

1699   Did you hear about the man who complained that his wife didn't appreciate his gifts?
When she wanted a mink, he bought her a mink.
When she wanted a silver fox, he got her a silver fox.
Now the house is filled with foxy minks and minksy foxes.

Frog

1700   Did you hear about the man who swallowed a frog?
He's likely to croak any minute.

1701   As Confucius says, "A cat may have nine lives, but a frog croaks every night."

1702   Did you hear about the frog who wasn't in very good voice around the pond?
He wasn't what he was croaked up to be.

1703   Did you hear about the handsome prince?
He turned into a frog at the croak of dawn.

1704 What do you call a spy novel about frogs?
A croak-and-dagger story.

1705 What is a frog's favorite ballet music?
The Nutcroaker Suite.

1706 Did you hear about the cowardly frog?
He was a chicken croakette.

1707 What is a frog's favorite game?
Croquet.

1708 What is a frog's favorite snack?
French flies and a large croak.

1709 What is a frog's favorite flower?
A croakus.

1710 Did you hear about the crazy frog?
He was a real croakpot.

1711 What did the frog say when he split his trousers?
"Rip it! Rip it!"

1712 Did you hear about the new play titled *The Frog Prince*?
It's ribbeting.

1713 That reminds us of the frog shipbuilder who said to his workers, "Rivet! Rivet!"

1714 What did the frog say to the masseuse?
"Rub it! Rub it!"

1715 And what did the frog say to the hare?
"Rabbit! Rabbit!"

1716 Did you hear about the lady frog who was asked her age?
She decided to fibbit fibbit.

1717 What did the driver say to the hitchhiking frog?
"Hop in."

1718 *Patron:* "Waiter, do you have frogs' legs?"
Waiter: "Of course."
Patron: "Then how about hopping to the bar and getting me a drink?"

1719 What job did the frog have in the brewery?
He supervised the processing of hops.

1720 That reminds us of the employer who accused a worker
of drinking on the job.
"No," explained the employee, "I've been eating frogs' legs,
and what you smell are the hops."

1721 Did you hear about the frog who made beer without alcohol?
It was a hopless case.

1722 What's the favorite restaurant for frogs?
IHOP.

1723 What game is also the favorite
beverage of Scottish frogs?
Hopscotch.

1725 *Patient:* "Doctor, doctor! I keep
seeing frogs in front of my eyes."
Doctor: "Don't worry; it's only
a hoptical illusion."

1726 Why are frogs never thirsty?
*Because they can make a spring
anytime.*

1727 Why was the frog dishonorably
discharged from the Navy?
He kept jumping ship.

1728 As one frog said to another,
"Warts up, Doc?"

1729 What is the classic space adventure
movie about frogs?
Star Warts.

1724 What was the frog's job at the hotel?
He was the bellhop.

1730 *Patient:* "Doctor, doctor! I have a frog growing from my neck."
Doctor: "A real, actual frog just popped up?"
Patient: "Well, it started as a wart."

1731 A man with a frog on his head went to see a doctor.
"May I help you?" asked the physician.
"Yes," replied the frog. "Get this wart off my tail."

1732 *Mother frog to offspring:* "And stop calling your
brother a little wart!"

1733 How do frogs spread rumors?
By wart of mouth.

1734 Why couldn't the python talk?
Because it had a frog in its throat.

1735 Two frogs met on a street corner for an appointment.
"You're late," said one.
"I'm sorry," replied the other.
"I got stuck in somebody's throat."

1736 Or, as one coughing frog said to another,
"I must have a person in my throat."

1737 And as a toad asked the veterinarian, "What's the frognosis?"

1738 Did you hear about the frog jumping contest?
It was an unfrogettable experience.

1739 How do you get a toad off the window of your car?
Turn on the defrogger.

1740 *Sign in a pet store:* Go Frog Wild. Have One for the Toad.

1741 A frog went to a fortune-teller and was told that he'd soon meet an
attractive young woman who would get very close to him and who would
have an intense desire to learn more about him. "Where will I meet her?"
the frog asked excitedly. "In a singles bar?"
"No," replied the fortune-teller, "in biology class."

1742   A biology professor was about to demonstrate the dissection of a frog. He reached into his desk to pull out the specimen, but in its place he removed a paper bag containing a sandwich. "Oh, dear," he exclaimed. "I distinctly remember eating my lunch."

1743   Where do frogs make notes?
On lily pads.

1744   A test question about World War II was: "What was the largest amphibious assault of all time?" Expecting to see "the D-Day invasion" as the answer, the teacher found instead on one paper: "Moses and the plague of frogs."

1745   What happened when two frogs tried to catch the same fly?
They ended up tongue-tied.

1746   A frog named Kermit Jagger went to a bank for a second mortgage on his lily pad. He asked the mortgage officer, a Miss Patricia Whack, if he could borrow a certain sum of money. When she asked him for some collateral, the frog gave her a small trinket. She took the object into the manager's office, explained the whole story, and concluded by saying, "I'd love to let him borrow the money, but I don't know what this trinket is."

The manager replied, "It's a knickknack, Patty Whack. Give the frog a loan. His old man's a Rolling Stone."

Gander

1747 Why did the chicken and the goose cross the road?
So the chicken could take a gander on the other side.

1748 Did you hear about the pet gander named Proper?

1749 Why didn't the baby goose believe anything his father said?
He thought it was all papaganda.

1750 What did one Wisconsin goose say to another?
"Look at that Michigander."

1751 There was a young wife from Uganda,
Renowned for her coolness and candor.
When, during abuse,
Her husband said, "You goose!"
She quickly retorted, "U-ganda!"

1752 What's the motto of Kenya's neighboring country?
"What's good for the goose is good for Uganda."
(Kenya believe that?)

Gecko

1753 What is it called when an artist paints only lizards?
Art gecko.

1754 If a lizard squeaks into a bottle, does he hear a gecko echo?

Gibbon

1755 What's a popular song among apes?
"Tie a Yellow Gibbon 'Round the Old Oak Tree."

1756 Did you hear about the man who rescued a drowning
ape from frigid water?
The owner of the ape decided to award him the blue gibbon.

Giraffe

1757 What is worse than a centipede with corns?
A giraffe with a sore throat.

1758 What is worse than a giraffe with a sore throat?
One with a stiff neck.

1759 Zookeeper: "Can a giraffe get a sore throat from getting its feet wet?"
Veterinarian: "Yes, but not until the following week."

1760   What do you call a giraffe family reunion?
Necks of kin.

1761   Did you hear about the giraffe race?
It was neck and neck all the way.

1762   Zoo keepers chasing an escaped giraffe asked
a country bumpkin whether he'd seen it.
*The lad replied, "I didn't see no geeraff, but there was
a long-necked spotted pony chewing the tops off of trees."*

1763   Where do giraffes hang out?
At Giraffe-ic Park.

1764   What's tall and flowery?
A giraffodil.

1765   Did you hear about the writing on a tall wall at the zoo?
It was giraffiti.

1766   Why is the giraffe the smartest animal in the zoo?
It has a high level of intelligence.

1767   Why are giraffes the snobbiest animals in the jungle?
Because they look down on everything.

1768   Why do giraffes live in the jungle?
Because it's out of the high-rent district.

1769   A short poem on a tall subject:
Just think how long a tall giraffe
Would take to have a belly laugh.

1770   Why do giraffes have such small appetites?
Because a little goes a long way.

1771   Why do giraffes rarely apologize?
Because they find it difficult to swallow their pride.

1772   Did you hear about the nearsighted basketball player?
He asked a giraffe for a date.

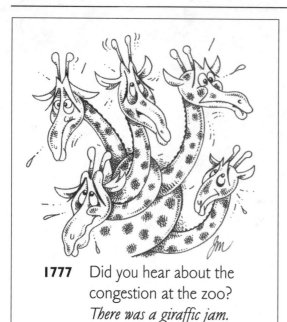

1777 Did you hear about the congestion at the zoo?
There was a giraffic jam.

1773 Why did the lion marry a giraffe?
Two other lions put him up to it.

1774 Did you hear about the African vineyard?
It's noted for making giraffes of wine.

1775 Who's the most famous giraffe baseball player?
Ken Giraffey, Jr.

1776 How did the animals escape from the shipwreck?
On a girraft.

Gnat

1778 What did King Arthur call his pet insects?
The Gnats of the Round Table.

1779 Who was a popular musical insect?
Gnat King Cole.

1780 What is an insect's favorite flower?
A forget-me-gnat.

1781 What kind of bugs bother spacemen?
Astro-gnats.

1782 *Girl:* "What's the difference between a gnat and a gnatterbaby?"
Mother: "What's a gnatterbaby?"
Girl: "Nothing. What's a gnatter with you?"

1783 One fisherman complained to another, "The mosquitoes, and not the fish, are biting."
"They're gnats, not mosquitoes," corrected the other.
"Big deal," replied the first. "Mosquitoes to me and gnats to you."

Gnu

1784 Why are gnus cleverer than dogs?
Because you can't teach an old dog gnu tricks.

1785 What is it called when you feel as if you've seen
a strange-looking horned animal before?
Déjà gnu.

1786 *Boy (at zoo):* "What's underneath
that funny-looking animal, Dad?"
Father: "There's nothing, son, under the gnu."

1787 The gnu's a bit shaggy, it's true,
But well known and quite popular, too.
    By the French he's adored,
    But Italians are bored,
And frequently ask, "What's a gnu?"

1788 What did Santa Claus tell his reindeer?
*"If you don't stop misbehaving,
I may get a gnu sleigh."*

1789 Or, as one antelope said to another on January 1, "Happy Gnu Year!"

1790 *Patron:* "I'd like a gnu steak."
Waiter: "How about something as good as gnu?"

1791 Why did the antelope?
Nobody gnu.

1792 Old antelope breeders never die.
They just begin a gnu.

1793 Why did Noah take four gnus on the ark?
Because he had some good gnus and some bad gnus.

1794 What do antelopes read every
morning at breakfast?
The daily gnuspaper.

1795   A herd of antelope invaded the Netherlands and headed straight for the famous Dutch cheese factory. This headline appeared on the front page of the morning newspaper: "Gouda gnus."

1796   What do you call an African antelope corral?
A gnus roundup.

1797   An African antelope called the circulation department of the Sahara Gazette and said, 'Please re-gnu my subscription.'"

1798   What do you call some African antelopes that are capable of operating copying equipment?
All the gnus that are fit to print.

1799   One day, while in search of their evening meal, two lions, each the leader of a pride, spotted two unsuspecting gnus and devoured them. "That," announced one of the kings of the jungle, "is the end of the gnus. And here, once again, are the head lions."

1800   One day I went to the zoo,
For I wanted to see the old gnu.
          But the old gnu was dead,
          And the new gnu, they said,
Surely knew as a gnu he was new.

1801   A bricklayer had a pet gnu that assisted him in his construction work, the gnu's favorite activity being the laying of tile floors in new homes. A prospective homeowner expressed amazement at the animal's prowess. The contractor replied, "He's a typical gnu and tiler, too."

1802   What do you call an average African antelope that makes or alters clothes?
A typical gnu and tailor, too.

1803   What did the father gnu say when his wife asked him to spank their baby for misbehaving while he was at work?
"I'm too tired. You paddle your own gnu."

Goat

1804 What is the best butter in the world?
A goat.

1805 Did you hear about the rabbit that
was eaten by a goat?
It was a hare in the butter.

1806 Why is it hard to talk with a goat?
Because he always butts in.

1807 Two acquaintances met in an elevator.
"What's up (besides this elevator)?" asked one.
The other replied, "I've been working on a farm
where they raise hornless goats."
"But—" began the first.
The second interrupted, "There are no butts."

1808 Or, as the mother goat scolded her kid, "I don't want
to hear another word. No ifs, no ands, and no butts."

1809 Did you hear about the goat farmer who married a poet?
He married her for butter or for verse.

1810 Two goats wandered into an alley behind a movie theater in search of
dinner. One of them found an old can of film, which he devoured.
"How was it?" asked his companion.
The first one replied, "The book was better."

1811 Or, as one goat said to another, "Eaten any good books lately?"

1812 Why did the goat eat fluorescent tubes?
He wanted a light lunch.

1813 Why did the farmer teach his livestock to play poker?
He wanted to see the three billy goats bluff.

1814 Did you hear about the angry farmer?
Someone got his goat.

1815   Or, as another farmer warned a neighbor,
"Watch out for that poacher; his tricks will get your goat."

1816   Did you hear about the dyslexic guy at the costume party?
He went to a toga party dressed as a goat.

1817   A schoolteacher asked her students for some examples of goats. The usual responses were received, such as billy goats, nanny goats, and mountain goats, until a minister's son asked, "What about the holy goats?"

Goldfish

1818   Did you hear about the fish with a desperate urge to paint itself gold?
It had a gilt complex.

1819   What kind of fish is kept by employees at Fort Knox?
Goldfish.

1820   As one goldfish said to another while swimming in a bowl, "See you around."

1821   Why does a goldfish travel more than any other animal?
Because it swims around the globe.

1822   Why did the man surround his goldfish bowl with postcards?
So the fish would think they were going somewhere.

1823   *Mom:* "Have you given the goldfish fresh water today?"
Son: "They haven't finished what I gave them yesterday."

1824   Two goldfish were swimming around in their bowl when one announced that he had become an atheist. "That's ridiculous," said the other. "Who do you think changes the water in this bowl?"

1825   What is stranger than seeing a horsefly?
Seeing a goldfish bowl.

Goose

1826   What is unique about a goose?
It's the only animal that grows down as it grows up.

> **1827**   *Pillow maker:* "I'd like to buy some goose feathers."
> *Feather supplier:* "Can you afford the down payment?"

> **1828**   As the baby goose said when it heard a car honk
> in the night, "Is that you, Ma?"

1829   What did the leader of a flock of geese say
to the birds that were following him?
"Stop that infernal honking! If you want to pass, then pass!"

> **1830**   Two geese were captivated by the formation of navy jets
> flying overhead. One commented to the other, "I admit they're
> pretty clever, flying without flapping their wings. But they
> needn't roar about it."

> **1831**   Did you hear about the two geese that had a midair collision?
> *Fortunately, all they got were goose bumps.*

1832   That reminds us of the goose that flew over a drive-in theater that was showing
a horror movie. He was so scared that he got people bumps.

> **1833**   Why is a goose like an icicle?
> *Because it grows down.*

> **1834**   Did you hear the one about the potato chip factory that
> fried its product in goose grease?
> An alert inspector noted that some goose feathers had
> somehow fallen into the works. Which just goes to show that he is
> a good man to have around when the chips are down.

1835   *Diner No. 1:* "I want something light for lunch."
Diner No. 2: "How about a plate of feathers?"
Diner No. 1: "No. Then I'd be down in the mouth."

> **1836**   What happened when a goose ran into a duck?
> *It was just a feather bender.*

1837   *Hunter No. 1:* "I shot ten geese."
Hunter No. 2: "Were they wild?"
Hunter No. 1: "No, but you should've seen the lady who owned them."

1838   Did you hear about the man who was charged with
stealing geese from wildlife preserves?
He was accused of leading police on a wild goose chase.

1839   Did you hear about the lame-duck politician?
His goose has been cooked.

1840   What kind of birds live in Lisbon?
Portugeese.

1841   One goose turned to another one at the back of a large formation and
asked, "Why do we always have to follow that same leader?"
"Because," the other replied, "he's the one with the map."

1842   Did you hear about the goose that made a broad jump?

1843   If a French infant is raised on a formula made from
goose livers, at what age should he be paté trained?

1844   If you and a goose are trapped on a roof
with no ladder, how can you get down?
Pluck the goose.

1845   What is it called when Mother Goose drives
her children around in a large, non-fuel-efficient car?
Gas gosling.

Gopher

1846   As the boy rodent said to the girl rodent, "I could really gopher you."

1847   *Teenager No. 1:* "I got a job as a gopher."
Teenager No. 2: "Oh, you mean you go for things?"
Teenager No. 1: "No, I dig holes in the garden."

1848   In searching for more animal puns, we gopher broke.

Gorilla

1849 Why did the ape join the Marine Corps?
He wanted to learn about gorilla warfare.

1850 What do you call chest-thumping
and limb-swinging?
Gorilla tactics.

1851 What is the favorite romantic song of apes?
"Gorilla My Dreams."

1852 Why did the female ape go on a diet?
To keep her gorillish figure.

1853 What did the gorilla call his wife?
His prime mate.

1854 What did Judy Garland sing to a big ape?
"King Kong, the witch is dead."

1855 What musical is about a gorilla?
The Kong and I.

1856 What do you call apes that barbecue in a light rain?
Grillers in the mist.

1857 Then there was the gorilla that invented a bell
that rings whenever a point is made in table tennis.
It's called the King Kong Ping Pong Ding Dong.

1858 As King Kong said after meeting Godzilla, "Small world, isn't it?"

Grasshopper

1859 What is an insect on a pogo stick?
A grasshopper.

1860 What lives in a store and jumps over shelves?
A grass shopper.

1861　　A biology student conducted a scientific experiment. He shouted, "Jump!" at a grasshopper, and the insect jumped. He then removed one of the grasshopper's legs and shouted, "Jump!" and the insect jumped. The results were identical with each of the ensuing four amputations. However, when he cut off the sixth leg and shouted, "Jump!" the insect lay motionless. The student concluded that when all six legs have been removed, a grasshopper becomes deaf.

1862　　While vacationing in Australia, a typical Texan was bragging about his big state when a kangaroo hopped by. The Texan was visibly impressed and drawled, "I must admit that your grasshoppers are bigger than ours."

Great Dane

1863　　Why was the theatrical dog cast for the lead part in the play Hamlet?
Because he was a Great Dane.

1864　　Did you hear about the Great Dane that was purchased by an unsuspecting family?
He had the house broken before he was.

1865　　*Man:* "Doctor, doctor, my Great Dane does nothing but chase sports cars."
Vet: "That's only natural. Most dogs chase cars."
Man: "Yes, but mine catches them and buries them in the backyard."

Greyhound

1866　　When is a black dog not a black dog?
When it's a greyhound.

1867　　What animal shows amorous affection by kissing?
The greyhound; it's always good for a buss.

1868 Did you hear about the funny-looking greyhound dog
that had a bus painted on its side?

1869 One flea to another: "I'm taking a Greyhound to the city."

1870 That reminds us of the guy who went
to the bus terminal to watch the Greyhounds race.

1871 What did the thirsty greyhound
do during the race?
He lapped the field.

Groundhog

1872 Did you hear about the rodent that bought
a thousand acres of farmland for development?
He was a real ground hog.

1873 Did you hear about the woman who saw her shadow on
Groundhog Day and predicted six more weeks of dieting?

Grouse

1874 What is the grumpiest of birds?
A grouse.

1875 How do birds measure their economic well-being?
By the Grouse National Product.

1876 Two guys were hunting grouse when a bird flew high over them. The
first guy took aim, fired, and brought down the grouse with a single shot. "You
didn't have to shoot it," said the other. "The fall alone would have killed it."

Haddock

1877 Two guys were fishing when one of them caught a fairly
large fish and exclaimed, "I think I got a haddock."
    The other fellow replied from the opposite end of the boat,
    "Then why don't you take an aspirin?"

1878   There once was a bonnie Scotch laddie,
        Who said as he put on the plaidie,
           "I've just had a dish
            Of some very good fish."
    What had he had? Had he had haddie?

1879   Many years ago a Jewish man named Kahn owned a fish market in the center of a Catholic area of town. Business, however, did not thrive. Thinking that his prospects might improve if he were a Catholic, Mr. Kahn went to the local priest and asked to be converted. The clergyman said it was a simple matter. He sprinkled some water over Mr. Kahn's head, did some fancy gesticulations, and said, "Kahn, Kahn, Meccon." The priest then informed the man that he was a Catholic and that his name had been changed from Kahn to Meccon.

Miraculously, Mr. Meccon's business boomed, and he soon added a meat section to his fish market. Several months later, the Meccons invited the priest to their home for dinner, and Mrs. Meccon prepared a delightful duck dinner, complete with all the trimmings. The priest spoiled the mood, however, when he said, "I'm afraid we can't have this duck. As good Catholics, we're not supposed to eat meat on Friday." "Don't worry," replied Mr. Meccon, "it's a simple matter." He then made some fancy gesticulations, poured his glass of water on the duck, and said, "Duck, duck, haddock."

Halibut

1880   What did the flatfish wife say when her husband
asked why she stayed out all night?
"Just for the halibut."

Hamster

1881   Hamsters are gangster pigs.

> **1882**   What kind of pets are pigs when they wake up from a nap?
> *Ham stirs.*

1883   Did you hear about the boy who found himself with ten hamsters?
His female hamster's "sister" turned out to be a himster.

1884   That reminds us of the entrepreneur who decided to raise hamsters, after seeing how rapidly they proliferated. Unfortunately, a rare disease killed his entire stock of over 100 of the little creatures. The man was about to dispose of the hamsters when his wife had an idea. She had read somewhere that if you mashed up the carcasses and boiled them, it yielded a jelly-like preserve suitable for serving on toast or in peanut butter sandwiches. However, the concoction tasted horrible, so the man spread the sticky substance in his garden for use as a fertilizer. Incredibly, beautiful roses began growing out of this miracle mixture. "That's truly amazing to get roses," exuded the man's wife. "I'd expect to get tulips from hamster jam."

Hare

1885   What do you call a row of rabbits walking backward?
A receding hare line.

1886   Did you hear about the bald rabbit?
He wore a harepiece.

1887   What do bald rabbits optimistically use?
Hare tonic and hare spray.

1888   A happily hopping rabbit suddenly collapsed in front of a barbershop. The barber grabbed one of his many cans of spray and emptied it on the furry little animal.

The rabbit was rapidly resuscitated and, in a seeming show of gratitude, repeatedly gesticulated with its paw as it hopped away, which shows that the can had the right solution, for the label read: "Hair spray. Restores life in dead hair. Adds permanent wave."

1889   How can you recognize old rabbits?
By the gray hares.

1890   Why shouldn't you wash your rabbit's fur with goat's milk?
Because you're not supposed to use that greasy kid stuff on your hare.

1891   What do you call donning long ears and a cotton tail?
Hare dressing.

1892   Why was the rabbit owner disappointed?
Because she washed her hare and couldn't do a thing with it.

1893   Did you hear about the pet rabbit that bit its owner?
It was a bad hare day.

1894   Little Jeannie wanted a real Easter bunny, so her dad shopped until he found just the right one. Now, dad proudly shows everyone a picture of "Jeannie with the light brown hare."

1895   Did you hear the one about the intoxicated man who accidentally swallowed a baby rabbit?

The unfortunate gent's wife put him in a tub of scalding water and scrubbed him until he coughed up the bunny. As she scrubbed, she sang, "I'm gonna wash that hare right out of my man."

1896   How did the rabbit become a wrestling champion?
It used a lot of hare pins.

1897   What airline do rabbits use?
U.S. Hare-ways.

1898   *Sign in pet shop:* Hare Ye!
Hare Ye! Easter Bunnies. Hop to It!

1899   Rabbit fur is hare hair.

1900   How did the magician's wife know that
he was up to his old tricks again?
Because she found a hare on his shoulder.

1901   As the magician said when he couldn't find the
rabbit he put in his hat, "Hare today, gone tomorrow."

1902   There's a box with a hole at each end and there's a rabbit in the box. The rabbit sticks his head out of the hole in one end, and a minute later he sticks it out the other end. Half a minute later, his head appears at the opposite end, a fourth of a minute later it appears at the end opposite to that one, an eighth of a minute later, etc., etc. How long will it take before the rabbit sticks its head out of both ends of the box at the same time?

In theory, two minutes. In practice, no answer is possible unless you split hares.

1903   *Customer:* "May I purchase just half of a rabbit?"
Butcher: "No, we don't split hares."

1904   What do you call an ugly rabbit that sits on
someone's forehead?
Unsightly facial hare.

1905 Did you hear about the bed-and-breakfast manager
who raised a baby rabbit as a pet?
It was an inn-grown hare.

1906 As the rabbit said to the baby goat,
"Hare's looking at you, kid."

1907 Or, as one baby goat said to another after seeing
a rabbit nuzzling a female sheep, "Hare's lickin' a ewe, kid."

1908 Did you hear about the man whose pet bunny kept breathing down
his neck and preventing him from concentrating on important events?
The man missed out on many things in life by a hare's breath.

1909 How did the close race between the rabbit and the turtle end?
It was won by a hare.

1910 Before baseball parks had lights, it often got so dark the players couldn't
see what they were doing. Once, when a ball was hit to an outfielder, the player
lost it in the darkness. Fortunately, a rabbit, running by at the time, grabbed the
ball and threw it to first base for the out. That was the first time anyone was
thrown out by a hare.

1912 Did you hear about
the rich rabbit?
He was a millionhare.

1911 What type of exercises
do rabbits enjoy?
Hareobics.

1913 What was the Playboy Bunny Club
in Dallas called?
The best little hare house in Texas.

1914 *Patron:* "Waiter! There's a hair
in my soup."
Waiter: "That's not surprising.
It's rabbit soup."

Hart

1915 What do you call a dialog
between deer?
Hart-to-hart talk.

1916   Did you hear about the staid stag that sauntered into a backyard cocktail party, sauntered to the punch bowl, and drank its absinthe-laden contents?

The stag staggered and fell into the swimming pool, proving that absinthe makes the hart go founder.

1917   What do you call a meal with deer and fish?
Hart and sole.

Hartebeest

1918   Did you hear about the president and vice president of a tiny Central African country who wanted to promote big game hunting?

They were to be filmed on safari, but the president, a bad shot, wounded a large antelope that charged the shooter. The guide was just barely able to save the president, but for a moment the frightened vice president was only a hartebeest from the presidency.

1919   What happened when a hungry lion raced after an African antelope?
The lion's breath made the hartebeest faster.

Hawk

1920   Did you hear about the wife who does bird imitations?
She watches her husband like a hawk.

1921   What bird has a funny-looking haircut?
A Mohawk.

1922   What bird has no wings?
A tomahawk.

1923   Why do hawks watch M*A*S*H?
They identify with scenes in which Hawkeye peers.

Heifer

1924   *Tourist:* "How many cows do you have?"
Farmer: "About heifer dozen."

1925 A farmer once called a cow Zephyr
'Cuz she seemed such an amiable hephyr.
　　　But when the farmer drew near,
　　　She kicked off his ear,
Which made him considerably dephyr.

1926 What did the bull groom say to his cow bride?
"I will love you for heifer and heifer."

1927 What is a bull's favorite love song?
"If Heifer I Should Leave You."

Hen

1928 Why did the dating agency for chickens
go bankrupt?
They couldn't make hens meet.

1929 Why was the chicken farmer unhappy?
Because he was henpecked.

1930 Or, as we always say, "Show us a man whose wife
chooses his clothes, and we'll show you a man
who dresses hen-peccably."

1931 That reminds us of the husband who suspected that there would be a peck of
troubles after he was married. But he never expected a henpeck of troubles.

1932 *Woman No. 1:* "If you think your hairdo is nice, wait till you see my hendo."
Woman No. 2: "What's a hendo?"
Woman No. 1: "It lays eggs."

1933 What wild warlike nomad laid eggs?
Attila the Hen.

1934 The Reverend Henry Ward Beecher
Called the hen a most elegant creature.
The hen pleased with that
Laid an egg in his hat—
And thus did the hen reward Beecher!
Oliver Wendell Holmes

1935 What famous chicken crossed the Alps?
Hennibal.

1936 Why did soldiers throw eggs at the enemy?
Because they were hen grenades.

1937 What's covered in feathers and tells jokes?
A stand-up comedihen.

1938 What's the favorite publication of chickens?
The National Henquirer.

1939 Two customers were standing in a checkout line when one of them said, "You have a henway on your back."
"What's a henway?" asked the other.
"Oh," replied the first customer, "about three pounds."

1940 A tourist saw a farmer carrying a plump hen and asked, "Isn't that huge hen heavy?"
"No," the farmer replied. "She ain't heavy. She's my brooder."

1941 That reminds us of the literature buff who raised hens.
He named one the Brooder Karamazov and another one Chickov.

1942 A farmer had a wife who was sick in bed. A passing neighbor saw the farmer in the backyard and stopped to inquire about the wife. After saying hello and nodding toward the house, the neighbor asked, "Is that her coughin'?"
"No," replied the farmer, putting down his hammer.
"I'm building her a henhouse."

1943 A beggar asked a farmer for an egg every day for a month. The farmer eventually inquired why the poor man didn't request a large number at one time. The man replied, "You shouldn't put all your begs in one ask it."

1944 Why did the hen eat a box of tacks?
So she could lay a carpet.

1945 *Poultry farm sign:* "Better laid than never."

1946   "It is not in my nature to fiddle,
And thumbs I am lacking to twiddle,"
           Said the hen with pride
           As she laid sunny-side
Two eggs on a piping hot griddle.

1947   As the hen said to the scrambled eggs,
"You crazy mixed-up kids!"

1948   Did you hear about the time it was so windy that one
hen laid the same egg four times?

1949   *Grocer:* "Eggs are going up."
Distracted Customer: "Hens must have lost all sense of direction."

1950   Why does a hen lay eggs?
Because if she dropped them, they would break.

1951   Did you hear about the hen that stopped
in the middle of the highway?
She wanted to lay it on the line.

1952   What is a motto for chefs?
"If at first you don't fricassee, then fry, fry a hen."

1953   Did you hear about the hen that received amorous
advances from a rooster?
She egged him on.

1954   And did you hear about the lovesick hen smitten
by the metal rooster atop the barn?
"You're so vane," she clucked.

1955   Why was the hen disliked by her colleagues?
Because she was always playing practical yolks.

1956   When do hens start laying?
When they've passed their eggs-am.

1957   Did you hear about the hen that misbehaved in school?
She was eggspelled.

It must be eggasperating and eggscruciating reading all these eggscentric and eggsotic puns on eggs. We could try to eggsplain that they are really eggscellent and eggsceptional eggsamples of eggsclusive, eggsquisite, eggsalted, eggstatic, and eggshilarating literary genius, but we just eggspress our hope that you don't become eggscessively eggshausted and eggspire!

1958 Or, as the French chef said about all these egg puns,
"All right already! *Un oeuf is un oeuf!!*"

Heron

1959 Did you hear about the partially deaf ibis?
He wore a heron aid.

Herring

1960 Did you hear about the partially deaf fish?
She was hard of herring.

1961 What do you call politicians on a fishing expedition?
A congressional herring.

1962 What happened to the man who dropped some Scotch into a fishbowl?
He got pickled herring.

1963 *Patient:* "Doctor! Doctor! Every bone in my body hurts."
Doctor: "Well, just be glad you're not a herring!"

1964 Did you hear about the stingy man who was told by his doctor that his wife needed some sea air?
He fanned her for a week with a herring.

Hippopotamus

1965 What's worse than a giraffe with a stiff neck?
A hippopotamus with chapped lips.

1966 A hippopotamus went to the doctor and complained of a failing appetite.
"I just peck at my food these days. A peck of this and a peck of that."

1967   What do you call a hippopotamus with chicken pox?
A hippospottymus.

1968   What weighs over a ton and has flowers in its hair?
A hippie-potamus.

Heh! Heh! Heh!

1969   What animal is always laughing?
A happy-potamus.
(But he doesn't like hippo-crits.)

1970   What do you call jumbo-sized fishing attire?
Hip-boot-potamus.

1971   What weighs over a ton, feels cold to the touch, and comes on a stick?
A hippopsicle.

1972   What weighs over a ton and thinks it's always sick?
A hippochondriac.

1973   *Chef No. 1:* "Have you ever seen hippopotami cook deer, elk, or moose?"
Chef No. 2: "I've never seen a hippo pot a moose."

1974   All of these horrible puns remind us of Shakespeare's Hamlet, who once said, *"Oh, what a rogue and hippopotami."*

1975   There once was a jolly fat hippo
That jumped in the sea for a dippo.
It would have been wise
Had he opened his eyes,
But he didn't and flattened a ship, oh!

1976   Three Indian women were sitting outside their teepees, two of them with their young children. The first mother was sitting on a deerskin and had a boy who weighed 60 pounds. The second mother was on a buffalo skin and had a boy who weighed 70 pounds. The third woman, who was childless, sat on a hippopotamus skin and weighed 130 pounds. This proves the mathematical theorem that the squaw on the hippopotamus equals the sons of the squaws on the other two hides.

1977   Where can you find hippos?
It depends where you hide them.

Hog

1978   Did you hear about the pigs at
a fraternity party?
They went hog wild.

1979   Why is a football called a pigskin?
Because the players like to hog the ball.

1980   Did you hear about the pig
that was driving a car?
He was a road hog.

1981   What is a racist pig?
A hog on wheels.

1982   Speaking of road hogs reminds us of the man in the hospital who
had a reputation for being one. When the doctor asked the nurse how the
patient was doing, she replied that the man kept sticking out his left arm.
"Good," commented the doctor, "he's turning the corner."

1983   One hog said to another, "Stop talking manwash!"

1984   Did you hear about the politician who
campaigned that the country needs a taller
hog—for people to live higher off?

1985   There once was a lazy green frog
That rode on the back of a dog.
        But the dog wasn't big,
        So he moved to a pig,
And that's how he went whole hog.

1986   Did you hear about the squealing TV actor Larry Hogman?

1987   How are hogs like trees?
They root for a living.

1988   What did the carpenter exclaim after his pigsty was broken into?
"I don't have mahogany more."

> **1989**   A long-lost Elvis Presley song about a pig swept
> away in a flood was just discovered.
> *It's called "You Ain't Nothing but a Drowned Hog."*

Horse

Once a pony time, there lived a coltish lass who wore a ponytail. Although she often said neigh, she never bridled or kicked up her heels at authority. We've herd that she was a real warhorse who champed at the bit to get back into harness each day. She was nobody's foal, and she never beat a dead horse or looked a gift one in the mouth. That's her story, straight from the horse's mouth. And remember that to err is human, but to make horse puns, equine.

1990   What do you call a veterinarian with a sore throat?
A hoarse doctor.

> **1991**   How about a pony with a sore throat?
> *A hoarse horse.*

> > **1992**   Did you hear about the thespian pony?
> > *It was a little horse play.*

> > > **1993**   What is a head cold?
> > > *The hoarse and buggy daze.*

1994   As one horse said to another, "I forgot your mane, but your pace is familiar."

> **1995**   How do jockeys determine which
> racehorses are the favorites?
> *By taking a gallop poll.*

> > **1996**   That reminds us of what you call a Warsaw native
> > who enjoys riding fast horses.
> > *A gallop Pole.*

1997   What kind of horse has trouble keeping track of his Macintosh?
An Appaloosa.

1998   What equine likes to cut in line?
A sawhorse.

> **1999**   Why was Dick Clark a favorite star with horses?
> *Because he was a disk jockey from Filly.*

> > **2000**   Spanish equestrians guide their horses with so
> > much slack in the reins that they actually hang down
> > across the horses' necks. That echoes the song:
> > "The reins in Spain fall plainly on the mane."

2001   Why did the artist put on a show of horse paintings?
He wanted to mount an exhibit.

> **2002**   What is a jockey's motto?
> *Put your money where your mount is.*

> > **2003**   Speaking of mounts reminds us of the novice who asked
> > a jockey, "What's the best way to mount a horse?"
> > "How should I know?" replied the irritable jockey.
> > "I'm not a taxidermist."

2004   *Owner:* "Did you find my horse well-behaved?"
Guest: "Yes, indeed. In fact, whenever we encountered a fence,
he let me go over first."

> > **2005**   Speaking of fences reminds us of the man who bought
> > a horse but then went back to the farmer and complained,
> > "I thought you said this horse you sold me could jump as high
> > as an eight-foot fence."
> >   "I did, and he can," said the farmer.
> >   "Well," replied the man, "he can't jump at all."
> > The farmer added, "Neither can a fence."

2006   What happened to the man who
used to own a riding academy?
Business kept falling off.

> **2007**   What made another stable owner successful?
> *He knew how to stirrup a lot of interest.*

2008   The novice asked the instructor, "What's the hardest
thing about learning to ride a horse?"
The instructor replied, "The ground."

2009   *Sign on a rodeo gate:* "Bronco riders needed immediately.
Big bucks possible."

2010   *Man No. 1:* "I went riding today."
Man No. 2: "Horseback?"
Man No. 1: "Yes, he got back an hour before I did."

2011   Richard Nixon was galloping to the White House,
but down by the mill house he broke into a water gait.

2012   If you want your troubles off your mind, go horseback riding.

2013   The stallion and the mare were going to get married,
but when the time came, the stallion got colt feet and failed to appear.
The mare hoofed indignantly, "The beast! He left me at the
halter and is probably out there with some cheap filly, horsing around.
But if he is that fickle, I'm better off not being saddled with him for life.
I can do without the bridle bouquet!"

2014   In what part of the barn did the newlywed horses stay?
The bridle suite.

2015   How did the horse avoid participating in a joust?
It got the knight off.

2016   Where did the Knights of the Round Table
park their horses?
In the Sir Lance Lot.

2017   *Guest:* "I'd like to rent a horse."
Farmer: "How long?"
Guest: "As long as you've got. There will be five of us."

2018   What made Teddy Roosevelt mean to horses?
He was a Rough Rider.

2019   Did you hear about the overweight woman who
took up horseback riding as exercise?
In a month the horse lost twenty-five pounds.

2020   A major with wonderful force,
Called out in the park for a horse.
All the flowers looked 'round,
But no horse could be found;
So he just rhododendron, of course.

2021   Did you hear about the man who works like a horse?
But only when his boss rides him.

2022   The ancient Norse mythological god of thunder went for a horse ride.
"I'm Thor," he thundered.
His horse replied, "No wonder you're Thor.
You forgot the thaddle, thilly."

2023   Speaking of saddles reminds us of dark horse candidates.
The problem with them is that you can't find out about their
track records until you're saddled with them.

2024   Why was the horseman fired from his job
of testing saddles?
He was always standing up on the job.

2025   Why did the horseman put a saddle on a large loaf of bread?
Because it was a crusty steed.

2026   Why is the old, decrepit horse named Flattery?
Because it gets you nowhere.

2027   What's the easiest way to make a slow horse fast?
Don't feed it.

2028   What was the tow truck doing at the racetrack?
It was trying to pull a fast one.

2029   Why are chorus girls like barge horses?
They have to tow the line.

2030 Why are clouds like jockeys?
Because they hold the reins.

2031 When he left his horse at the stable, the cowboy got a rein check.

2032 As Mrs. Paul Revere said to her husband, "I don't care who is coming. I'm using the horse tonight."

2033 We know about a horse in Hollywood that's made ten films.
He's not a star, though. He just does bit parts.

2034 Then there was the sad horse that felt a bit down in the mouth.

2035 A horse eats best when it doesn't have a bit in its mouth.

2036 Did you hear about Sugar Ray Robinson's horse?
It got angry and bit at the champ.

2037 What goes into the mouth of a quarter horse?
Two bits.

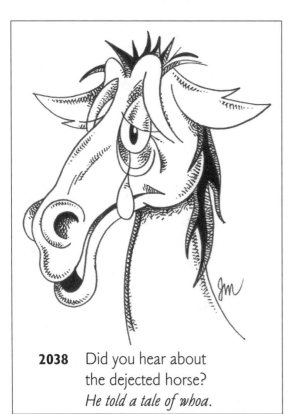

2038 Did you hear about the dejected horse?
He told a tale of whoa.

2039 What is a horse's favorite sport?
Stable tennis.

2040 *Mother to daughter:* "Just because we live in a ranch house is no excuse for your room to look like a stable."

2041 That reminds us of the student who got a part-time job at the horse stables. His work is really piling up.

2042 What is horse sense?
Stable thinking—and the ability to say neigh.

2043 What well-known person strives to ensure safety for horses?
Ralph Neighder.

2044 Did you hear about the horse with a negative attitude?
It always said, "Neigh."

2045 If you hear it from the horse's mouth,
then you're listening to a neigh sayer.

2046 Schubert had a horse named Sarah,
He rode her to a big parade.
And all the time the band was playing
Schubert's Sarah neighed.

2047 What domestic animals were
raised at Walden Pond?
Thoreau-bred horses.

2048 Why did the horse cross the road?
To visit his neighbor.

2049 A serious thought for today
Is one that may cause us delay.
Just what are the forces
That bring little horses
If all the horses say nay?

2050 She was only a jockey's daughter,
but she didn't know how to say nay.

2051 Or, she was only a stableman's daughter, but all the horsemen knew 'er.

2052 Why did the horses line up at a theater box office?
They wanted two stalls for the evening show.

2053 How is an egg like a young horse?
It can't be used till it's broken.

2054 Why did the horse stir his cereal with his hoof?
Because he wanted to feel his oats.

2055 Did you hear about the guy whose diet contained
nothing but oat bran?
He fell in love with the winner of the Kentucky Derby.

2056   What got one horse all charged up?
Eating haywire.

2057   Why did one horse go hungry?
His dinner plans went haywire.

2058   Two horses were chatting before a race, and one said, "I don't know why we try so hard to win. It's only money for the owner."
"Not this time," replied the other. "My owner told me he'd give me twenty-five bales of hay if I win today."
The first horse exclaimed, "Hay! That ain't money!"

2059   Or, as the horse said upon eating all of its hay,
"That's the last straw!"

2060   How is manna from heaven like the horse's hay?
Both are food from aloft.

2061   Did you hear about the horse
that ate all of his hay?
He had a bale-full look about him.

2062   Then there was the horse that was assigned
to pull a VIP's carriage in the big parade.
It went without a hitch.

2063   What young couple rode a horse
up a hill to fetch a pail of water?
Jockey and Jill.

2064   What do you call a horse that plays the violin?
Fiddler on the hoof.

2065   What happened when the horse
swallowed a dollar bill?
It bucked.

2066   How much money did
the bronco have?
Only a buck.

2067   What did one bookie say to another as they left a church service?
"You embarrassed me in there. It's hallelujah, not Hialeah."

> **2068**   What goes "clip"?
> *A one-legged horse.*

> **2069**   *Patron:* "I'm hungry enough to eat a horse."
> *Waiter:* "You came to the right place."

2070   Did you hear about the dumb guy who couldn't tell the difference between his two horses?
> *A friend suggested measuring the two, which is how the guy discovered that the brown horse was two inches taller than the white one.*

> **2071**   As Groucho Marx told his son in *Horse Feathers,*
> "I'd horsewhip you, if I had a horse."

> **2072**   Then there was the guy who named his horse Radish.

2073   Why did the farmer call his horse Baseball?
Because it's covered with horsehide.

> **2074**   Did you hear about the guy with five keen senses?
> *What he lacks, however, is common and horse.*

> **2075**   What dynamic duo was famous for stealing horses?
> *Bonnie and Clydesdale.*

2076   Why was the gambler hiding in the shrubbery next to the racetrack?
He was hedging his bets.

> **2077**   Why was the racehorse named Raspberry Ice?
> *He was a sherbet.*

> **2078**   Why was the racehorse named Bad News?
> *Because Bad News travels fast.*

2079   Why did the superstitious jockey compete at only one racetrack?
He had a one-track mind.

2080   *Overheard at a racetrack*: "I bet on a horse yesterday at
twenty to one. It didn't come in until quarter past two."

2081   A man explaining to his wife why he was home late
from the racetrack said, "I bent down to tie my shoe and
some nearsighted guy put a saddle on me."
           "What did you do?" asked the wife.
           The man replied, "I came in tenth."

2082   What is the strongest of all animals?
*A racehorse. It can take hundreds of people
for a ride simultaneously.*

2083   Did you hear about the horse player who woke
up at seven o'clock one morning, had seven dollars in his
billfold, was the seventh person in line to bet, and saw
there were seven horses in the race?
           *Inspired, he bet on the seventh horse—
and watched it come in seventh.*

2084   A bookie called his client and said, "I've got some
good news and some bad news. The good news is that your
horse came in first in the seventh. The bad news is that he
was racing in the sixth."

2085   *One bettor to another*: "You said he was a great
horse, and he sure is. It took eleven other
horses to beat him."

2086   Why did the man name his racehorse Fleabag?
Because the horse was often scratched.

2087   A guy bet on a horse merely because he saw a priest
blessing it before the race. When the horse lost, the man told
the priest, "So much for your blessing!"
           The priest replied, "I wasn't blessing the horse.
I was giving it last rites."

2088   Did you hear about the horse that was so slow in one
race that the jockey kept a diary of the trip?

2089   Why is horse racing romantic?
*Because the horse hugs the rail, the jockey puts his arms
around the horse, and you kiss your money good-bye.*

     2090   Did you hear about the racehorse that was so late
         coming in they had to pay the jockey time and a half?

          2091   Did you hear about the aristocratic horse?
            He was the last of his race.

2092   There once was a fake vet named Morse,
Brought in to inspect a sick horse
      Soon scheduled to race,
      So he kept a straight face
And said, "Just let this thing run its course."

         2093   How is a leaking faucet like a racehorse?
           It's off and running.

          2094   "Will I ever be able to race my horse again?"
            the owner asked the veterinarian, following a serious
            operation on his prize filly.
               "I'm sure you will," replied the vet, "and
            you'll probably beat her, too."

              2095   Did you hear about the Englishman who
                 thought the Kentucky Derby was a hat?

2096   "All you ever think about are horses and racetracks," the woman
complained to her husband. "I bet you don't even remember the date
when we got married."
     "Yes, I do," countered the husband. "It's the day Man o' War won
the Kentucky Derby."

         2097   Two men were discussing a mutual friend's bad luck
            at the racetrack when one said, "Isn't it funny how John is so
            lucky at poker but does so poorly at the racetrack?"
               "Funny, nothing," countered the other. "They won't let
            him shuffle the horses." (Not only that, but it's hard to hide a
            horse up your sleeve.)

2098 Why are racehorses like lollipops?
Because the more you lick them, the faster they go.

2099   On his way back from the racetrack, a man saw one
of those road signs that said Speed Kills. The man commented,
"If that's true, then I bet on a horse that's going to live forever."

2100 How is a racehorse like a letter?
They both begin a trip at the post.

2101 Did you hear about the man who received a hot
tip on a horse called Cigarette?
He didn't have enough tabaccer.

2102 Then there was the guy who crossed a horse with a fish.
He put a fin on its nose.

2103   *Owner:* "Wow! You whispered in the horse's ear before
the race, and he won. What did you say?"
Jockey: "Roses are red; violets are blue; horses that don't
win are turned into glue."

2104 What is a famous painting of a racehorse?
"Whistler's Mudder."

2105 What do you call a horse that's been
all around the world?
A globe-trotter.

2106 What do you call it when a gang of militant
jockeys with diarrhea takes over the government?
Coup d'etrots.

2107 What's another name for
an assistant stable cleaner?
Co-pile-it.

2108 That reminds us of the hapless fellow who
follows the horses—with a pail and shovel.

2109 There were two horses on a ship including a sick bay.

2110   Show us a pink polka-dot pony, and we'll show you a horse of a different color.

> **2111**   Did you hear the one about the horse that enjoyed eating doughnuts for dessert?
> A neighbor came over one evening and tried to feed the horse some cake, but the finicky critter refused to eat.
> "What's wrong with your horse?" asked the visitor.
> "Nothing," replied the owner. "This is just a horse of a different cruller."

> > **2112**   What did the wife say to the undertaker when he started hitting his stalled car?
> > *"Stop beating a dead hearse."*

2113   Why did the tennis pro leave his wife's funeral early to play a match?
To put the court before the hearse.

> **2114**   Why did the philosopher have such a stable marriage?
> *Because he always put Descartes before divorce.*

> **2115**   People who drink and drive put the quart before the hearse.

2116   As the man told his loafing horse, "Quit stallion."

> **2117**   What cavalry division defended the vast onion fields of Tuscany?
> *The Italian Scallion Stallion Batallion.*

> > **2118**   Did you hear about the former Soviet officials who decided to castrate the statue of a horse carrying one of their national heroes?
> > *It was an example of destallionization.*

2119   Why is it difficult to identify horses from the back?
They're always switching their tails.

> > **2120**   *Wife to husband:* "Let's play horse. I'll be the front, and you be yourself."

2121   What did the lower-middle-class cowboy say to urge on his horse?
"Hi ho, Stainless."

2122   What did the horse say when he slipped on wet grass?
"Help! I've fallen and I can't giddy-up."

2123   A cowboy ran out of a saloon, made a graceful running
jump, and landed smack on the ground.
        "Are you injured?" asked a passerby.
        "No," replied the cowboy. "But I want to get my hands
on the guy who moved my horse!"

2124   *Bumper sticker:* Roy Rogers Was Trigger Happy.

2125   Did you hear about the woman who says she feels like a young colt?
Actually, she looks more like an old .45.

2126   What do you call a claim to
determine a colt's father?
A palomino suit.

2127   Why was the man sued by his horse?
For palomino-mony.

2128   As one horse said to another, "Any friend of yours is a palomino."

2129   Why did the (fill in your favorite nationality)
water polo team come in last?
Because all the horses drowned.

2130   Did you hear about the girl who worked
like a horse to get a groom?

2131   Why is the tongue like a horse?
Because it runs fastest when it carries the least weight.

2132   When does a horse neigh?
Whinny wants to.

2133   An Englishman was visiting an American horse
farm and asked, "How does one go about hiring
a horse?"
        The owner replied, "Give it two pairs of stilts."

2134 You can lead a horse to water, but a pencil must be lead.

2135 As the blacksmith said after getting the wrong part of a horse on the anvil, "Let's forge ahead."

2136 Who did the breeder summon when his horse was possessed by the devil?
An exhorsist.

2137 Did you hear about the Paul Revere cocktail?
Two drinks and you wake the neighbors and start horsing around.

2138 What did the stallion say to the mare?
"Your pace or mine?"

2139 Why was Lady Godiva considered a sports gambler?
Because she put everything she had on a horse.

2140 What happened when Lady Godiva's horse saw she had no clothes on?
It made him shy.

2141 As Lady Godiva said toward the end of her ride, "We're nearing our clothes (of the horse chapter)."

2142 And what was the result of Lady Godiva's famous horse ride?
She didn't win, and she didn't place. But she surely did show.

Hummingbird

2143 Why do hummingbirds hum?
Because they don't know the words.

2144 As a matter of fact, you show us a nightingale that forgets the words to its song, and we'll show you a humming bird.

Hyena

2145 Two hyenas were talking by that usual talking place, the water fountain.
"How was your vacation?" asked one.
"It was a lot of laughs," the other replied.

2146 Why did the man cross a parrot and a hyena?
So he could ask what it was laughing about.

2147 Did you hear about the poor stand-up comedian who couldn't even make a hyena laugh?

2148 What is a hyena's favorite motorcycle?
A Yamaha-ha.

2149 What happened when the hyena swallowed a bouillon cube?
He made a laughing stock of himself.

2150 Did you hear about the rich hyena that swam across the river?
She laughed all the way to the bank.

2151 What do hyenas fill their cars with?
Laughing gas.

Ibis

2152   As one heron said to another, "Ibis seeing you later."

Iguana

2153   *Tourist:* "Do you have any lizards on this island?"
Native: "I guana show you one."

Inchworm

2154   How many night crawlers are there in a foot?
Twelve inchworms.

2155   What is a drawback of adopting the metric system?
Figuring out what to call the inchworm.

Jackal

2156   An unfunny beast is the jackal,
Which seems, indeed, to lack all
      Sense of humor;
      Well, that's the rumor,
For it's never been known to cackle.

      2157   How do jackals in the jungle see at night?
         They use jackal lanterns.

Jackass

2158   As Confucius says, "Nonchalance is the ability to look
like an owl when you have acted like a jackass."

2159   A couple was chatting one evening when the wife asked
her husband what the differences were between a sigh, a car, and
a jackass. When the husband couldn't guess, the wife said, "A sigh
is 'Oh, dear!' and a car is too dear."
       "Then what's a jackass?" he asked.
       She replied, "You, dear."

2160   Of what importance are animals to a woman?
*She wants a Jaguar in the garage, a tiger in bed,
a mink in the closet, and a jackass to pay for it all.*

2161   *Tennis player:* "Is my style reminiscent of Arthur Ashe?"
Tennis coach: "No, you're more like his brother, Jack Ashe."

2162   *Speaker to heckler:* "Please be quiet, sir. I have only thirty minutes
to make a jackass of myself. You have a whole lifetime."

2163   Then there was the speaker who turned to
a heckler and said, "Do you know what type of fruit
you'd be if you were sitting next to a jackass? A pear."

2164   That reminds us of the speaker who said of a heckler, "When I was
growing up on a farm, I accidentally ran over my pet donkey with the tractor,
and my father said that someday that donkey would come back to haunt me.
Well, there's that jackass now!"

Jaguar

2165   A venerable dame in Nic'raguar
Had her hair nipped off by a jaguar.
       The lady gasped, "Ah!"
       The jaguar said, "Bah,
What a false, artificial old haguar."

2166 Did you hear about the woman who incessantly nagged
her husband to buy her a Jaguar?
He did. And it ate her.

Jellyfish

2167 What is a marine policeman's favorite snack?
A jellyfish doughnut.

2168 Where do jellyfish get their jelly?
From ocean currants.

2169 What connection is there between jellyfish and
members of congress creating a budget?
None, except that the budgeters are like a group
of nearsighted people sitting in a dark room, wearing
boxing gloves, and trying to measure the thickness of
a jellyfish with a pair of rubber calipers.

Kangaroo

2170 What did the kangaroo tell his psychiatrist?
"Nothing I do makes me feel jumpy."

2171 Later, the kangaroo added,
"Sometimes I feel as if I've run out of bounce."

2172 Why did the kangaroo hesitate?
He didn't want to jump to a conclusion.

2173 Why would kangaroos make unreliable sailors?
Because they'd always be jumping ship.

2174 Why did the judge jump up and down?
It was a kangaroo court.

2175 What is a kangaroo's favorite season?
Spring.

2176 What do you call a baby kangaroo that can't jump yet?
An offspring.

2177 When does a kangaroo jump the highest?
In leap year.

2178 Did you hear about the fast-growing baby kangaroo?
He grew by leaps and bounds.

2179 How can a zookeeper tell when a kangaroo is getting old and run-down?
When it's frequently out of bounds.

2180 Did you hear about the obese kangaroo?
It left potholes all over the countryside.

2181 Did you hear about the angry kangaroo?
It was hopping mad.

2182 What's the main ingredient of Australian beer?
Kangaroo hops.

2184 Did you hear about the kangaroos that got married?
They lived hoppily ever after.

2183 Who was a famous cowboy kangaroo?
Hopalong Cassidy.

2185 Did you hear about the cheerful kangaroo?
It was a hoptimist.

2186 What sounds do kangaroo Rice Krispies make?
Snap, crackle, and hop.

2187 Why did the kangaroo throw her
daughter out of the pouch?
She was eating crackers in bed.

2188 *One kangaroo to another:* "It's going to rain today, which
means that the kids will have to play inside again."

2189 Why was the kangaroo so depressed?
She was left holding the bag.

2190 Why did the baby kangaroo refuse
to hop into a neighbor's pouch?
Because it wasn't his bag.

2191 Did you hear about the baby kangaroo
that was kidnapped?
The mother had her pocket picked.

2192 When a sailor in San Diego's zoo
Snatched a tiny baby kangaroo,
Its mother said, "Jack,
You can put it right back.
You know picking my pocket's taboo."

2193 Why do politicians appeal to kangaroos
to make campaign contributions?
Because they have deep pockets.

2194 What do kangaroos like to read?
Pocket Books.

2195 *One young kangaroo to another:* "When
I leave home, Mom's turning my room
into a briefcase."

2196 Where do kangaroos eat breakfast?
They hop to IHOP with the frogs.

Kid

2197 *Patient:* "Doctor, doctor! I feel like a baby goat."
Doctor: "You've got to be kidding."

2198 Or, as one goat said to another, "I kid you not."

2199 Did you hear about the couple that is perfectly matched?
He's a funny old goat, and she's a great kidder.

2200 *Commercial on TV:* "Attention, goats! It's late at night.
Do you know where your kids are?"

2201 How should you treat a baby goat?
With kid gloves.

Kipper

2202 A herring and a whale were fine fanatic (and finatic) friends, and they even traveled in the same school. On a rare occasion, another fish noticed the herring swimming alone and asked where his compatriot was. "How should I know?" replied the herring. "Am I my blubber's kipper?"

2203 What did Cain say when Abel asked
him to make soup from his herring?
"Am I my kipper's broth-er?"

2204 Or, as the female herring told her
escort on a date,
"Kipper hands to yourself!"

2205 "What are we going to eat," asked one woman,
"now that the Day of Atonement fasting is over?"
Her friend replied, "Oh, yum! Kipper!"

Kitten

2206 Why did the cat join the Red Cross?
She wanted to be a first aid kit.

2207 What do you call a cat
that does tricks?
A magic kit.

2208 What happened
when the
poker player's cat
swallowed a dime?
*There was money in
the kitty.*

2209 Did you hear about the
pet kitten named Kaboodle?

2210 What do you call newborn kittens
passed from owner to owner?
A chain litter.

2211 What do English cats
drink in the afternoon?
Kit-tea.

2212 Why are kittens such good TV announcers?
They have wee paws for station identification.

2213 Where did the three little
kittens find their mittens?
In the Yellow Pages.

2214 If dogs go to obedience school,
where do cats go?
Kittygarten.

2215 Why does the man call his wife Kitty?
Because she has dyed nine times.

2216 Did you hear about the two punsters
who told multiple jokes about kittens?
*"We won't tell any more," they said.
"And we're not kitten, either."*

Koala

2217   Did you hear about the Australian family?
They spend a lot of koality time together.

2218   What's the favorite drink
of Australian bears?
Coca-Koala.

2219   What is a koala from outer space?
An Austr-alien.

2220   Did you hear about the family that applied to the Australian
government to raise a native bear as a pet?
Their application was denied because they didn't koalafy.

2221   A special beverage, given to patients at Australia's Mercy
Hospital, is named after a native bear. The drink contains a fair
amount of ursine sediments, however, which proves that
the koala tea of Mercy is not strained.

Labrador

2222 What did the generous Labrador say when
he gave away his bones?
"It is better to give than to retrieve."

2223 What goes "ring-knock-woof"?
A labradoor.

2224 Then there was the woman at a dog show
who asked an usher, "How do I get to the Labradors?"
The usher replied, "The ladies' room is straight ahead."

2225 What dog is the most popular
with scientists?
A laboratory retriever.

Ladybug

2226   *Patron:* "Waiter, what is that crawling up my menu?"
Waiter: "That's a ladybug, sir."
Patron: "You have amazing eyesight."

Lamb

2227   What's woolly and plays jazzy music?
A Dixie lamb band.

2228   A Texas sheep rancher's wife was dyeing some clothes in a large vat. A tiny lamb gamboled over for a look and fell in, thereby turning a lovely shade of blue. The woman placed the lamb in a small fenced-in area near the road to dry and was surprised when a tourist stopped and offered a large sum of money for the rare blue lamb.
         It didn't take the sheep rancher long to realize that he was on to something big. In fact, to this day, he is the biggest lamb dyer in the state of Texas.

2229   Why was the baby sheep afraid to appear in public?
Because he had to take it on the lamb.

2230   What is a baby sheep that swallows a light bulb?
A lamp.

2231   Did you hear about the boxer who entered the ring like a lion?
He went out like a lamp.

2232   How do sheep protect their drivers' licenses?
By having them lambinated.

2233   *Patron:* "Waiter, I'd like a lamb chop, and please make it lean."
Waiter: "Which way?"

2234   *Lamb chop about to be placed on a skewer:* "Oh, spear me!"

2235   Did you hear about the thief who was caught in a butcher's store?
He was chop-lifting.

2236   Two businessmen were having a roast dinner at a restaurant
when one said, "I think the lamb is a bit tough."
The other replied, "Let's not talk chop."

2237   How can elderly people with no teeth enjoy eating lamb?
*By licking their chop*s.

2238   *Patron:* "Waiter, I'd like lamb chops au gratin."
Waiter (calling the order to the chef): "Cheese it, the chops!"

Lark

2239   What do you call a bashful songbird that
slyly appropriates food stolen by other birds?
A shylark.

2240   As Confucius says, "One robin doesn't make a summer,
but one lark is often the cause for a fall."

Lemming

2241   Why was the lemming so hesitant?
He didn't want to jump to a conclusion.

2242   What is a rodent's favorite drink?
Lemming-ade.

Lemur

2243   As one monkey-like mammal said to another,
"Lemur know if there's anything I can do for you."

Leopard

2244   As the leopard said after eating a meal,
"That really hit the spot."

2245   Why is it hard for a leopard to hide in the jungle?
Because it's always spotted.

2246   Why was a leopard hired by
a television news team?
He did on-the-spot reports.

2247   Why couldn't the proficient
leopard baseball player
excel in basketball?
*Because a leopard can't
change his sports.*

2248   How can a leopard
change his spots?
By moving.

2249   A leopard went to see an optometrist because he thought
he needed an eye exam. "Every time I look at my wife," he worriedly
told the optometrist, "I see spots before my eyes."
   "So what's to worry about?" replied the doctor.
"You're a leopard, aren't you?"
   "What's that got to do with anything?" replied the patient.
"My wife is a zebra."

2250   What happened to the leopard that
took a bath three times a day?
After a week he was spotless.

2251   What happened to the lion that developed
measles and became very spotty?
The other lions sent him to a leopard colony.

2252   There once was a handsome young shepherd,
Who was eaten at lunch by a leopard.
         Said the leopard, "Egad!
         You'd be tastier, lad,
If you had been salted and peppered."

2253   As Rev. Spooner might say,
"The Lord is a shoving leopard."

Lion

2254   Did you hear about the man who was sitting on the steps
in front of the New York City Public Library?
He was reading between the lions.

2255   Why is it difficult to telephone the King of the Jungle?
The lion is often busy.

2256   As the man said to his friend who was going on a safari in Africa,
"Don't forget to drop me a lion."

2257   Did you hear about the circus truck driver
who was fired because he refused to tow the lion?

2258   Did you hear about the German
who named his pet lion Frau?

2259   Where did the zookeeper hang his laundry to dry?
On the clothes lion.

2260   After losing his two watchdogs to a hungry coyote, a sheep
farmer obtained two lions and had them rotate their watch-standing
duties. The next time a coyote tried to have a sheep for dinner, it was
devoured by the lion on watch. The local game warden could tell that
a coyote was missing from that area and asked the farmer where the
coyote was. The farmer replied, "It's all in the lion of duty."

2261   Two military officers, one Army and one Navy,
were on a safari in Africa, and they bet a round of ale on
who would shoot the first lion. The Army man immediately
headed into the jungle, but the Navy pilot found a jet and
shot a lion from the air. That proves that a strafed lion
is the shortest distance between two pints.

2262   Did you hear about the latest safari recipe?
*Take a couple of pounds of the King of the Jungle and
soak it in brandy for two days. Then dine on the sotted lion.*

2263   A farmer decided to raise lions to attract tourists. His place, which
was near an intersection, became so popular that cars clogged the roadway.
He finally had to erect a sign that said, "The lion farm's to the right."

2264 What happens when a lion runs into an express train?
It's the end of the lion.

2265 Did you hear about the inept Chinese chef who frequently got drunk?
He couldn't wok a strayed lion.

2266 How much do animal trainers in a circus make?
They earn the lion's share of the money.

2267 *Hunter No. 1:* "I once shot a lion that was 20 feet long."
Hunter No. 2: "Some lyin'."

2268 Daniel was the only man who was not spoiled by being lionized.

2269 Why is the King of the Jungle the laziest animal?
Because he's always lion down on the job.

2270 Did you hear about the fellow who mowed his lawn
while brandishing a whip?
He was the dandelion tamer.

2271 What do you call a lion wearing a cravat
and a flower in its mane?
A dandy lion.

2272 What if the tiger is fed and the lion is not?
The lion gets a roar deal.

2273 How do lions like their meat cooked?
Medium roar.

2274 What does a lion brush his mane with?
A catacomb.

2275 Did you hear about the new lion entree
at the restaurant with a jungle theme?
It's the mane dish.

2276 What do you call a show full of lions?
The mane event.

2277 Did you hear about the circus employee who entertained
visitors by sticking his right arm into a lion's mouth?
His friends now call him Lefty.

2278 That reminds us of the circus stuntman who used to stick
his left arm AND left leg into a lion's mouth. He's all right now.

2279 An unemployed man went home and excitedly told his
wife that he had just been hired by the circus to stick his head
into a lion's mouth.
His wife asked, "Isn't that hard on the lion?"
"No," replied the husband, "his part of the act is a snap."

2280 What happened to the man who tried to cross a lion with a goat?
He had to get a new goat.

2281 What did the lion trainer look for in his contract with the circus?
A protection claws.

2282 What was the name of the film about
a killer lion that swam underwater?
"Claws."

2283 Did you hear about the new book titled *Lion Taming?*
It's by Claude Bottom.

2284 Did you hear about the best-selling jungle book
titled *Never Make a Lioness Angry?*
It's by Sheila Tack.

2285 *Ad in newspaper:* "Lion tamer wants tamer lion."

2286 A man applied for a job as an assistant lion tamer with
the circus. The main lion tamer was a gorgeous lady in a skimpy
bathing suit, and she gave the aspiring applicant a brief
demonstration of her abilities.
As she entered the lion's cage, the mighty beast kissed
her on the cheek and lay down at her feet. "Do you think you
can do that?" she asked.
"No problem," the man replied. "But you'll have to get
that lion out of there first."

2287   *Hunter No. 1:* "I went hunting in Africa and bagged a lion."
Hunter No. 2: "You bagged a lion?"
Hunter No. 1: "Yes. I bagged him and bagged him to please go away."

2288   A hunter on a safari in Africa stepped out of his tent, and,
as fate would have it, a lion was there waiting for him. He fell to the
ground in terror, covered his head with his arms, and waited for the
worst. He looked up a minute later and was astonished to see the lion
lying on the ground beside him.
           "Aren't you going to eat me?" the terrified man asked.
           "Quiet," retorted the lion. "Can't you see I'm saying grace?"

2289   Or, as one lion said to another, "Let us prey."

2290   What is a lion's favorite food?
Baked beings.

2291   How can you get a set of teeth put in at no charge?
Smack a lion.

2292   How does a lion greet the other animals in the field?
"Pleased to eat you."

2293   On which day do lions eat people?
Chewsday.

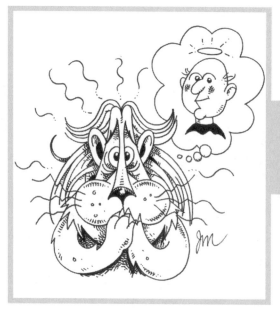

2294   Why did the lion eat the
tightrope walker?
*Because he wanted to have
a balanced meal.*

2295   Why did the lion feel sick after
he ate the minister?
*Because it's hard to keep
a good man down.*

2296   A mother lion scolded her
child for chasing a hunter around
a tree. "How many times must I
tell you not to play with
your food?"

2297 Two lions escaped from the zoo and went in separate directions. When they met about a month later, one of them was emaciated while the other was quite plump. The thin one asked his friend how he managed to stay so healthy-looking.

"It's easy," the other replied. "I've been hiding out in the Pentagon. Every day I eat an admiral or a general, and so far no one has noticed."

2298 Why did the lion eat a man reading a book instead of one working at a word processor?
Because he knew that readers digest but writers cramp.

2299 Why did Roman newspaper reporters rush back to their offices after a Christian was victorious at the Coliseum?
Because there were dead lions.

2300 Why did the Romans give up their money-losing major holidays?
Because the lions ate up all their prophets.

2301 Did you hear about the lion that was killed during one of the ancient Roman games?
He forgot to wear his after-slave potion.

2302 *Roman Christian No. 1:* "I'm going into the arena soon to face the lion."
Roman Christian No. 2: "Yes, we're here today and gone to martyr."

2303 What do you call an armed king of the beasts?
A cat with lion knives.

2304 A man took his wife and mother-in-law on a safari and somehow managed to get the latter lost. The couple soon located her, but she was cornered by a huge, roaring lion. "What are we going to do?" screeched the wife.
"Nothing," replied the husband. "The lion got himself into that predicament. Now let him get out of it."

2305 Did you hear about the man who was ordered to take his pet lion to the zoo?
He did, and the next day he took his pet to the movies.

2306 Why was the king of the jungle not worried about the weather?
Because there was only a 10% chance of its reigning.

2307 Why did the lion cross the jungle?
To get to the other pride.

2308 What happened when the lion became a cannibal?
He had to swallow his pride.

2309 What did the animal trainer think about her lion family?
It was her pride and joy.

2310 Why do groups of lions tend to migrate just before the autumn?
Because pride goeth before the fall.

2311 Why do other lions wait until winter
to migrate to seasonal hunting grounds?
Because the fall goeth before the pride.

2312 A fan of astrology built his own telescope to better study the
constellations. One day he met a girl who claimed she was born under
a certain sign, but he suspected she was lion. For long hours each
evening he charted the heavens to answer a burning question:
"Is that gal a leo?"

Lizard

2313 What has a long tongue and walks on yellow brick roads?
The Lizard of Oz.

2314 Then there was a smarmy-looking little reptile that spent
a lot of time in a hotel lobby.
The manager referred to it as "Our resident lounge lizard."

2315 A Caribbean cruise ship captain made an announcement:
"I have some good news and some bad news. The bad news is that
the refrigeration system failed, the food has spoiled, and we have nothing
to eat except lizards. The good news is that there aren't enough lizards
to go around."

Llama

2316 What South American animal likes girls' toys?
The dolly llama.

2317 What do you call a cart that's used by a chief Tibetan monk to carry around a large South American animal?
The Dalai Lama's llama dolly.

2318 Are llamas skittish animals?
Yes, it's easy to a llama them.

2319 What do South American animals use to help them wake up?
A llama clock.

2320 How does a tourist make a plan for traveling through the mountains of Peru?
By the process of a llama nation.

2321 A sailing vessel carrying South American animals caught fire. As the spar burst into flames, the captain exclaimed, "There goes the mast of the red-hot llamas!"

2322 There was once a herd of llamas that lived next to a herd of cows. The animals were separated by only a small fence. Daily, the cows tricked the young llamas into moving near the fence; then, when they got close enough, the cows grabbed one and pulled it over to their side. The cows used the llama like a soccer ball. They kicked it around for a few hours until they tired of it. The moral of the story? Llamas, don't let your babies grow up to be cow toys.

2323 Or, as we always say, "If life gives you llamas, make llamanade."

Lobster

2324 Who is the principal doctor in a fish hospital?
The chief lobstertrician.

2325 A cannibal's daughter asked, "Mommy, is an airplane good to eat?" The mother replied, "It's like lobster. You eat only what's on the inside."

2326 What did the lobster say when placed in a boiling pot?
"I'm in hot water now!"

2327 Did you hear about the lobster that
got hot under the collar?
But only when he was steamed.

2328 *Patron:* "I'd like a nice lobster tail."
Waiter: "Once upon a time there was a nice lobster . . ."

2329 *Patron:* "Waiter, this lobster has only one claw."
Waiter: "He was probably in a fight."
Patron: "Then bring me the winner."

2330 The tennis team representing Boston
is called the Boston Lobsters.

2331 Why did the lobster blush?
It saw the salad dressing.

2332 Why did the other lobster blush?
Because the seaweed.

2333 Did you hear about the organization
that catches illegal lobsters?
It's a claw enforcement agency.

2334 *Waiter:* "Our special tonight is twin lobsters."
Patron: "How can they tell?"

Locust

2335 What insect cursed in a quiet voice?
A locust.

2336 How do some insects save money?
They live in locust housing.

2337 What do you call an insect that performs magic?
A hocus-pocus locust.

Loon

2338 Where do geese invest their money?
In a savings and loon.

    2339 Did you hear about the crazy birdwatcher?
    He was a raven loonatic.

        2340 What do you call a French dessert cake
        that's filled with bird meat?
        Eclair du loon.

Louse

2341 Did you hear about the young woman who thought
she was bitten by the love bug?
It was only a louse.

    2342 Friar Tuck returned to camp riding a donkey that
was infested with lice. A few days later, a peasant took a sheep
to Robin Hood and complained that "The lice of Tuck's ass are
upon ewe."

2343 Why does rubbing your hair with vinegar
give you head lice?
Because he who acetates is loused.

Lox

2344 Why did the salmon fishermen
stay on strike for several weeks?
They were dead-loxed.

    2345 How are fish kept imprisoned in jail?
    With strong lox.

        2346 What do you call a mixture of imported
        and domestic salmon?
        Combination lox.

2347 Some birds flew over the Panama Canal, prompting
a deli owner to name an entree after them.
He called it locks and bay gulls.

2348 An entrepreneur purchased some smoked salmon and
some steaks and then had those fine foods packed in a large
cylindrical container. You might say that he bought it all, lox,
stock, and barrel.

2349 Or, as one salmon said to another, "Lox of luck."

2350 Did you hear about the deli that became so successful
that the owner renamed it Fort Lox?

2351 Workers in a deli were permitted to eat anything during
their scheduled spare time except smoked salmon. Thus, these
became the world's first anti-lox breaks.

Lynx

2352 Did you hear about the wildcat that escaped from the zoo?
It was a missing lynx.

2353 Did you hear about the pet lynx named Miss Sing?

2354 *Sign at a furrier's store:* Be Our Miss in Lynx.

Mackerel

2355 As the minister said when he caught a large fish, "Holy mackerel!"

2356 What is a favorite song among fish?
"Mackerel the Knife."

2357 What is a difficult science class for fish?
Mackerel Economics.

Magpie

2358   What dessert can fly?
A magpie.

2359   Did you hear about the guy whose wife does bird imitations?
She talks like a magpie.

> **2360**   What is baked into a score of British magpies?
> *Foreign twenty blackbirds.*

Manatee

2361   An aquatic, seaweed-eating mammal named Hugh began swimming very close to a man's waterfront property. The man tried to get rid of the creature by clubbing it, but he was arrested. In court, the man's lawyer argued that assault against a marine mammal is not an offense.
          The judge disagreed, however, stating,
"This is a crime against Hugh manatee."

Mare

2362   Did you hear about the horse that kept late hours?
It was a nightmare.

> **2363**   Haiku:
>   A sausage-eating
>   Armored soldier on horseback:
>   It's my wurst knight mare.

> > **2364**   What kind of race does a female horse enter?
> > *A mare-thon.*

> > **2365**   What is the song "The Old Gray Mare" about?
> > *A politician who runs a city.*

2366   A mare joined a poker game for horses, and one
of the players asked, "How about a little stud?"
The mare replied, "Yeah! Where is he?"

Mink

2367 What exclusive clothing was worn
by the ancient Chinese people?
Ming coats.

    2368 Why are minks such charitable animals?
They give people the shirts right off their backs.

        2369 Did you hear about the ex-convict who
gave his wife a mink stole for her birthday?
*It may not have been genuine mink,
but it certainly was stole.*

2370 Did you hear about the mink farm that hired a veterinarian?
The farmer's wife began to wear the vet's patients.

    2371 *Customer:* "Is it harmful to wear a mink coat in the rain?"
Salesman: "Have you ever seen a mink carrying an umbrella?"

        2372 *Man to salesclerk:* "I'd like something in mink—your model."

2373 A man eventually gave in to years of badgering by his wife
and bought her a mink coat. She was obviously happy, but she
commented on how sorry she was for the poor creature that got
skinned for it. Her husband replied, "Thanks, I appreciate your sympathy."

    2374 *Woman No. 1:* "That's a beautiful mink."
Woman No. 2: "Oh, it's just a little conversation piece
I picked up. My husband never stops talking about it."

    2375 A diplomat is a man who can convince his wife
she looks bad in a mink coat.

        2376 If your wife feels bad
And is really sad
At finding another wrinkle,
It's hard to know
What will make her glow,
But somehow I think a mink'll.

2377 How did the woman who wanted a mink coat and her
husband who wanted a car reach a compromise?
They bought the coat and kept it in the garage.

2378 Did you hear about the man who bought
his wife a complete mink outfit?
He got her a trap and a rifle.

2379 As the man said to his wife while she ogled a mink coat
in a display window, "There are other ways to fight a cold."

2380 There's nothing like a mink coat to thaw a cold shoulder.

2381 *Secretary No. 1:* "My boss gave me a mink coat."
Secretary No. 2: "To keep you warm?"
Secretary No. 1: "No, to keep me quiet."

2382 *Or to put it another way:* "When I threatened to tell
his wife, you should have seen the furs fly."

2383 Did you hear about the Hollywood starlet who was kind to animals?
She'd do anything for a mink.

2384 Did you hear about the woman who took
four years to get a sheepskin?
It took her only one day to get a mink.

2385 Why is a knowledge of animals important in obtaining a mink?
*The way to get a mink is to be like a fox
and play cat-and-mouse with a wolf.*

2386 There was an old woman of Lincoln
Who made a considerable stink on
The subject of furs,
For a young niece of hers
Had run off with nothing but mink on.

2387 Did you hear about the woman whose hobby is magic?
She gets mink from an old goat.

2388 She was only a mink farmer's daughter, but she muffed it every time.

2389 Did you hear about the hippie mink?
She was fur out, man.

2390 *Sign in a mink coat boutique:*
Furs Come, Furs Served.

Mite

2391 What is the favorite book of arachnids?
Of Mites and Men.

2392 A prison was infested with very small arachnids, while a hospital was devoid of any bugs. This proves that the pen is mite-ier than the ward.

2393 What happened when arachnids from a pigsty infested the backyard grass?
The pen was mite-ier than the sward.

2394 What was the arachnid judge's motto?
Mite makes right.

2395 What is a buggy fling?
A one-mite stand.

Mockingbird

2396 What animal is the most impudent?
The mockingbird.

2397 If you had a ton of songbirds, how many would you have?
Two kilo mockingbirds.

2398 How many margaritas did the woman pour into her birdbath?
Enough tequila mockingbird.

Mole

2399   Why are moles such uninteresting company?
Because they're always boring.

2400   What animal makes molehills out of mountains?
Moles.

2401   What is a Wonderbra?
An invention designed to make mountains out of molehills.

2402   What happened when a frustrated homeowner stuck his garden hose into one of the numerous mounds in his backyard?
He made a fountain out of a molehill.

2403   Did you hear about the guy who's always making mountains out of molehills?
Whenever he makes a mistake, it's a real butte.

2404   As the male mole said to his mate, "I worship the ground you tunnel under."

2405   Or, as one mole asked another, "Did the earth move for you, too?"

2406   Why did the mole build a new house?
He was fed up with the hole thing.

2407   A family of moles was tunneling underground with papa mole in the lead and mama mole and baby mole close behind. Progress was impeded when they hit a patch of heavy clay, which made them slower than molasses in January.

2408   What is a mole's favorite author?
Molière.

Mongoose

2409   A farmer who was bothered by marauding snakes wrote a note to the city zoo: "Please tell me how I could acquire a pair of mongeese."

The word didn't seem right, so he wrote another note: "Please tell me how I could acquire a pair of mongooses."

By then, neither word seemed right, so he wrote: "Please tell me how I could acquire a mongoose and a second one to keep the first one company."

2410   What extremely large animal eats cobras?
A humongoose.

2411   *Jamaican No. 1:* "What is that little animal that eats snakes?"
Jamaican No. 2: "A mongoose, mon."

Monkey

2412   What do you get if you run over a monkey?
Rhesus pieces.

2413   How did the chimpanzee escape from its cage?
He used a monkey wrench.

2414   Did you hear about the chimpanzees whose stag party was broken up?
Someone threw a monkey wrench into the works.

2415   What do monkeys eat on Independence Day?
Star-spangled bananas.

2416   What were King Kong's last words?
"Don't monkey around with me."

2417   Why did the clever simian cross the line?
To engage in a little monkey business.

2418   Did you hear about the monkeys in the zoo that were playing poker?
They were playing for peanuts.

2419 A young woman was traveling with her infant son on a train when a man walking down the aisle abruptly halted in front of her, did a double take, and exclaimed, "That's the ugliest baby I've ever seen."

The woman burst into tears, and the conductor who heard her crying tried to console her. "Don't worry about what inconsiderate people have to say; they're just being uncouth. Here, here's a banana for your monkey."

2420 Two professorial men were visiting the zoo when a monkey looked at them and said, "Forget the theory of evolution! You're not going to make a man out of me."

2421 The best way to make a monkey out of a man is to ape him.

2422 *Man No. 1:* "Well, I'll be a monkey's uncle."
Man No. 2: "Actually, there is a family resemblance."

2423 What do you call a farm
that raises chimpanzees?
A monkey ranch.

2424 Why do chimpanzees like
potato chips?
Because they're chip monks.

Moose

2425 What do you call an antlered animal's dessert?
A moose mousse.

2426 Did you hear about the
antlered animal that tells lies?
It's a bull moose.

2427 What do moose do at a concert?
They make moosic.

2428 Did you hear about the (fill in one from your favorite group) who shot a moose and put its head on the wall in the family room?
The rest of the moose was on the other side of the wall in the next room.

2429   What has antlers and eats cheese?
Mickey Moose.

2430   Be kind to the moose.
He may be of some use
For hanging your hat
Or something like that.

2431   A Scottish visitor was in Maine for the first time.
Spotting a large antlered animal, he asked his host
what manner of beast it was.
"That's a moose," the native replied.
"In that case," added the Scotsman,
"I wouldna like to see one of your rats!"

2432   How can you distinguish
a male elk from a female?
By his moosetache.

2433   A reddish-colored stallion was trained to hunt large
Maine deer, but thieves took it. This proves the old proverb
that a stolen roan gathers no moose.

2434   As the Mainer shouted to the stately antlered
animal that sauntered into his backyard, "Vamoose!"

Moray

2435   As the male eel sang to his girlfriend, "That's a moray!"

2436   During a debate, one eel said to another,
"I'd like to get moray to the point."

Mosquito

2437   Why was the mosquito limping?
He went in through a screen door and strained himself.

2438   That reminds us why the young mosquito was so happy.
He passed his first screen test.

2439 Did you hear about the new book titled *Jungle Fever?*
It's by Amos Quito.

2440 What did the police department do to combat the infestation of mosquitoes?
They formed a SWAT team.

2441 A pair of mosquitoes was watching an acupuncturist "needle" a patient. One mosquito shook his head and said, "And for our little puncture, we get swatted."

2442 What insect lives in Russia?
A Moscowito.

2443 How is a mosquito like the government?
Both bite the hand that feeds them.

2444 What is a mosquito's favorite hobby?
Skin diving.

2445 What makes mosquitoes annoying?
They get under your skin.

2446 · The new CEO of a financially troubled corporation was asked how he felt about his new duties. "I feel like a mosquito in a nudist camp," he replied. "I know what I have to do, but I don't know where to begin."

2447 *Greta Garbo:* "There's a mosquito in my room."
Hotel manager: "Is he bothering you?"
Greta Garbo: "No, but I vant to be alone."

2448 Two mosquitoes were lunching on Robinson Crusoe when one said to the other, "I'm leaving now, but I'll see you on Friday."

Moth

2449 How do scale-winged insects communicate?
By word of moth.

2450 What likes to spend the summer in a fur coat
and the winter in a woolen bathing suit?
A moth.

2451 Why didn't the baby moth cry after being spanked?
Because it's hard to make a moth bawl.

2452 Why didn't the butterfly go to the dance?
Because it was a moth ball.

2453 When a moth in a closet saw camphor,
He said, "That's one thing I don't give a damphor."

2454 Why did the elephant eat a can of camphor balls?
He wanted to keep moths out of his trunk.

2455 Did you hear about the woman who is like a moth?
She's always chewing the rag.

2456 Two actresses were comparing their wardrobes.
One said, "I choose my own clothes."
The other replied, "A moth chews mine."

2457 Why did the moth in a theater chew a hole in the rug?
It wanted to see the floor show.

2458 William Shakespeare once asked his wife to check
whether moths had done any damage to his favorite coat.
After a thorough inspection, she announced, "No holes, Bard."

2459 A moth of the cloth named Clint
Didn't eat any wool for a stint.
He acts really holy;
'Fore Easter, just solely
'Cause he gave up his woolens for lint.

2460 Did you hear about the golf moth?
It makes eighteen holes a day.

2461 Why did the tightfisted miser keep a moth as a pet?
Because it only ate holes.

2462   A moth went to the doctor, complaining of recurring bellyaches. "You must stop eating overcoats," advised the doctor. "You're getting an ulster of the stomach."

2463   How did the overworked moth get away from it all?
It spent the winter in a tropical worsted suit.

    2464   That reminds us of the moth who wanted a wool suit in the worsted way. (There certainly moth be a better pun than that!)

2465   Max Moth and Maggie Moth discovered some wool spats in a shoe closet. After devouring that unexpected meal, they retired for the evening. At work the next day, Max told his coworkers, "I had a spat with my wife last night."

    2466   What are a butterfly's favorite subjects in school?
Mothematics and Greek mothology.

      2467   What is the world's largest insect?
A mammoth.

2468   A boy asked the bookstore clerk for the book *Advice to Young Mothers.*
"Is the book for your mom?" asked the curious clerk.
"No," replied the lad, "it's for me. I collect moths."

    2469   A rolling stone gathers no moths. It squashes them.

    2470   Did you hear about the farmer who attached an insect trap to the back of his horse?
When he checked it a few hours later, it was empty. This proves the old adage that a strolling roan gathers no moths.

Mouse

2471   Why did the mouse take a bath?
Because he wanted to be squeaky clean.

    2472   The angry wife snapped at her husband, "Are you a man or a mouse? Squeak up!"

2473 A woman awakened her husband during the night and exclaimed, "I heard a mouse squeak."

"What do you want me to do," the husband replied, "oil it?"

2474 Which mice are poverty-stricken?
The ones that just squeak by, living a hand-to-mouse existence in a hole in the wall.

2475 What is the favorite game of mice?
Hide and squeak.

2476 Where did mice go to drink during Prohibition?
To a squeakeasy.

2477 How is Mickey Mouse like a comet?
He's a star with a tail.

2478 Why did Mickey Mouse go on a rocket to outer space?
He wanted to find Pluto.

2479 *Patient:* "Doctor, doctor! I keep seeing images of Mickey Mouse."
Doctor: "Don't worry. You're just having Disney spells."

2480 Where does Minnie Mouse keep her husband's baseball trophies?
On Mickey's mantelpiece.

2481 What is Mickey Mouse's favorite kind of calculator?
A Minnie computer.

2482 Why did Mickey Mouse take his girlfriend's computer?
Because he wanted to leave Minnie Apple-less.

2483 Why did Walt Disney's famous rodent have only one girlfriend?
Because Mickey was monogamouse.

2484   Where do computer mice reside?
In a mouse pad.

2485   What's gray, buzzes, and eats cheese?
A mouse-quito.

2486   A mouse that was mad about cheese
Developed a terrible sneeze.
         His problem was this:
         The holes in the Swiss
Admitted too much of a breeze.

2487   What famous mouse lived
in ancient Rome?
Julius Cheeser.

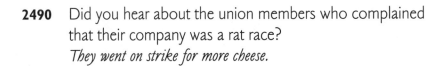

2488   Why are mice's children so polite?
*They always say "cheese" and
"thank you."*

2489   Or, as the mouse photographer
said, "Say cheese."

2490   Did you hear about the union members who complained
that their company was a rat race?
They went on strike for more cheese.

2491   Why didn't the mouse enter the house
through the open window?
Because he's a dormouse.

2492   As Confucius says, "A modest girl never pursues a man.
Nor does a mousetrap pursue a mouse."

2493   How are mousetraps like the measles?
Both are catching.

2494   Did you hear about the new mousetrap
that tempts mice with music?
It plays a catchy, snappy tune.

2495   A man didn't have any cheese to put in his mousetrap, so he cleverly cut out a picture of cheese and used that as bait instead. The next day, the man saw with satisfaction that the trap had been triggered. And in the trap was a picture of a mouse.

2496   Did you hear about the inventor who built a better mousetrap?
Now he has better mice.

2497   As Confucius says, "Marriage is like a baited mousetrap. Those out of it can't wait to get in, and those in it can't wait to get out."

2498   A henpecked husband was asked by the marriage counselor, "Are you a man or a mouse?"
"I must be a man," replied the husband, "because my wife's afraid of mice."

2499   *Wife:* "My mother won't stay in our house unless we get rid of the mice."
Husband: "Well, let's get rid of the cat."

2500   The sultan got sore on his harem,
And invented a scheme for to scare 'em.
He caught him a mouse
Which he loosed in the house.
The confusion is called harem-scarem.

2501   Why is an old loaf of bread like a mouse dashing into its hole?
Because you can see it's stale.

2502   Did you hear about the cat that put an advertisement in the newspaper saying she would do light mouse work?

2503   Did you hear about the cat doctor who made mouse calls?

2504   A mouse went to a plastic surgeon and requested to be transformed into a gnome. As the doctor scooped a huge shovelful of the transforming leaven, he commented, "It takes a heap of leaven to make a mouse a gnome."

2505   What organization do mice attend to give up drinking?
Alcoholics Anonymouse.

2506   Or, as the shy female mouse said when she
joined the convent, "I want to be a nunny mouse."

2507   Why didn't the church mouse live in the steeple?
He didn't aspire that high.

2508   Hickory, dickory, dock,
Some mice ran up the clock.
The clock struck one,
And the rest escaped with minor injuries.

2509   Where did the mouse moor his sailboat?
At the hickory dickory dock.

2510   Did you hear about the Chinese pet rat named Mousey Tung?

2511   What city has the most
mice and cattle?
Mousecow.

2512   What do angry mice send
each other in December?
Cross-mouse cards.

2513   How do drowning rats save each other?
With mouse-to-mouse resuscitation.

2514   *One mouse to another in a laboratory cage:* "I've got that scientist
trained. Whenever I press this lever, he gives me food."

2515   *Another mouse to yet another one:* "I've got a brother
in cancer research and a sister in psychological testing."

2516   Two small mice were crouched under a table in the chorus girls'
dressing room of a big Broadway show. "Wow," exclaimed the first mouse,
"have you ever seen so many gorgeous legs in your life?" "Means nothing to
me," said the second. "I'm a titmouse."

2517   Did you hear about the snobbish French mouse?
He got too big for his Brie cheese.

2518   A family of mice once found a rare underground deposit of Brie cheese. It took three excavations before all of the cheese was removed. Which raises the question: Have you ever seen such a site in your life as Brie mined thrice?

2519   What has six eyes but can't see?
Three blind mice.

        2520   What is a cat's favorite breakfast?
        Mice Krispies.

                2521   What is a cat's favorite fast food?
                Minute Mice.

                        2522   What is a hot cat's favorite dessert?
                        Mice cream.

2523   What do cats like on their hot dogs?
Catsup and mousetard.

                2524   A mouse in her room woke Miss Dowd,
                      She was frightened, it must be allowed.
                            But a happy thought hit her:
                            To scare off the critter,
                      She sat up in bed and meowed.

2525   A mouse bragged to his friend that he crawled into an airplane's overhead storage compartment and relieved himself. The other mouse wasn't impressed and replied, "Bin there. Dung that."

                2526   What has gray skin, four legs, and a trunk?
                No, not an elephant—but a mouse on vacation.

Mule

2527   Did you hear the joke about the mule?
You'll get a real kick out of it.

                2528   Why was the Mule Rental Company fined?
                It was accused of accepting kickbacks.

2529 Will a mule laugh if you tickle him?
He may—but you'll get a bigger kick out of it.

2530 Mule in a barnyard, lazy and sick;
Boy with a pin on the end of a stick.
Boy jabbed mule; mule gave a lurch:
Services Sunday at the country church.

2531 *Customer:* "Do you stand behind your merchandise?"
Salesman: "No. I sell mules."

2532 *Farmer:* "Where's my mule that I told you to have shod?"
Worker: "Shod? I thought you said shot."

2533 Two wiseacres, Samuel and Thomas, met on
a street corner. The first one said, "How are you, Tom-ass?"
The other replied, "Just fine, Sam-mule."

Mullet

2534 As one fish said to another, "Before I make a decision, I'd like to mullet over."

2535 What is a famous college for fish?
The Mulletary Academy.

Mussel

2536 Why did the fisherman eat a lot of shellfish?
He did it for mussel tone.

2537 Or, as one macho clam said to another, "Feel that mussel."

2538 Did you hear about the guy who went to a seafood
gym? He pulled a mussel.

2539 There was a strong man named Russell,
Who liked getting into a tussle.
But he once lost face
At a seafood place,
When he struggled to open a mussel.

2540 Did you hear about the nuclear-powered shellfish?
It was a guided mussel.

Mynah

2541 Why wouldn't the bartender give a drink to the young bird?
He wasn't allowed to serve mynahs.

2542 Show us a keen-eyed talking and music-producing bird,
and we'll show you a see-sharp mynah.

2543 Did you hear about the Chinese talking bird?
It was named Asia Mynah.

2544 What was the aspiration of the talking bird
that was devoted to baseball?
To play in the mynah league.

2545 What birds wear helmets
down in the pits?
Coal mynahs.

2546 A marine biologist developed a potion for indefinitely extending the lives of porpoises, the key ingredient being mynah birds. Returning home from his lab late one night with a bag of these birds, he was puzzled to find a lion sleeping at his front steps. He shrugged and, keeping his eyes on the beast, carefully stepped over it, whereupon he was arrested by observant police and charged with transporting mynahs across a staid lion for immortal porpoises.

Nag

2547 As Confucius says, "A nag never seems to have enough horse sense to bridle her tongue." (Or, as one horse said to another, "Don't be a nag.")

2548 Did you hear about the long-suffering husband who really feels at home at the racetrack?
It's always nag, nag, nag.

2549 That reminds us of the man who met his future wife at the racetrack. He went there to bet on a nag and wound up saddled with one for life.

Newt

2550 She was only a salamander's daughter, but no one newt.

2551 The first President Bush must have overheard this exchange between a salamander breeder and a mathematician.
Salamander man: "My business would get a boost if I could show you posing with two of my amphibians as a living graph."
Mathematician: "No newt axes."

2552 *Boy No. 1:* "Why do you call your pet salamander Tiny?"
Boy No. 2: "Because he's my newt."

2553 You can't teach an old dog new tricks, but you can teach an old salamander newt tricks.

2554 What great amphibian football player had to retire when his joints hardened?
Newt Rock-Knee.

2555 Some slimy salamanders slithered out of their tank in the aquarium, but the keeper was able to lure them back by tempting them with some dark-purple berries. They moved very slowly, however, which prompted the keeper to comment that he was having a sloe newts day.

2556 Why did the newspaper sports editor interview several salamanders for his article on animal track teams?
He wanted all the newts that's fit to sprint.

Nightingale

2557 What singing birds did King Arthur value highly?
Knightingales, because their singing drowned out the lyres at court. (Of course, it also made for many sleepless knights).

2558 A retired diva was asked to perform at a party. She glanced at her new rich husband and replied, "I'm now a nightingale. It doesn't sing after it's made its nest."

Ocelot

2559 Who was King Arthur's favorite knight?
Sir Ocelot. (Who liked to ocelot of other knights to swordfight.)

Octopus

2560 Did you hear about the octopus soldier?
He went into battle well-armed.

2561 Did you hear about the two octopuses that fell in love?
They walked arm in arm in arm in arm . . .

2562 What is an octopus's favorite song?
"I want to hold your hand, your hand, your hand . . ."

2563 Why did the octopus buy several telephones?
*So it could reach out and touch someone . . . and someone else . . .
and someone else . . .*

2564 Did you hear about the clever marketing manager?
He sold a family of octopuses a supply of underarm deodorant.

2565 Did you hear about the clumsy octopus
that played football?
He still managed to fumble the ball.

2566 What mathematical formula describes the area
formed by four cephalopods and their partners
as they join tentacles in a barn dance?
Octopi are squared.

2567 What did the octopus take with
him on a camping trip?
Tent-acles.

2568 Did you hear about the squid sheriff?
It formed an octoposse.

2569 *Zoo visitor to octopus:* "What's
it like to have eight arms?"
Octopus: "Pretty handy."

2570 What does an octopus wear?
A coat of arms.

2571 An octopus has two pairs of forearms.

2572 How do you confuse an octopus?
Tell it to count to nine on its fingers.

2573 How do squids get to work?
On an octobus.

2574 What kind of cat likes water?
An octopuss.

Opossum

2575   As one marsupial said to another,
"Opossum by your house and decided to stop for a visit."

2576   What is an opossum?
An Irish possum.   See also Possum

Orca

2577   Where do killer whales play
their musical instruments?
In the orca-stra.

2578   Where do killer whales go
to get their teeth straightened?
To the orca-dontist.

Ostrich

2579   Did you hear about the long-necked bird that
was a social outcast?
It was ostrichized.

2580   A nine-member family was asleep when a tornado
swept through their yard. Just as the house was about to
collapse, they were awakened by the squawking of their pet
bird. The headline the next day read:
"Ostrich in Time Saves Nine."

2581   *Doctor:* "How do you limber up every day?"
Patient: "Ostrich first thing in the morning."

2582   What happened to the ostrich that kept his head
buried in the sand too long?
He got burned in the end.

2583   An ostrich arrived late for a beach party at which all the other guests
had their heads buried in the sand. The latecomer looked around and then
called out, "Where is everybody?"

2584 Did you hear about the ostrich that became a gangster?
He liked to bury someone else's head in the sand.

Otter

2585 What is the Golden Rule for web-footed mammals?
Do unto otters as you would have them do unto you.

2586 As the web-footed mammal said when he got back on the merry-go-round, "One good turn deserves an otter."

2587 Did you hear about the unique furry aquatic creature?
He was unlike all the otters.

2588 Why was the furry aquatic creature bewildered?
He suffered from otter confusion.

2589 That reminds us of the visitor to a Chinese zoo who facetiously asked whether the web-footed mammals spoke pidgin English.
"No," replied the zookeeper, "they speak otter Confucian."

2590 Said the otter to his daughter,
"Daughter, don't go near the water."
Said the daughter to her pater,
"I'm an otter, not a squatter."
Should he slap or maybe swat her?
Suppose a rotter otter spot her?
A slicker swain, a surly plotter,
A cad, a reputation-blotter?
The more he thought, he grew the hotter.
But all he said was "You shouldn't oughter."

2591 *Sign at the zoo:* "Out of Otter."

2592 What kind of vehicles do web-footed mammals drive?
Otter mobiles.

2593 As one aquatic mammal said to another, "You really otter try harder."

2594 Why did the furry aquatic creature cross the road?
To get to the otter side.

Owl

2595   As the English teacher said when she corrected her
owlish student, "It's whooo, not whoooom."

2596   Or, as the father owl said to his son,
"It's not what you know but whooo you know."

2597   Did you hear about the book on detective owls?
It's a whooodunit.

2598   What book is about famous owls?
Who's Whooo.

2599   *Patient:* "Doctor, doctor! I know a man who thinks he's an owl."
Doctor: "Who? Who?"
Patient: "Now I know two people."

2600   Did you hear about the indifferent owl?
He just doesn't give a hoot.

2601   What is a gourmet owl's
favorite meal?
Hoot cuisine.

2603   Why was the Scottish owl
upset with his parents?
*Because they wouldn't let him
go hoot at night.*

2604   What is an owl's favorite web site?
www.YaHOOT.tree

2605   As Confucius says, "Many a
woman tries to change her
night owl into a homing
pigeon."

2602   Did you hear about
the comedian owl?
He was a real hoot.

2606   As the sea captain announced to
his bird passengers, "Owl aboard!"

2607   What does an owl in the daytime have in common
with the sixteenth president of the United States?
They're both a-blinkin'.

> **2608**   As a wise old owl once said,
> "Nothing is certain except death and taxidermists."

2609   Or, as the male spotted owl said to his wife one evening,
"You can't have a headache! We're an endangered species."

> **2610**   What is a palindromic owl's summer complaint?
> *"Too hot to hoot."*

2611   Did you hear about the two owls whooo refrained
from courting because it was raining?
They just sat in a tree and repeated, "Too wet to woo. Too wet to woo."

> **2612**   That reminds us of the very funny owl. He was too wit to woo.

Ox

2613   Why did the ox run away from the
wise-cracking farmer?
Because he couldn't take a yoke.

2614   Or, as one ox said to another,
"I guess the yoke's on me."

2615   What do you call a photocopy
of a drawing of a male bovine?
A Xerox.

2616   What is the favorite Bible verse of
cattle and sheep?
"Ox and ewe shall receive."

2617   What university is also the favorite
car of cattle?
Oxford.

2618   What is the formal attire
of male bovines?
Black oxbow tie.

2619   Did you hear about the two beasts of burden that bumped into each other?
It was just an oxident.

Oyster

2620   A noise annoys an oyster.

2621   As the oyster said while contemplating whether or not to
make a pearl necklace, "To bead or not to bead, that is the question."

2622   Or as the manager counseled an employee, "Be like an
oyster. It can make a pearl of great value if it has the grit."

2623   A man went to see a doctor because he swallowed an oyster that
contained something more than succulent seafood. The doctor removed
the object and said, "A gritty pearl is like a malady."

2624   A man can get a pearl out of an oyster, but it takes
a pretty girl to get a diamond out of an old crab.

2625   As the diver said when he opened an ugly oyster,
"What's a nice pearl like you doing in a place like this?"

2626   A happy little grain of sand became lodged inside an oyster shell,
and somehow he ended up confined to a wheelchair. He was pearlized
and became a pearlaplegic.

2627   The Browns and the Smiths had dinner at a popular seafood
restaurant. Mrs. Brown and Mr. Smith both ordered oysters.
Next day, at the water cooler, Smith commented on the food
and asked, "Did the oysters disagree with your wife?"
"They wouldn't dare!" replied Brown.

2628   *Waiter:* "Sir, are you looking for a pearl in your oyster stew?"
Patron: "No, I'm looking for oysters."

2629   Why is the Fourth of July like oyster stew?
It's no good without crackers.

2630   Did you hear about the angry oyster?
It found itself in a stew.

2631   An oyster met an oyster, and they were oysters two;
Two oysters met two oysters, and they were oysters, too;
Four oysters met a cup of milk, and they were oyster stew.

2632   Did you hear about the oyster joke?
It's too raw.

2633   *Patron:* "Waiter, are raw oysters healthy?"
Waiter: "I never heard one complain."

2634   Then there was the woman who was so polite
that she wouldn't open an oyster without knocking first.

2635   Did you hear about the shy oyster?
It crawled into its shell and clammed up.

2636   The world is your oyster, but only if you
have enough clams.

2637   What is chocolate and lies
on the bottom of the ocean?
An Oyster egg.

2638   Where do mollusks march in the springtime?
In the Oyster parade.

2639   As the English fisherman in Liverpool shouted
when a woman fell off the pier, "'Oyster up!"

2640   According to experts, the oyster
In its shell—or crustacean cloister—
May frequently be
Either he or a she
Or both, if it should be its choice ter.

Panda

2641   What do you call chaos among bears in the Himalayas?
Pandamonium.

2642   Where do many Tibetan bears live?
In pandaminiums.

2643   Did you hear about the mean old bear wrangler at the Bejing zoo
who inflicted pain on the bears? He was busted for causing panda moan-ium.

> **2644**   Why was another bear wrangler at the Bejing zoo busted?
> *For panda handling.*

> > **2645**   Did you hear about the spoiled baby bear?
> > *Its parents panda to its every whim.*

Parakeet

2646   What is a fidgety parakeet?
A fuss-budgie.

> **2647**   What do you call birds that love to recite poetry?
> *Parro-Keats.*

Parrot

2648   What did the parrot say when it saw a duck?
"Polly wants a quacker."

> **2649**   Or, as the parrot said to the frog, "Polly wants a croaker."
> (Which is also what the undertaker taught his parrot to say.)

> > **2650**   What did the parrot say on Independence Day?
> > *"Polly wants a firecracker."*

2651   What did the socialite's parrot say?
"Polly wants a cracker—with caviar on it."

> **2652**   What bright green Texas bird once ran for president?
> *H. Ross Parrot.*

> > **2653**   Why did the parrot always carry an umbrella?
> > *He didn't want to be Polly-saturated.*

2654   How can you tell whether a parrot is intelligent?
It speaks in Polly-syllables.

2655   What is a parrot's favorite game?
Monopoly.

2656   What are a parrot's favorite literary characters?
Mr. Macawber and Pollyanna.

2659   What do you call birds that like to attack ships?
Parrots of the Caribbean.

2657   What is a macaw's favorite song?
"I Love Parrots in the Springtime."

2658   What is the favorite operetta of singing birds?
The Parrots of Penzance.

2660   Did you hear about the parrot that swallowed a watch?
Now it goes tick-talk-tick-talk— and all it ever talks about is Polly tics.

2661   Why is politics for the birds?
Because politicians always parrot the same old lines.

2662   A man gave his wife a parrot for her birthday, complete with ribbons attached to the bird's legs. When the woman pulled one ribbon, the parrot said, "Happy Birthday." When she pulled the other ribbon, the parrot said, "I love you."

The woman then mused, "I wonder what would happen if I pulled both ribbons at once."

The parrot replied, "I'd fall off my perch, you silly twit."

2663   A parrot never said a word until past its seventh birthday. Then, one day during a meal it blurted out, "This piece of fruit is rotten!"

The parrot's owner exclaimed, "You can talk! Why haven't you spoken before?"

The parrot replied, "Well, so far everything's been okay."

2664   That, in turn, reminds us of the father parrot that punished his son—for not talking back.

2665   A parrot made some rude comments to its owner. As punishment, the parrot was put into the freezer for several minutes ("to cool its heels," in the owner's words). When the shivering parrot was removed, it pointed to the freezer and asked, "What did the chicken do to deserve that?"

2666   A man's parrot was having difficulty talking. A veterinarian diagnosed the problem as a misalignment of the upper and lower beaks and suggested that the man might file down the upper beak. The man went to a hardware store and told the manager what he wanted. The manager warned the man that such filing could interfere with the bird's ability to peck its food and that the parrot could die of starvation.

A few weeks passed, and the man went to the hardware store for something else.

"How's your parrot?" asked the manager.

"Oh, he died," replied the man.

"I told you he would starve," reprimanded the manager.

"Oh, he didn't die of starvation," countered the man. "He was already dead before I took his head out of the vise."

2667   After a woman purchased a parrot at an auction, she asked the auctioneer, "Are you sure this parrot talks? I've bid an awful lot of money on it."

The man replied, "I'm quite sure. It was the parrot that was bidding against you."

2668   A parrot is a wordy birdy.

2669   Did you hear about the parrot noise?
All the neighbors squawked.

2670   A minister had a parrot that always said, "Let us pray." A young couple had a parrot that always said, "Let's kiss." In hopes of converting the wayward winged one, the minister lent his parrot to the young couple. When the two birds met for the first time, the worldly one said, "Let's kiss."

The preacher's parrot replied, "My prayers have been answered."

2671   Did you hear about the talking birds who were concerned about population growth?
They were members of Planned Parrothood.

2672 Why did the mother bird go to Junior's school?
For a parrot-teacher conference.

> **2673** Why did the talking bird join the Army?
> *He wanted to be a parrot-trooper.*

> > **2674** What's orange and sounds like a parrot?
> > *A carrot.*

2675 What did the man say to his parrot when he
learned that the bird's original owner was an earl?
"Polly, you're a thane."

> **2676** Why don't parrots owned by math teachers have breakfast?
> *Because they are poly-no-meals.*

Partridge

2677 Did you hear about the guy who played
golf on Christmas and accidentally hit a bird?
He got a partridge on a par three.

> **2678** Or the fellow who put a bullet in a Christmas
> tree that had shed all its needles?
> *He had a cartridge in a bare tree.*

> > **2679** Did you hear about the bird that went on
> > an infrequent drinking bout?
> > *It was a partridge in a rare spree.*

Peacock

2680 Why did the librarian recommend
A Peacock's Life by Ima Bird?
It's a beautiful tale.

> **2681** What makes peacocks unreliable?
> *They're always spreading tails.*

> > **2682** How is the figure 9 like a peacock?
> > *It's nothing without its tail.*

2683 Did you hear about the time a farmer's son used left-over Easter egg dye on all of the eggs in the chicken coop?
The rooster saw the colorful collection and killed the peacock.

Pekingese

2684 Why were miniskirts once called "dogs"?
Because you could peek on knees.

2685 When do small dogs commute to work?
During the peke hour.

2686 What was the favorite TV show of small dogs?
"Twin Pekes."

Pelican

2687 As the pelican said after a huge fish dinner, "Well, that certainly fills the bill."

2688 Why did the pelican refuse to pay for his meal?
His bill was too big.

2689 What a wonderful bird the pelican:
His beak can hold more than his belican.
He can hold in his beak
Enough food for a week,
And I don't know how in the helican.

2690 What do you call a big-billed bird with a negative attitude?
A pelican't.

2691 Why did the pelican put a leg in his beak when he ate in a restaurant?
He wanted to foot the bill.

2692 How does a lawyer resemble a pelican?
In the length of his bill.

Penguin

2693   What's black and white and black and white and black and white?
A penguin rolling down a hill (or in a revolving door).

2694   What three birds are black and white and red all over?
*A penguin with the measles, a blushing penguin, and
a sunburned penguin. (Yes, we know about the gnuspaper,
but that's an animal of another breed.)*

2696   Did you hear about the guy who used a computer dating service and requested someone who was short, liked water sports, and wore formal attire?
The computer set him up with a penguin.

2697   That reminds us of the formal dance at the zoo. The penguins arrived in tuxedos, and the monkeys wore tails.

2698   What lives at the South Pole and smiles?
A pengrin.

2695   What's black and white and has eight wheels?
A penguin on roller skates.

2699   Where do penguins keep their money?
In a snow bank.

2700   What is a penguin's favorite vehicle?
An ice-cycle.

2701   What do penguins wear to keep their heads warm?
Polar ice caps.

Perch

2702   What is an arrogant fish?
A lofty perch.

2703 *Patient:* "Doctor, doctor! I feel like a fish."
Doctor: "Just perch there for a minute."

2704 Which fish have historic recognition?
The 1803 Louisiana Perches.

Pheasant

2705 As one game bird said to another, "Pheasant greetings to you."

2706 Why would a bird be offended if you called him a pheasant?
Because you'd be making game of him.

2707 Why was the hunter arrested for trying
to aid two injured game birds?
He was charged with mal pheasants.

2708 What is a pheasant under glass?
A small bird with a large bill.

2709 A flea once lived on a pheasant
Who was royally vain and unpleasant
Till the flea, on a whim,
Bit the h out of him,
And now he is only a peasant.

2710 What do you call an eastern Mediterranean bird
that wears a brimless felt hat with a tassel?
A fez-ant.

Phoenix

2711 Why did the mythological bird go to a psychiatrist?
It had phoenix envy.

Pickerel

2712 Did you hear about the fish in a predicament?
He was in a real pickerel.

Pig

Once upun a time, a little girl grew up with pigs as her pen pals in a rural hamlet. She wore cute little pigtails and porkpie hats and was happy as a pig in spit when her family carried her around piggyback.

Devoted to the classics, the pig gal spoke pig Latin and squealed with delight at the works of Francis Bacon.

She abboared swine that live high off the hog of pork barrel politics. Snout the right thing to do. It just isn't kosher.

It is, therefore, not a pigment of our imagination when we say, "To err is human; to make pig puns, porcine."

2713   Did you hear about the pig golfer?
He plays on sausage links.

2714   Show us a sausage factory that covers an entire acre, and we'll show you a lot of baloney.

2715   What do you call a sausage that has been stolen?
A missing link.

2716   As one pig said to another on a very hot day, "I never sausage heat."
The other pig replied, "Yeah, and I'm almost bacon."

2717   Did you hear about the acting pig?
He performed so well that he brought home Kevin Bacon.

2718   Did you hear about the actor who had a pet pig named Hamlet?

2719   *Patron:* "Waiter, are you sure this ham was cured?"
Waiter: "Yes, sir."
Patron: "Well, it's had a relapse."

2720   Did you hear about the pig that was taken by a pawnbroker?
It was a ham hock.

2721   What do you call someone who steals pigs?
A hamburglar.

> **2722**   What were Miss Piggy's last words?
> *"I'm pink; therefore, I'm ham."*

> > **2723**   That reminds us of what a philosophical pig says:
> > "I stink; therefore, I ham."

2724   Or, as the pompous pig said, "I ham what I ham."

> **2725**   A pig and a chicken went to a restaurant for breakfast.
> The chicken ordered ham and eggs, which prompted the pig to
> pontificate, "I don't like that choice of meal. For you, it may be
> a mere contribution, but for me, it means a total commitment."

> > **2726**   Did you hear about the pig that was ground into
> > sausages by a lady butcher?
> > *The pig's last act was to give his seat to a lady.*

2727   Why did the butcher make his sausages with meat at one end but
only corn meal at the other?
Because in hard economic times, it's difficult to make both ends meat.

> **2728**   Or, as the pig said when the butcher cut off his tail,
> "That is the end of me."

> > **2729**   Did you hear about the butcher who backed into
> > the bacon slicer?
> > *He got a little behind in his work.*

2730   Why is getting up at four o'clock in
the morning like a pig's tail?
Because it's twirly.

> **2731**   Did you hear about the new book
> titled *Off to Market*?
> *It's by Tobias A. Pigg.*

> > **2732**   Did you hear about the pig that built himself a home?
> > *He made a knot in his tail and called it a pig's tie.*

2733   Where do good pigs go when they die?
To a sty in the sky.

2734   When did the farmer overlook his pigs?
When he had a sty in his eye.

2735   Did you hear about
the perplexed pig?
He was sty-mied.

2736   Why did the pig go to see a psychiatrist?
He was having a mud-life crisis.

2737   What is a favorite book of pigs?
The Wizard of Ooze.

2738   *Bumper sticker:* Pigs Do It Sloppily.

2739   Where do pigs enjoy vacationing?
In Wallow Wallow, Washington.

2740   A pig author writes with a pig pen.

2741   Why did the boy call his pet
pig Ballpoint?
It was just a pen name.

2742   Why was another pet
pig named Ink?
Because it kept running out of the pen.

2744   What state has the most pigs?
Pennsylvania.

2745   Did you hear about
the pigs' dinner?
It was real swill.

2743   That reminds us of the
criminal pig.
He did time in the pen.

2746   Or, as one pig said to another,
"Where there's swill there's whey."

2747   Did you hear about the chef's favorite pig recipe?
It was his strong suet. (And it sueted him just fine.)

      2748   Why should you never confide in a pig?
      Because pigs squeal a lot.

            2749   Did you hear about the farmer's truck that carried a dozen and a half pigs?
            It was an eighteen-squealer.

2750   Did you hear about the squealing Spanish artist: Pablo Pigasso.

      2751   What is a porker's favorite stage play?
      Pygmalion.

            2752   Did you hear about the farmer who raised midget hogs?
            They were pygmies.

2753   A smart aleck asked a butcher for a yard of ham. Not to be outsmarted, the butcher gave him three pig's feet.

      2754   Speaking of pig's feet reminds us of the couple at a restaurant. The wife said to her husband, "See whether the chef has pig's feet."
      The husband replied, "I can't tell. He has his shoes on."

            2755   How did the psychic guess the color of the hog?
            By pigmental telepathy.

2756   There was a young wife from Antigua,
Who said to her husband, "What a pigua!"
      He responded, "My queen,
      Is it manners you mean?
Or do you refer to my figua?"

      2757   Stubborn hogs are pigheaded.

            2758   Where do hogs keep their money?
            In piggy banks.

2759   Did you hear about the time that France sent the
United States a huge shipment of hot dogs?
They paid off a debt of several million franks.

2760   A traveling salesman was stranded during a tornado and went
to a nearby farm. The farmer offered the guest his choice of entree
for dinner: ham, hot dogs, or sausages. The visitor replied,
"Any pork in a storm."

2761   Where do pigs like
to picnic in New York City?
In Central Pork.

2762   Did you hear about
the squealing composer?
It was Cole Porker.

2763   What is a pig's favorite game?
Stud porker.

2764   *Man No. 1:* "How'd you get that lump on your head?"
Man No. 2: "From my wife. I said if she could cook breakfast without
burning it, pigs would fly. She said pigs would fly—and threw a pound
of frozen sausages at me."

2765   Two pigs were playfully wrestling when one
asked the other, "Do you give up? Say oinkle."

2766   What was the name of the pig
farmer's corporation?
Oink, Inc.

2767   How do pigs transmit top secret messages?
With invisible oink.

2768   Why are pig farmers so easygoing?
They take things for grunted.

2769   Why was the pig farmer angry?
He was disgruntled.

2770   Did you hear about the gorgeous pig from gay Paris?
She was famous for saying "oui-oui oui-oui" all the way home.

Pigeon

2771   Did you hear about the girl who is rather dovelike?
She's not soft and cooing, but she's pigeon-toed.

2772   Why did the guy put bread crumbs in his shoes?
So he could feed his pigeon toes.

2773   Did you hear about the guy
who named his pet pigeon Toad?

2774   A family of pigeons was traveling on vacation when the youngest
offspring complained of tiredness. The father offered to pull the youngster
along with a string attached to him, but the young one said, "I don't want
to be pigeon-towed."

2775   Did you hear about the father pigeon that
chided his offspring for walking people-toed?

2776   How can you tell when a recession is ending on Wall Street?
There are more pigeons than stockbrokers on window ledges.

2777   Did you hear about the pigeon family
that wanted to buy a house in the suburbs?
They didn't have enough money, so they put down a deposit.

2778   A small-town mayor was asked what he was going to do about
the abundance of pigeon droppings. "For one thing," replied the mayor,
"I'm not going to dodge the issue."

2779   Or, as one British pigeon said to another when they saw the railroad station,
"Let's fly over it and do a little train spotting."

2780   A group of immigrants was in the process of becoming U.S.
citizens, and the judge was expounding on the history of Old Glory.
When he completed his tutorial, the judge asked one applicant, "What
flies over the Capitol?"
The immigrant replied, "Pigeons."

2781 *Patient:* "Doctor, doctor! My wife insists on keeping
a goat in the bedroom, and the smell is terrible."
Doctor: "Why not open a window?"
Patient: "What? And let all the pigeons out?"

2782 During an extended visit to her daughter's home,
a mother commented, "I can imitate any bird you mention."
The son-in-law said, "Let's see a homing pigeon."

2783 Did you hear about the bird that landed
on an electrical wire?
It was an ohming pigeon. (It couldn't resist.)

2784 Did you hear about the guy who was so mean
that he sent his homing pigeon out and then moved?

2785 It is extremely difficult for a homing pigeon to construct
its house. It requires a dedicated effort of piling up layers of
material. You might say that it takes a love of heaping to make
a homer house.

2786 What is the language of birds?
Pigeon English.

2787 What kind of bird is the least trustworthy?
A stool pigeon.

Pike

2788 Why did the snail release itself from the trout's fin?
He thought he could travel faster on the pike.

2789 A swimmer appeared at a diving competition with a fish.
When asked what dive he was going to attempt, he replied, "A
somersault with pike."

Pinscher

2790 What did the vet ask the woman's husband?
"Why did the Doberman pinscher?"

2791   What do you call a dog that loves bowling?
A Doberman tenpinscher.

Plaice

2792   *Customer:* "Waiter, this fish is very rude."
Waiter: "It doesn't know its plaice."

2793   As one fish said to another,
"Your plaice or mine?"

2794   Or, as one parasite said to another after meeting
in a flatfish, "What's a nice girl like you doing in
a plaice like this?"

Platypus

2795   Have you heard about the cat
that swallowed a mallard?
It was a duck-filled fatty puss.

2796   Or, as the elephant said to the platypus,
"I never forget a face. But with yours I'll make an exception."

Pointer

2797   *Military cadet:* "I'm a West Pointer."
Young woman: "I don't care if you're an Irish setter."

2798   Did you hear about the well-behaved
hunting dog that was so polite he didn't point?
He just nudged.

2799   Did you hear about the sheepdog bra?
*It herds them up and points them in
the right direction.*

2800   That reminds us of the bird-dog bra.
It turns setters into pointers.

Polar Bear

2801   What's the most popular drink in Alaska?
Polar beer.

2802   An Alaskan saloon is a polar bar.

2803   Did you hear about the magnet
that was drawn into a polar bar?

2804   Why is one polar bear
attracted to another one?
Animal magnetism.

2805   What is a polar bear's favorite food?
Icebergers.

2806   Where do white bears vote?
At the North Pole.

2807   What did the dentist see
at the North Pole?
A molar bear.

2808   Then there was the hard-of-hearing Alaskan who thought
he was being asked to be a polar bear at a funeral.

2809   Did you hear about the two bears that were in a debate?
They became polarized.

2810   What is an Arctic bear's favorite sport?
Polar vaulting.

2811   What do Arctic bears get from
sitting on the ice too long?
Polaroids.

2812   Did you hear about the photographer who took
a picture of a large white Alaskan bear?
It was a Kodiak moment.

2813 Why did the polar bear go to the South Pole?
To visit Aunt Arctic.

2814 Did you hear about the baby bear that was
happy some days and sad on others?
He was a little bipolar.

2815 A Texan grew weary of living in merely the second largest state, so he went to Alaska, stopped in a bar, and asked how he could become an Alaskan. The bartender, deciding to have a little fun with the visitor, said, "You can't become an Alaskan until you've downed a pint of whiskey in one gulp, danced with an Eskimo, and shot a polar bear." The Texan guzzled the pint of whiskey in one gulp and with glazed eyes staggered out of the saloon. Several hours later the Texan stumbled through the door all scratched and bloody. "I'm just about to be an Alaskan," he gasped. "Now where's that Eskimo I'm supposed to shoot?"

Polliwog

2816 Did you hear about the parrot that married a frog?
They had a pollywog.

2817 A princess who lived near a bog
Met a prince in the form of a frog.
   Now she and her prince
   Are the parents of quints:
Four girls and one polliwog.

Pony

2818 How is a drama teacher
like the Pony Express?
He's a stage coach.

2819 Did you hear about the impersonator who
stole a horse and went on the mail run?
He was a phony express rider.

2820 As Confucius says, "A dark horse is often
the one that is willing to pony up."

Poodle

2821   How can you tell when it's raining cats and dogs?
When you step into a poodle.

2822   Why did the man call his dog a miniature poodle?
Because the miniature turn your back, it does a poodle.

2823   Did you hear about the dog that enjoys
having its hair washed every day?
He's a shampoodle.

2824   There once was a man with two poodles
Whose names were Doodles and Toodles.
Their favorite dish
Was neither meat nor fish
But oodles and oodles of noodles.

2825   What do you call a French poodle
on which fleas live?
A Parisite.

2826   What did the rich attorney call his French poodle?
Fee-Fee.

Porcupine

2827   Show us a porcupine, and we'll show you a thorny matter.

2828   Did you hear about the nervous porcupine?
He's always on pins and needles.

2829   As the baby porcupine said when it bumped into
a cactus plant during the night, "Is that you, Mom?"

2830   Did you hear about the two porcupines that fell in love?
They got stuck on each other. (And they were in prickly heat.)

2831   How do porcupines kiss?
Very carefully.

2832   What did the two porcupines say when they kissed each other?
"Ouch!"

2833   We're reminded of the old Burma Shave roadside sign:
No lady likes to dance or dine
Accompanied by a porcupine.

2834   As the father porcupine said to the son he
was about to spank, "This is going to hurt me
more than it's going to hurt you."

2835   How do we know that King Solomon was very kind to women and animals?
The Bible says that he had seven hundred wives and three hundred porcupines.

2836   Did you hear about the fight between a porcupine and a wolf?
The porcupine won on points.

2837   What does a porcupine like
to do when playing volleyball?
Spike.

2838   What's worse than a rhinoceros on water skis?
A porcupine on a rubber raft.

2839   What kind of tree has the sharpest needles?
A porcu-pine.

2840   What is a porcupine's favorite vegetable?
Prickled beets.

Porpoise

2841   Did you hear about members of the school debating team that went
to the aquarium on a field trip and found themselves in front of several angry
dolphins? They were at cross porpoises.

2842   A Boy Scout troop was on a camping trip near an ocean beach.
Every evening friendly dolphins swam toward shore for their meal. The
Scout leader called everyone to dinner by shouting, "It's chow time for
all in tents and porpoises."

2843 As one dolphin said after accidentally swimming into another one, "I didn't do it on porpoise."

2844 Old fishermen never die; they just lose their porpoise in life.

2845 *Bumper sticker:* Porpoises Do It Flippantly.

2846 Did you hear about the shark named Robin Hood?
He robbed richpoises to feed porpoises.

Possum

2847 Did you hear about the two marsupials
talking on the telephone?
It was a possum-to-possum call.

2848 Did you hear about the marsupial author
that died prematurely?
His works will be published possumously.

2849 What did amorous Pete say to unresponsive Patty?
"Are you playing possum again tonight?"

See also Opossum

Prawn

2850 Why did one shrimp swim into another one?
Because he was accident-prawn.

2851 Where can you find good deals on shrimp?
At a prawn shop.

2852 Did you hear about the bashful high school shrimp?
She didn't have a date to the senior prawn.

2853 *Patron:* "Waiter, what are the prawns like today?"
Waiter: "The same as yesterday—little pink shrimp."

2854 What do you call an obscene book about shrimp?
Prawnography.

Praying Mantis

2855 Did you hear about the religious insect?
It was a praying mantis.

2856 How do praying mantises gather?
In sects.

Puffin

2857 What do you call a male seabird that wears
a dress and can do card tricks?
Drag the Magic Puffin.

2858 A breathless bird is a puffin.

Puma

2859 A jolly young fellow from Yuma
Told an elephant joke to a puma.
Now his skeleton lies
Under hot Western skies.
The puma had no sense of huma.

Puppy

2860 Where do baby dogs sleep on camping trips?
In pup tents.

2861 Did you hear about the baby dog
that was ill from being chilled?
He was a pupsickle.

2862 Why are dogs spayed?
To decrease the Pupulation.

2863 What sound does a baby dog's
favorite breakfast make?
Snap, crackle, and pup.

2864   What is a baby dog's favorite dinner?
Puppy chow mein.

2865   What is a baby dog's
favorite pizza?
Pupperoni.

2866   How is an ink blotter like a lazy baby dog?
*A blotter is an ink-lined plane, an inclined plane
is a slope up, and a slow pup is a lazy dog.*

2867   What type of food
keeps a dog quiet?
A hush puppy.

2868   What did the minister say when he saw the damage
done to his favorite flowers by his young dog?
"What I grow, my pup runneth over."

2869   Did you hear about the homeowners who complained
because their puppy was at the gnaw-it-all stage?

2870   Or, as Confucius says, "Puppy love
is the beginning of a dog's life."

2871   Did you hear about the couple who owned a small nursery that was
renowned for its chrysanthemums as well as for a small kennel?
It was a mum-and-pup operation.

2872   Then there was the time when some folks in San
Francisco described hippiness as a warm poppy.

Python

2873   Did you hear about the two snakes
that talked on the telephone?
It was a python-to-python call.

2874   What reptile enforces the law in Canada?
A Mountie Python.

Quahog

2875 Did you hear about the clammer who was crazy about bivalves?
He went quahog wild.

Quail

2876 What did the cowardly bird do when challenged to a fight?
He quailed at the idea.

2877 As Confucius says, "A quail is a flinch or cowherd."

Rabbit

2878 What do you get when you pour boiling
water down a rabbit hole?
A hot, cross bunny.

2879 Did you hear about the rabbit that wouldn't
take a shot of Novocain from the dentist?
It was an ether bunny.

2880 Did you hear about the initial migration of rabbits from
California to the East Coast?
*When a young female reached New York,
she became the first East her-bunny.*

2881 And did you hear about the egg-laden rabbit that jumps off bridges?
He's called the Easter Bungee.

2882 What do you call a rabbit that works in a bakery?
A yeaster bunny.

2883 Where do newlywed rabbits go?
On a bunnymoon.

2884 Did you hear about the young rabbit that shaved his whiskers and was consequently rejected by his peers?
It just proves that a bunny shaved is a bunny spurned.

2885 As Bugs Bunny said to the pier, "What's up, dock?"

2886 Or, as the electric rabbit said, "Watts up, doc?"

2887 Did you hear about the Parisian priest who raised rabbits?
He kept them in the hutch back of Notre Dame.

2888 What is a rabbit's favorite vehicle?
A hutchback car.

2889 What is a payoff to rabbits called?
Hutch money.

2890 Speaking of rabbits' habitats, what do you call a man with several rabbits on his head?
Warren.

2891 What legal document must a policeman have before apprehending a sleeping rabbit?
An arrest warren.

2892 Did you hear about the insomniac who kept running out of sheep to count?
He switched to counting rabbits.

2893 What did the customer say to the pet store owner after buying a bunny?
"Rabbit up nicely. It's a gift."

2894 How do bunnies commute to work?
By rabbit transit.

2895 Then there was the boxer who had an incredible rabbit punch.
Unfortunately, his manager only let him fight people.

2896 A very large number of rabbits once occupied the grassy center area of the expressway. There were so many that the highway department workers referred to it as the hoppy median.

2897 What is a rabbit's favorite dance style?
Hip-hop.

2898 What do bunnies do when they see hawks?
They hop and pray.

2899 An infant rabbit was orphaned. Fortunately, though, a family of squirrels took it in and raised it as if it were one of their own. This adoption led to some peculiar behaviors on the part of the rabbit, including a tendency for it to eschew jumping and instead embrace running around like its stepsiblings.

As the rabbit passed through puberty, however, it faced an identity crisis (don't we all). It went to its stepparents to discuss the problem. It said it felt different from its stepsiblings, was unsure of its place in the universe, and was generally forlorn.

Their response was "Don't scurry; be hoppy."

2900 Did you hear about the new gasoline ad that tells you to put a rabbit in your tank?
It's for short hops.

2901 As the little bunny said to the first robin of spring and her two sheep friends, "Hoppy birdy two ewes!"

2902   What is a rabbit's favorite college?
Johns Hopkins.

> **2903**   Why did the rabbit have trouble hopping?
> *Because he always kept one foot in his pocket for good luck.*

2904   Rabbits' feet aren't so lucky for rabbits.

> **2905**   Or, as Confucius says, "Rabbits' feet are
> poor substitutes for horse sense."

2906   Why are rabbits so quiet at formal dances?
Because they have cotton balls.

> **2907**   Why did the rabbit go to the jewelry store for vegetables?
> *Because he heard the store had carats.*

2908   Why did the rabbit arrange two dozen lunches in a circle?
He wanted a twenty-four-carrot ring.

> **2909**   What does the word lettuce mean to a rabbit?
> *It's either a salad or a proposition.*

> > **2910**   Why did the rabbits go on strike?
> > *They felt they deserved a better celery.*

2911   Speaking of rabbit food reminds us of the night security guard who went to see an optometrist because he was having trouble with night vision. The guard was told to eat plenty of carrots to improve his eyesight. The good news is that his vision actually became keener. The bad news, however, is that he began tripping over his ears.

> **2912**   What's invisible and smells like carrots?
> *Bunny breath.*

> **2913**   Where do rabbits settle their legal disputes?
> *In a pellet court.*

2914   *Father rabbit:* "Why is our son so happy today?"
Mother rabbit: "He learned how to multiply in school."

2915 That reminds us of this newspaper headline:
"Father of Seventeen Shot. Mistaken for Rabbit."

> **2916** The habits of rabbits are such, it's agreed,
> That dozens of cousins are common indeed.

>> **2917** Did you hear about the pet store owner who went crazy?
>> *He was trying to take an inventory of the rabbits.*

2918 A nuisance and pest is the rabbit:
When he spies your best lettuce, he'll grab it.
>> In smarts he's not high,
>> But oh my, oh my!
He surely knows how to cohabit.

>> **2919** *Mother rabbit to her daughter:* "A magician
>> pulled you out of a hat. Now stop asking questions."

>> **2920** Rabbits breed by leaps and bounds.

2921 Why did the printing press business name itself the Rabbit Company?
Because it wanted to be known for its fast reproductions.

>> **2922** Did you hear about the investor who
>> cornered the market on young hares?
>> *It was a leveret buyout. (The investor was just lapin it up.)*

2923 What are the three hats of a campaigning politician?
*One for throwing into the ring, a second for talking through, and
a third for pulling rabbits out of if elected.*

>> **2924** Why are some of the Texas highways closed?
>> *Because the Texas rabbits ate up the cloverleafs.*

2925 A man with a rabbit on his head went to see a psychiatrist.
The doctor asked, "May I help you?"
"Yes," replied the rabbit, "get this man off my tail."

2926 A husband asked his wife what she was cooking, and she said,
"I'm making a rabbit stew for dinner."
"Thank goodness," replied the husband. "I was afraid it was for us."

2927   "What are you doing in the washing machine?"
a woman demanded of her pet rabbit.
"It's a Westinghouse," replied the bunny, "and I'm westing."

2928   What do you call mobile homes for rabbits?
Wheelburrows.

2929   How did the turtle keep two jumps ahead of the hare?
He played him a game of checkers.

2930   Old Energizer bunnies never die. They just go on, and on, and on . . .

2931   Did you hear that the Energizer bunny was arrested?
He was charged with battery.

Raccoon

2932   Did you hear about the anecdote teller who named his pet raccoon Tour?

2933   Then there were the kids who went to
a costume party as a masquerade of raccoons.

2934   What happened when three squirrels asked a raccoon to play cards with them?
He became a fourth to be raccooned with.

Ram

2935   What was the most important
animal to the ancient Roman army?
The battering ram.

2936   Did you hear what happened when wild
male sheep were provoked?
They went on a rampage.

2937   What is ewes' favorite football team?
The Rams.

2938   What domesticated animal has the best memory?
The RAM.

Rat

2939 What is a mouse's favorite vegetable dish?
Ratatouille.

> **2940** Why did the gambler bet on a rodent in a card game?
> *He wanted to baccarat.*

> > **2941** Did you hear about the rat with a toothache?
> > *He went to a rodentist (who gave the rat rodentures).*

2942 What car magazine do mice like the best?
Rodent Track.

> **2943** What did the stuttering cat say when
> he looked out of Noah's ark?
> *"Is that Ararat?"*

2944 Then there was the Southern architect who named his pet rat Frank Lloyd.

> **2945** What did the Soviet citizen
> call his pet mouse?
> *Comrat.*

> > **2946** Did you hear about the psychiatrist
> > who pulled habits out of rats?

2947 Why did the research scientist replace his lab rats with lawyers?
*He didn't become as attached to them, there's no shortage
of lawyers, and there are some things a rat just won't do.*

> **2948** Why did the research scientist claim that old episodes
> of NBC's Tonight Show are dangerous to one's health?
> *A study done on rats found the show to be Carsonogenic.*

2949 As Confucius says, "The problem with rat races is
that even if you win, you're still a rat."

> > **2950** As the police sergeant said to the suspect, "Don't
> > be a man or a mouse. Be a rat."

2951 Why did the mouse become depressed?
He learned that his father was a rat.

2952 Did you hear about the stubborn laboratory rat that resisted performing his assigned tasks?
He was given some cheese and promptly wended his maze.

2953 A New Englander was vacationing in the South and checked into a charming bed-and-breakfast establishment. The host asked, "Do you want to eat rat now?"

The repulsed visitor replied, "Not now. And not later, either."

"Well, that's all rat," said the native. "Just let me know when you get hungry."

Rattlesnake

2954 What snakes along the desert but bounces in baby's crib?
A rattler, of course.

2955 What does a snake have that Baby throws?
Snake eyes. (Did you think we'd say rattler?)

2956 Did you hear about the guy who had a rough childhood?
When his parents gave him a rattle, it was still attached to the snake.

2957 Why do rattlesnakes make good politicians?
They always speak with forked tongues.

2958 A scandalmonger is a prattlesnake.

2959 Before embarking on his first camping trip, the cautious camper asked his doctor what he should do if a rattlesnake bit him in the arm.

"Have a friend cut open the wound and suck out the poison," advised the medical man.

"Suppose I get bitten in the leg?" asked the man.

"Follow the same procedure," added the doctor.

"What should I do," persisted the pragmatist, "if I happen to sit down on a rattlesnake?"

"In that case," responded the doctor, "you'll find out who your real friends are."

2960 How do you make a baby or a snake cry?
Take away its rattle.

Raven

2961 Did you hear about the crazy crow?
It was a raven lunatic.

> **2962** There was an old gent from New Haven,
> Whose whiskers had never been shaven.
> He said, "It is best,
> For they make a nice nest—
> A haven to keep my pet raven."

2963 Did you hear about the bird lover
from Missouri?
*His name and address are: Quoth D.
Raven, Never, Mo.*

2964 As I was paddling down the Po,
A raven kept me on the go.
For every time I rowed to shore,
Quoth the raven, "Never moor."

2965 Soon after Edgar Allan Poe's famous
poem appeared, everybody was raven
about it.

Reindeer

2966 *Wife:* "How is a cloud like Santa Claus?"
Husband: "It holds rain, dear."

2967   In the days of the Soviet Union, a couple was having lunch
when the husband glanced out the window and commented,
"It's starting to rain."
        The wife looked out and said, "I beg to differ;
that's sleet, darling."
        "You're wrong," he countered. "Rudolph the Red
knows rain, dear."

2968   It was Chanukah, and the small town was in fear of not having any latkes because they had run out of flour. Rudi, the Rabbi, was called upon to help solve their problem. He said, "Don't worry. You can substitute matzo meal for the flour, and the latkes will be just delicious!"

A wife asked her husband, "Bernie, do you think it'll work?"

"Of course, it will. After all, Rudolph the Rab knows grain, dear."

2969   That somehow reminds us of Olive, the other reindeer.

2970   *And then there was Santa's nastiest reindeer:* Rude Oft.

2971   Why did Santa use only seven reindeer last year? *Comet stayed home to clean the sink.*

2972   As Santa Claus said to one of his joke-telling reindeer, "You sleigh me."

Retriever

2973   Why wouldn't the yellow dog fetch the thrown stick? *Because it was irretrievable.*

2974   Did you hear about the baseball player's pet dog? *It's a good retriever that chases flies and runs for home trying to avoid the catcher.*

2975   Did you hear about the pretty golden retriever? *She had a fetching face.*

Rhea

2976   Did you hear about the zookeeper who collapsed from exhaustion after trying to change the color of a large flightless South American bird? *He suffered from dye-a-rhea.*

Rhinoceros

2977   What happens to a rhino's armor when it gets wet? *It rhinocerusts.*

2978 Did you hear about the inebriated rhino?
He was a wine-oceros.

Roan

2979   Did you hear about the red-colored horse that picked up scraps of oral hygiene supplies outside a dentist's office?
        A recycling center owner "borrowed" the horse one night in hopes of using the clever animal in his business. But it was all to no avail because a stolen roan gathers no floss.

2980 As the cowboy said to his eighteen-year-old boy after presenting him with a saddle and a red horse, "Son, you're on your roan now."

Robin

2981 Did you hear about the criminal bird?
He was always robin banks.

2982 Did you hear about the sheriff who named his pet robin Hood?

2983 Why did Batman go to the pet store?
To buy a Robin.

2984 Why was Batman so depressed?
Because Robin flew south for the winter.

2985   A man went home from work, and his wife greeted him happily, "I just spotted the first robin of spring."
        "You're lucky," the husband replied. "He spotted me first."

Rook

2986 As one literary crow said to another, "Bred any good rooks lately?"

2987 How can you distinguish one soaring crow from another?
You can always tell a rook by its hover.

2988 What is a crow's favorite kind of music?
Rook 'n' roll.

Rooster

2989 What famous bird once lived in the White House?
Teddy Roostervelt.

2990 But as one hen said to another,
"Things aren't what they rooster be."

2991 There was an old cat from Wooster
Who used to crow like a rooster.
But we cut off his head
And killed him dead;
Now he can't crow like he useter.

2992 Did you hear about the chef who named his pet rooster Shire Soss?

2993 What does a lazy rooster say?
"Cock-a-doodle-don't."

2995 *Bumper sticker:*
Roosters Do It Cockily.

2994 What is a rooster's
favorite drink?
A cocktail.

2996 Why did the islander name his
pet rooster Robinson?
Because he Crusoe.

2997 What did the boss rooster tell
his employee?
"Don't be a cluck watcher."

2998 As Confucius says, "It's harder for a man
to keep a secret from his wife than to
sneak the dawn past a rooster."

2999 That reminds us of the guy who bragged
to his friends that he ruled the roost.
Unfortunately, his wife rules the rooster.

3000 Did you hear about the conceited rooster?
He stood on top of a roof, whether vane or not.

3001   What did the rooster crow when Humpty Dumpty fell off the wall?
*Crack-a-doodle-do. (And the pet rooster of the first signer of the
Declaration of Independence crowed, "John Hancock-a-doodle-do.")*

3002   What animals took the most and the least luggage on Noah's ark?
The elephant took his trunk, but the rooster had only his comb.

Saint Bernard

3003 Did you hear about the socially conscious Saint Bernard?
He knows how to hold his liquor.

3004 A Saint Bernard is a dog with a liquor license.

3005 Why did the mountain-climbing
rescue team fire its Saint Bernard?
*Because he figured out how to get
the cork out of the keg.*

3006 Did you hear about the kind old lady who had the face of a saint?
Unfortunately, it was Saint Bernard.

Salmon

3007 What is a pink-fleshed fish's favorite song?
"Salmon Chanted Evening."

3008 What is a young fish's favorite game?
Salmon says.

3009 Did you hear about the new
recruiting poster for the fish navy?
It has a picture of a bearded Uncle Salmon.

3010 Where do fish study to become ministers?
At a salmonary.

3011 What is a fish's favorite author?
Salmon Rushdie.

3012 Did you hear about the collection of poetry written by a talking salmon
named Rusty and discovered on the *Titanic* by divers?
It was published under the title Salmon Rusty's Titanic Verses.

3013 Where can you find good deals on salmon?
At a spawn shop.

3014 What is smoked salmon?
Herring with high blood pressure.

Sand Dollar

3015 How did the sea urchin pay for his meal?
With a sand dollar.

Sardine

3016 What is the world's most crowded island?
Sardine-ia.

3017 What is the head of a fish school called?
The sar-dean.

3018   What can you say about workers at a busy sardine factory?
They're really packing them in.

> **3019**   That reminds us of the sardines on a subway during rush hour.
> *They were packed in like commuters.*

> > **3020**   Did you hear about the unlucky Texan?
> > *He couldn't find oil even in a sardine can.*

3021   Or, as the mother sardine said to her daughter after spotting a submarine, "Don't worry. It's just a can of people."

> **3022**   The survivor of a shipwreck told reporters,
> "I had to live for a week on a can of sardines."
> A voice in the back asked, "Weren't you afraid of falling off?"

3023   What happened to the sardine factory
employees who were poor performers?
They were canned.

> **3024**   What geographical location would be the best place
> to set up a sardine processing plant?
> *The Cannery Islands.*

Scallop

3025   Did you hear about the frightened Pilgrim fishermen
who saw Indians coming toward the beach?
> *They thought the natives were after their scallops.*

Scrod

3026   A patron in a seafood restaurant developed severe food poisoning after having just a small portion of fish. As he lay doubled in agony on the floor, the victim saw another customer leave after a satisfactory meal.
> *The pitiful patron moaned, "There but for the trace of scrod go I."*

> **3027**   Did you hear about the patron who went to the
> Oar House seafood restaurant to get scrod?

Seagull

3028   Did you hear about the seabird that landed on a channel marker?
Buoy meets gull.

> **3029**   *That reminds us of the signs on a seafood*
> *restaurant's restrooms:* Buoys and Gulls.

3030   What do you call musical birds flying in formation over the ocean?
Chorus gulls.

3031   What kind of birds live near rain forests?
Jun-gulls.

> **3032**   Who was a famous seabird astronomer?
> *Gullileo.*

> > **3033**   What bird enjoys soccer?
> > *A gull keeper.*

3034   Where can you find seabird paintings?
In an art gullery.

> **3035**   Did you hear about the new book on vacation trips to the
> Atlantic coast to view and study seabirds?
> *It's called* Gull Lovers' Travels.

3036   A marine biologist developed a potion for indefinitely extending the lives of porpoises, the key ingredient being seagulls. While returning home from his lab late one night with a bag of these birds, he was puzzled to find a lion sleeping on his front porch. As he carefully stepped over the dormant beast, the man was arrested by the police. He was charged with transporting gulls across a staid lion for immortal porpoises.

> **3037**   If a seagull flies over the sea,
> what flies over the bay?
> *A bagel.*

> **3038**   Or, as one seagull said to another after easily deceiving him,
> "You're so gullible."

3039 What do you call a man with a seagull on his head?
Cliff.

> **3040** Two seagulls were flying over a packed beach on a hot holiday weekend when one said to the other, "It takes all the skill out of it, doesn't it?"

3041 Two men were walking along the beach when a seagull deposited a load right smack in one guy's eye.
The other fellow thoughtfully offered, "Let me get some toilet paper."
"Forget it," the victim replied. "It's probably a mile away by now."

> **3042** Or, as one seagull said to another when they flew over a casino, "This one's on the house."

3043 *Man No. 1:* "There's a job opening for someone to clean the stained glass windows in lighthouses."
Man No. 2: "Since when do lighthouses have stained glass windows?"
Man No. 1: "Ever since there have been seagulls."

3044 A pirate returned from the war with an eye patch and a wooden arm with a hook, and he was asked by a friend how it happened. "An enemy cannonball hit our mast," explained the pirate, "causing a huge piece of wood to come flying and sever my arm."
The friend then asked, "Is that also why you're wearing an eye patch, because a splinter from the mast pierced your eye?"
"No," said the pirate, "it was because a seagull deposited a load right smack in my eye."
"You mean," said the friend, "that the seagull's load landed with such force that you lost your eye?"
"No," replied the pirate. "You see, it was the first day that I had my hook."

Seahorse

3045 Why did the sportsman buy a seahorse?
He wanted to play water polo.

> **3046** Did you hear about the performing seahorses?
> *They get wave reviews.*

3047 What is a sawhorse?
The past tense of a seahorse.

Seal

3048 Two sea animals were conversing, and one asked,
"Can you keep a secret?"
"Yes," replied the other, "my lips are sealed."

3049 What sea animals pose
no hazards for kids?
Childproof seals.

3050 Why wouldn't Scrooge buy any Christmas Seals?
Because he didn't know how to feed them.

3051 What is a seal's favorite
subject in school?
ART-ART-ART.

3052 Did you hear about the guy who went on a raw fish diet?
*He didn't lose much weight, but he sure can balance a ball
on his nose and bark like a seal.*

3053 Then there was the guy who's so bad at financial
matters that not even a seal could balance his checkbook.

3054 Did you hear about the woman who has
the seal of her husband's approval?
And she has the mink, also.

3055 Once upun a time, when seals had tremendous political clout, Dianne
Feinstein was running for governor. An opposing candidate had a nightmare in
which he lost the election, thanks to the convincing campaigning of some savvy
seals. When the loser awoke, he saw a seal seated by his windowsill and sang
out to it, "You picked a Feinstein to lead me, you seal!"

3056 A baby seal walked into a saloon, and the bartender
asked, "What'll you have?"
The seal said, "Anything but a Canadian Club."

Sea Lion

3057 Why did the seal get only average grades in school?
Because he was a C-lion.

Seeing-Eye Dog

3058 Did you hear about the two seeing-eye dogs that went on a blind date?

3059 A blind man went into a bookstore, grabbed his
seeing-eye dog by the hind legs, and swung the poor pooch
back and forth. An astonished salesclerk asked,
"May I help you, sir?"
"No, thanks," replied the man. "I'm just browsing."

3060 Did you hear about the major
league baseball umpire who retired?
His seeing-eye dog died.

3061 Why don't blind people like to skydive?
Because it scares the heck out of the dog.

3062 But one man found a way. There he was, standing in
the plane, outfitted to dive, and wearing dark glasses, carrying
a white cane, and holding a seeing-eye dog by a leash.
A seasoned veteran of many dives expressed his
admiration for the blind man's courage and then asked, "By the
way, how do you know when the ground is getting close?"
"Easy," the blind man replied. "The leash goes slack."

3063 In the early 1700s, the captain of a Spanish pirate ship was very proud
of his mongrel pet for its ability to bark once for "si" and twice for "no." After
being captured by a British commander, the dog was taught the same trick in
English. He thereby became the world's first "si" and "aye" dog.

Setter

3064 What is a bowling alley
attendant's favorite dog?
A setter.

3065 Did you hear about the dog that continually walks back and forth?
He's a pace setter.

> **3066** That reminds us of the dog that frequently
> travels overseas. He's a jet setter.

> > **3067** Speaking of English setters, what do the British
> > use for buying canine food?
> > *Dog pounds.*

3068 Did you hear about the man who used his dog as a tea tray?
Mind you, the dog was often upset.

Shark

3069 Did you hear about the money-lending fish?
He was a loan shark.

> **3070** As Confucius says, "Loan sharks attack
> only those who go beyond their financial depth."

> > **3071** What happened when a shark
> > swallowed a set of keys?
> > *He got lockjaw.*

3072 What new horror movie costars the
Loch Ness monster and a shark?
Loch Jaws.

> **3073** What did the sharks do when the Weight
> Watchers class went for a swim nearby?
> *They chewed the fat.*

> > **3074** What happened when a shark tried to eat
> > an entire crate of bubble gum?
> > *He bit off more than he could chew.*

3075 Did you hear about the southern shark from Tennessee?
He was a Chattanooga chew chew.

3076 Why did the gambler frighten all of the swimmers out of the ocean?
Because he was a card shark.

3077 Did you hear about the underwater billiard player?
He was a pool shark.

3078 Two sharks were swimming near the shore when one suddenly asked, "What was that two-legged thing that just came into the water?"
"I don't know," replied the other. "I'll bite."

3079 Did you hear about the new seafood restaurant named Jaws?
It costs an arm and a leg to eat there.

3080 What is a shark's favorite hobby?
Anything he can sink his teeth into.

3081 If a married couple fell overboard into shark-infested waters, who would escape?
The wife—because she's among man-eating sharks.

3082 Two coworkers were talking when one commented, "I saw a man-eating shark at the aquarium."
"Big deal," replied the other. "I saw a man eating mahi-mahi in a restaurant."

3083 *Shark No. 1:* "Who was that lady I saw you with last night?"
Shark No. 2: "That was no lady. That was dinner."

3084 Why won't a shark attack a lawyer?
Because of professional courtesy.

3085 What do you call those rubber bumpers on yachts?
Shark absorbers.

3086 Shark carpenters are hammerheads.

Sheep

3087 To err is human; to make sheep puns, ovine.

3088 Did you hear about the boss who acted like
a lamb when an employee asked for a raise?
He responded, "Baaa!"

3089 What do you call a sheep that
runs around with forty thieves?
Ali Baaa Baaa.

3090 Where is a sheep's favorite vacation spot?
The Baaahamas.

3091 Where do Mexican
sheep go on vacation?
To Baaaja.

3092 *Sheep farmer No. 1:* "Do you know the favorite song of sheep?"
Sheep farmer No. 2: "No. Hum a few baaas."

3093 What do you call a dancing sheep?
A baaallerina.

3094 Did you hear about Shep Sheep, the comedian?
He was a master of baaad jokes.
In fact, he was a regular knit wit.
His idol among comedians was Harry Shearer.
His trademark line was, "Take my wife's fleece."
His theme song was "When the Sheep Go Marching In."
Once a heckler called out, "Hey, you got any new jokes?"
Shep shot back, "Yes sir, yes sir, three bags full."
His sign-off line was, "If I don't see you in the future,
I'll see you in the pasture."

3095 Did you hear about the sheep that fell into a vat of chocolate?
He became a Hershey baaa.

3096 *Little girl:* "Baaa, baaa, black sheep, have you any wool?"
Black sheep: "What do you think this is? Nylon?"

3097 What is the most boring animal?
Blah, blah, black sheep.

3098   Or, as Scrooge said to the shop owner when looking for
a sweater, "Bah, bah, humbug. Have you any wool?"

> **3099**   What is "sis boom baaa"?
> *The sound made by an exploding sheep.*

> > **3100**   Or, as one sheep said to another, "I've got
> > some good news and some baaad news."

> > > **3101**   Where do sheep get shorn?
> > > *At the baaa-baaa shop.*

3102   Did you hear about the two sheep that were shorn identically?
It was shear and shear alike.

> **3103**   Or, as we always say, "Show us a farmer who raises sheep
> for their wool, and we'll show you a shear cropper."

> > **3104**   That reminds us of the two lambs that fell
> > in love while being shorn. It was shear ecstasy.

3105   Speaking of shearing reminds us of the lamb clipper who worked
a double shift one day and consequently was bedridden with an aching back.
The man's assistant filled in for him, and thereby became known as the sore
shearer's apprentice.

> **3106**   Why was the lamb clipping company such
> a popular place to work?
> *Because it offered a profit-shearing benefit.*

> > **3107**   Here's a lamb-poon of a poem.
> > He gambols to the shearer's shear
> > And soon his woolies disappear.
> > And thus he gets his just deserts,
> > For gambolers always lose their shirts.

3108   Did you hear about the group of lambs that gathered in a meadow?
It was a meeting of Gambolers Anonymous.

> **3109**   *Tourist:* "Those are lovely-looking sheep. Romanov?"
> *Farmer:* "Yes, all over the field."

3110 Did you know that Shakespeare wrote a play about lamb stew?
It's called Much Ad Ewe About Mutton.

3111 What sets sheep apart from other animals?
They have mutton in common.

3112 What is a lamb's favorite comic strip?
Mutton Jeff.

3113 As one sheep said to another, "You're the black sheep of the family, you muttonhead."

3114 Did you hear about the car with a license plate that read "BAA BAA?"
It belonged to the black Jeep of the family.

3115 What was the name of the sheep that was cloned in a Central American country?
El Salvador Dolly.

3116 And here's another poetic lamb-poon:
Mary had a little lamb,
She fed it kerosene.
The little lamb sat near a fire,
Since then it's not benzene.

3117 An Arab sheik fell off a Ferris wheel at an amusement park and was instantly devoured by the second of three starving sheep. The attendant turned to the voracious animal and said, "Middle lamb, you've had a dizzy Bey."

3118 Did you hear about the investor who was neither bullish nor bearish?
He was sheepish.

3119 What is a ewe's second favorite football team (after the Rams)?
Navy, since everything is kept sheep-shape.

3120 As the sailor said after seeing a boat loaded with ewes, "Sheep ahoy!"

3121   Or, as the ex-navy-captain-turned-shepherd shouted
when confronted with a rampaging flock, "Abandon sheep!"

3122   Did you hear about the ewe that enjoyed a sheep thrill?

3123   How was the ewe launched into space?
In a rocket sheep.

3124   Did you hear about the guy who named his sheep One-Upman?

3125   Why did the sheep call the police?
Because he'd been fleeced.

3126   If dogs have fleas, do sheep have fleece?

3127   What is a sheep's favorite painting?
The Mona Fleesa.

3128   How do shepherds greet each other on Christmas?
"Fleece on Earth; good wool to men."

3129   Did you hear about the bashful sheep that
wouldn't dance with anyone at the prom?
She was a wool flower.

3130   What is a sheep's favorite newspaper?
The Wool Street Journal.

3131   Why did the couple put sheep rugs throughout their new home?
They wanted wool-to-wool carpeting.

3132   Why did the bargain-hunting sheep shop
at a discount department store?
Because she knew she'd get her Woolworth.

3133   Did you hear the tragic story about the shepherd
who was trampled by a flock of sheep?
He dyed in the wool.

3134   Why did the farmer feed his sheep iron-enriched vitamins?
He wanted to get steel wool.

3135   As the famous sheep playwright once said, "All's wool that ends wool."

> **3136**   As Confucius says, "A man who casts sheep's eyes
> at a woman has had the wool pulled over them."

> **3137**   Why did the farmer drive lambs across a frozen lake?
> *He wanted to pull wool over the ice.*

3138   What's wrong with pulling the wool over people's eyes?
After a while, they begin to recognize the yarn.

> **3139**   A customer was complaining about the high cost of
> a sweater, and the shop owner replied, "The cost is not really
> steep when you consider that the wool was shorn from a special
> strain of sheep in a rugged island off Scotland and then
> hand-woven. It is indeed a beautiful yarn."
> "Yes, it is," added the customer, "and you tell it well, too."

> **3140**   Did you hear about the sheep that joined
> a private club?
> *The members are a tightly knit group.*

3141   What kind of wool do you get
from dirty, down-to-earth sheep?
Nitty-gritty.

> **3142**   A tourist asked a farmer how many sheep he had.
> "I don't know," was the reply. "Every time I try to
> count them, I fall asleep."

> **3143**   A psychiatrist suggested that a boxer with
> insomnia try counting sheep.
> "I've already tried that," replied the punchy
> pugilist. "And every time, just before I reach ten, I stand up."

3144   A sheep with insomnia went to a psychiatrist for help.
"Do you have any suggestions?" asked the sheep. "And please, no wisecracks!"

> **3145**   As Confucius says, "Many men count sheep at night
> because they counted calves by day."

3146   Did you hear the one about the jewel thieves who were arrested while trying to fence their ill-gotten gains?

They tried to escape through a nearby farm but were hampered by a huge flock of sheep. To this day, they have recurring dreams of seeing fences jump over sheep.

3147   Two shepherds leaned on their crooks at the end of a long day, and the first asked the second, "So, how's it going?" The second one sighed and shook his head, "Not well. I can't pay my bills, my health isn't good, my kids don't respect me, and my wife is mad at me." The first replied, "Well, don't lose any sheep over it."

3148   What happened to Little Bo Peep's sheep?
They were stolen by a crook.

3149   Or, as the shepherd said to his staff, "I am not a crook."

3150   How do Scottish sheep stay warm in the winter?
With central bleating.

3151   Did you hear about the shepherd who took a day job in a coat factory?
He watched his flock by night.

3152   A little boy told his parents that in Sunday School he learned about the shepherds who cleaned their clothes in the dark. When his parents asked him for more information, he said the story was about the shepherds who washed their socks by night.

3153   A shepherd is a person all kids flock to.

3154   As the alarmed shepherd said to another shepherd, "Let's get the flock out of here."

3155   Thank you for letting us pull your eyes over the wool.

Sheepdog

3156   Did you hear about the two shaggy sheepdogs that were madly in love? One moonlit night, the male was feeling romantic and gushed, "My matchless Melissa, I dare say that I cannot live another day without you. Ah, you are Melissa, aren't you?"

Shellfish

3157   Why was the crustacean so unpopular?
He was always promoting his own shellfish interests.

3158   Here's an old tongue twister (repeat five times rapidly): *selfish shellfish.*

3159   As Confucius says, "A shellfish is not the only one that has a crab for a mate."

Shrew

3160   As the male of the species said to Cousin Hedgehog, "You think it's easy being married to a shrew?"

3161   Did you hear about the astute mouse-like mammal?
He was very shrewd.

Shrimp

3162   *Patron:* "Waiter, how do you serve shrimps here?"
Waiter: "We bend down."

3163   How did short Pilgrims arrive in the American colonies?
They came in shrimp boats.

3164   That reminds us of one of the classic oxymorons: *jumbo shrimp.*

3165   What is a music teacher's favorite Japanese food?
Shrimp tempo-ra.

3166   Did you see the Western film about shrimp?
It's called "The Brinestone Cowboy."

Skunk

3167   What happened to the skunk that failed his swimming lesson?
He stank to the bottom of the pool.

3168   Did you hear about the argumentative skunk?
Made a stink everywhere he went.

3169   *Skunk mother:* "What do you want to be when you're older?"
Skunk kid: "A big stinker."

3170   Have you heard the ultimate skunk joke?
You don't want to; it really stinks.

3171   How can you tell when a skunk is angry?
It raises a stink.

3172   What is a skunk's
philosophy of life?
"Eat, stink, and be merry."

3173   As the famous skunk philosopher
said, "I stink; therefore, I am."

3174   How were the mother and
father skunks able to tell the
difference between their identical
twins named In and Out?
Instinct.

3175   How are skunks able
to avoid danger?
*By using their instincts
and common scents.*

3176   Why are skunks so smart?
Because they have a lot of scents

3177   Did you hear about the gambling skunk?
He played cards for a scent a point.

3178   What happened when a skunk backed into a fan?
It got cut off without a scent.

3179   Did you hear about the hunting dog that chased a skunk?
It will be a long time before he loses the scent.

3180 How many skunks does it take to make a big stink?
Quite a phew.

3181 What is the feeling that you've smelled a certain skunk before?
Déjà phew.

3182 What noise is made by a planeload
of skunks passing over Seattle?
Pew-jet sound.

3183 Why can't skunks keep secrets?
Because someone is always getting wind of them.

3184 As the forgetful skunk said when the wind suddenly
changed direction, "It's all coming back to me now."

3185 What's a skunk's favorite game in school?
Show-and-smell.

3186 How do you stop a skunk from smelling?
Hold its nose.

3187 Why are skunks so unpopular?
Because they put on awful airs.

3188 There was a young man from the city
Who met what he thought was a kitty.
He gave it a pat
And said, "Nice little cat."
They buried his clothes out of pity.

3189 Just how angry was the skunk?
He was incensed.

3190 What's black and white and red all over?
A skunk with diaper rash.

3191 Did you hear about the woman who was in a bizarre car accident?
*She claimed that she followed the white line. Odorously, however,
the white line turned out to be a skunk.*

3192 Why did the mother skunk take
her baby to see the doctor?
Because it was out of odor.

3193 Or, as the judge said when a skunk entered
his courtroom, "Odor in the court."

3194 The vicar of lovely Vouvray
Met a skunk who was passing his way.
The skunk gave a squirt,
So the smell's on the shirt
Of the vicar who said, "Let us pray."

3195 Or, as one skunk said to another when they were
cornered outside a church, "Let us spray."

Sloth

3196 Did you hear about the chef who won an award for his baked
sloth? The other contenders lost the contest because they prepared
it in a different way. Which just goes to show that too many cooks
broil the sloth.

Slug

3197 How is the snail housing market?
A bit sluggish.

3198 A slug is a snail with a housing problem.

3199 Did you hear about the two snails that got into a fight?
They really slugged it out. (And it was a veritable slugfest.)

3200 What did the slug say as he
slipped down the wall?
"How slime flies."

3201 Did you hear about the slug
that fell off the cabbage?
He went off his food.

Smelt

3202 *Sign at fish market:* Smelt to High Heaven.

> **3203** *Man No. 1:* "What kind of fish did you have for lunch?"
> *Man No. 2:* "Smelt."
> *Man No. 1:* "It sure did. But what kind of fish was it?"

Snail

3204   A snail bought his first automobile and was so proud of it that he painted a large *S* (for *Snail*) on each side. As he drove along the street, a neighbor exclaimed, "Look at the S-car go."

> **3205** How do the French transport their snails overseas?
> *In an escargo ship.*

> **3206** How do escargots cross the ocean from France?
> *By snail boat.*

> **3207** What is another term for the post office?
> *U.S. Snail Mail.*

> **3208** As one snail said to another, "Your pace or mine?"

3209 How fast does a mollusk travel?
At a snail's pace.

> **3210** Radio newscaster: "Dense fog has closed the airport and slowed snails to a traffic pace."

3211 Or, as the snail said to the turtle, "What's the rush?"

> **3212** *Patron:* "Waiter, where are my snails?"
> *Waiter:* "If you were in such a hurry, you shouldn't have ordered snails."

3213   At a fancy restaurant to celebrate their fifth anniversary,
the husband turned to the wife, pointed to escargots on the menu,
and asked, What's that?"
     She replied, "That's French for snails."
     "Then I'll pass," said the husband. "I prefer fast food."

3214   A man's wife ordered escargots in a fancy restaurant. When
the appetizer arrived, the husband stared at it for a moment
and then said, "I'd rather eat snails!"

3215   A waiter told a customer that snails were the specialty
of the restaurant. "And I notice," replied the patron, "that you've
got them dressed like waiters."

3216   A snail was gradually crawling up an apple tree during the winter.
A squirrel spied the slowly moving snail and said, "You're wasting your time.
There aren't any apples up there."
     The snail replied, "There will be when I get there."

3217   A snail was in the hospital recovering from an accident
in which he was run over by a turtle. A nurse asked him what
happened, and he replied, "I don't know. It all happened so fast."

3218   *Patient:* "Doctor, doctor! I feel like I'm a snail."
     Doctor: "Just try to come out of your shell."

3219   What is a gambling snail's favorite hobby?
     Playing the shell game with a turtle.

3220   What is the strongest animal?
The snail, because it carries its house on its back.

3221   Where can you find giant snails?
     At the end of giants' fingers.

3222   What do escargots use to paint their toes?
     Snail polish.

3223   What is expertise in escargots called?
     Snailsmanship.

Snake

3224   How do some snakes communicate with one another?
They make poison-to-poison phone calls.

3225   What did the baby snake say to his mother?
"I hope I'm not poisonous. I just bit my tongue."

3226   Or, as one snake said to another at the funeral of the man he bit,
"I knew that man poisonally. And he had a great poisonality."

3227   Did you hear about the deadly serpent
with a lovely singing voice?
It was a choral snake.

3228   What hymn did the serpent sing
to Eve in the Garden of Eden?
"A Bite with Me."

3229   Did you hear about the snake trainer who
married an undertaker?
They have towels marked Hiss and Hearse.

3230   What is a snake's favorite meal?
Hiss and chips.

3231   Did you hear about the snake that
had a fit of uncontrollable laughter?
It had hissterics.

3232   What is a snake's favorite
subject in school?
Hisstory.

3233   What medication do you give
a sneezing snake?
An anti-hiss-tamine.

3234   As one snake romantically said to another, "How about a little hiss, baby?"

3235   Did you hear about the poverty-stricken snake?
He didn't even have a pot to hiss in.

3236   What is long-bodied, limbless, and goes "hith"?
A thnake with a lithp.

3237   What do you call a snake
that sheds its skin?
Ssssnaked.

3238   Why did the boy name his pet snake Lava?
Because it was always moltin'.

3239   Why aren't worker snakes highly paid?
Because they work for scale.

3240   As the coach consoled his losing team of snakes,
"You can't venom all."

3241   What snakes are employed
by the federal government?
Civil serpents.

3242   Did you hear about the snake with false fangs?
He was an indentured serpent.

3243   What is used for getting
paint off snakes?
Serpentine.

3244   *Girl:* "Mommy, a snake just snapped at me."
Mother: "Snakes don't snap. They coil and strike."
Girl: "But this was a garter snake."

3245   How can you tell snakes are smart?
You can never pull their legs.

3246   When was the blame game first played?
*Adam blamed Eve, and Eve blamed the serpent. And the serpent
didn't have a leg to stand on.*

3247   *Boy No. 1:* "I saw a six-foot snake."
Boy No. 2: "I didn't think snakes had feet."

3248   Why did St. Patrick drive the snakes out of Ireland?
Because it was too far for them to crawl.

3249   Did you hear about the snake
that graduated from college?
He was a Phi Beta Copperhead.

3250   What is a snake's
favorite college?
Pitt.

3251   Did you hear about the nearsighted hiker?
He picked up a snake to kill a stick.

3252   That reminds us of the nearsighted snake. He fell in love with a rope.

3253   Did you hear about the snake
trainers who fell in love?
It's a charming story.

3254   Did you hear about the snake from Brooklyn?
*He married his coilfriend. They used to make a lot of
long-distance coils. Now they love to coil up with a good book.*

3255   What is a snake's
favorite vegetable?
Coily-flower.

3256   What is a cannibal's favorite meal?
Snake and pygmy pie.

3257   What is a snake's
favorite Italian opera?
Wriggletto.

3258   As one politician said to another, "Anyone who speaks with a forked
tongue is a snake in the grass."

3259 Did you hear about the political snake? It was a real party mamba.

Snapper

3260 Did you hear about the Chinese commissar who snapped
his fingers for service in his favorite seafood restaurant?
He was called the Red Snapper.

Sole

3261 Did you hear about the twins who like flatfish?
They're sole brothers.

> **3262** That reminds us of the two flatfish that were great friends.
> *They were sole mates.*

>> **3263** Did you hear about the Korean seafood restaurant?
>> *It specializes in filet of Seoul.*

3264 What do you call a lonely Korean fish spirit?
A sole Seoul sole soul.

> **3265** *Patron:* "Waiter, what is this leathery food you served me?"
> *Waiter:* "It's filet of sole."
> *Patron:* "In that case, I'd like a tender piece from
> the upper part of the shoe."

>> **3266** *Fish No. 1:* "Can you keep a secret?"
>> *Fish No. 2:* "I won't tell a sole."

3267 Did you hear about the fish that avoided the fisherman's nets?
He was the sole survivor.

> **3268** What book was written about a conservative
> British author who was an avid fisherman?
> *The Greatest Tory Ever Soled.*

>> **3269** Did you hear about the chef who inserted prongs
>> in fish and then cooked them by using an electrical current?
>> *They were the tines that fry men's soles.*

3270   Marcel Marceau once owned a fabulous restaurant on the coast of Maine that specialized in seafood. The particular specialty was a superb version of Filet of Sole. Customers went from near and far to enjoy the fine food and be greeted by the owner in pantomime. The kitchen staff was also adept at the art of pantomime.

A sign over the kitchen entrance read:
"These are the mimes that fry Maine's soles."

3271   What is a flatfish's favorite song?
"O Sole Mio."

3272   Did you hear about the deep-thinking fish?
It was sole-searching.

Sow

3273   How much is the owner of a hundred
female pigs and a hundred male deer worth?
Two hundred sows and bucks.

3274   Did you hear about the squealing
French philosopher, Jean Paul Sowtre?

3275   Or, as one pig said to another, "Sow's things?"

Spaniel

3276   Why did the dog wear glasses?
He was a cockeyed spaniel.

3277   Did you hear about the English
dog with a wrench?
He was a cocker spanner.

3278   Why did the Eskimo send his mail by dog sled?
He wanted it shipped by Airedale spaniel delivery.

3279   What kind of spaniel likes
to draw pictures with its paws?
A cocker doodler.

Sparrow

3280 Why didn't the little bird hurt himself
when he fell out of the tree?
Because he used a sparrow chute.

3281 What little bird used
to live in Washington, DC?
Sparrow Agnew.

3282 *Patron:* "Do you have asparagus?"
Waiter: "No, we don't have a sparrow.
And my name isn't Gus."

Spider

3283 Why did the fly fly?
Because the spider spied her.

3284 Why did the spider play baseball?
He liked catching flies.

3285 As one little creature said to another,
"You're very nice, spider what everyone says."

3286 Did you hear about the spiders
that just got married?
They're newlywebs.

3287 When do spiders go on their honeymoon?
After their webbing day.

3288 What is a spider's favorite food?
Corn on the cobweb.

3289 As the spider said when someone
broke his new web, "Oh, darn it!"

3290 As one techie spider said to another,
"Have you checked out my web site?"

3291　Why are spiders like toy tops?
Because they're always spinning.

3292　Did you hear about the spider that asked to test drive a car?
He just wanted to take it for a spin.

3293　Why was the anxious guy called Spider?
*Because he was always climbing the wall
and living in suspense.*

3294　Did you hear about the Irish spider?
He was a Paddy longlegs.

3295　Little Miss Muffet sat on a tuffet,
Eating her curds and whey.
Along came a spider who sat down beside her
And said, "That's lots of cholesterol on your tray."

3296　What did Miss Muffet say when
the spider asked her for a date?
"Ha! No whey!"

Sponge

3297　Why do sponges reproduce so rapidly?
Because there's a soaker born every minute.

3298　Would the water level in the ocean be higher
if there weren't so many sponges in it?

Springbok

3299　How can you tell when it's daylight saving time
in southern Africa by looking at a gazelle?
The springbok fall forward.

Squid

3300　Why did the octopus go to the psychiatrist?
He was a crazy mixed-up squid.

3301 Where do impoverished fish go?
To squid row.

3302 Who lives in the ocean, has
eight legs, and robs banks?
Billy the Squid.

3303 What happened to the traitorous fish?
He was executed by a firing squid.

3304 Who was the infamous
pirate octopus?
Captain Squid.

3305 What is the favorite expression
of an octopus studying Latin?
Squid pro quo.

3306 A British bookie was visited by a crab and an ill octopus.
The crab said, "Here's the sick squid I owe you."

Squirrel

3307 Show us a squirrel's home, and we'll show you a nutcracker's suite.

3308 Did you hear about the insane squirrel?
He went to the nuthouse.

3309 *Squirrel No. 1:* "I'm just nuts about you."
Squirrel No. 2: "You're nut so bad yourself."

3310 What is a squirrel's favorite flower?
Forget-me-nut.

3311 What is a squirrel's favorite
Shakespearean line?
"To be or nut to be."

3312 And what is a squirrel's favorite Shakespearean play?
Much Ado About Nutting.

3313 What was President Andrew Jackson's squirrel's favorite snack?
Old Hickory nuts.

3314 What do you call a crazy squirrel in a spaceship?
An astronut.

3315 How did the homeowner finally catch an elusive squirrel?
He climbed a tree and acted like a nut.

3316 Once upun a time there was a large squirrel family reunion in which everyone chipped in to gather pinecones for the winter. Non-family members were also invited and were even afforded the opportunity to be the first contributors.

Which echoes the New Testament admonition to let them that are without kin stash the first cone.

3317 As one squirrel said to her friend, "I'd go out on a limb for you."

3318 Two squirrels were living in an evergreen forest when one squirrel said to his mate, "Company is coming. We'd better spruce up the place."

3319 Why did the squirrel cross the road?
To see his flat mate.

3320 Did you hear about the squirrels that developed an assembly-line nut-gathering process?
They were autumn-mated. (And they were able to squirrel away many nuts at a time.)

3321 *British bumper sticker:* Squirrels Have a Cracking Good Time.

Stag

3322 As the doe said to the bleary-eyed buck, "How was the stag party?"

3323 It's a staggering thought, but the atmosphere at the stag party was quite stagnant.

Steer

3324 As the market analyst said, "Bulls and bears are responsible for fewer stock losses than are bum steers."

3325 Said a cow in the pasture, "My dear,
There isn't much romance around here.
    I start with high hopes
    But meet only dopes,
And I end with the usual bum steer."

3326 *Farmer No. 1:* "How's business?"
Farmer No. 2: "Cows continue to steer into a bull market."

3327 That reminds us of an old Burma Shave sign:
    Cautious rider to her reckless dear:
    "Let's have less bull and lots more steer."

3328 What is the favorite movie of cattle?
Steer Wars.

3329 What do you call a drug for cattle athletes?
Steeroids.

Stingray

3330 A radiologist and his wife saw the body of
a stingray washed up on the beach. "Is it dead?" she asked.
"Yes," the doctor replied, "it's an ex-ray."

Stork

3331 How are babies born?
Stork naked. (And it's a his-stork occasion.)

3332 As Confucius says, "Pity the poor stork. He gets blamed for
many things that some other bird is responsible for."

3333 Where do herons invest?
In the stork market.

3334   The zookeeper caught a man feeding the stork buckshot and demanded to know what he was doing. "I have a dozen children," the man explained, "and I want to ensure that this bird doesn't get off the ground again."

3335   What happened to the woman with a dozen kids?
She went stork raving mad.

3336   *Minister (to father of triplets):* "I hear the stork has smiled on you."
Father: "Smiled on me! He plumb laughed out loud!"

3337   Did you hear about the family that had another bundle deposited on their doorstep by a stork?
That's the good news. The bad news is that it wasn't a baby.

3338   There was a young man from New York
Whose morals were lighter than cork.
        "Spring chickens," said he,
        "Hold no terrors for me.
The bird that I fear is the stork."

3339   *One small boy to another:* "So that's how it's done!
I always suspected the stork had too short a wingspan to carry a six-to-nine-pound load."

3340   How did Aurelius get to Rome?
The Stoic brought him.

3341   Why does a stork stand on one leg?
Because if he lifted it, he'd fall down.

3342   Where does baby corn come from?
The stalk brings it.

Sturgeon

3343   Who's the main doctor in a fish hospital?
The chief sturgeon.

3344   What fish performs face-lifts?
A plastic sturgeon.

Swallow

3345   What bird is present at every meal?
A swallow.

3346   What did one tonsil say to another?
"Winter must be over, because here comes a swallow."

3347   As Confucius says, "One swallow does not make
a spring, but several swallows often make a fall."

3348   Did you hear about the guy who drank
so much that he was several hundred swallows
ahead of Capistrano?

3349   Did you hear about the new deli restaurant?
It's called the Swallows of Capastrami.

3350   *Patron:* "Waiter, my soup is cold."
Waiter: "Who told you that?"
Patron: "A little swallow."

3351   Did you hear the one about the sick little bird
whose mother gave one medication that had a sharp,
acrid taste and followed that with another tablet?
The youngster shook his head and said,
"That's a bitter pill, too, swallow."

3352   What is a small bird's favorite game?
Swallow the leader.

Swan

3353   Did you hear about the swan song?
If not, then that swan on you.

3354   What is a bird's economic guideline?
Two can live cheaply as swan.

3355   Or, as we always say, "It swan darn thing after another."

3356   Swans sing before they die;
         It'd be no bad thing
         If certain persons die
         Before they sing.

3357   If an old water bird sings its swan song, does
         a young water bird sing its cygneture tune?

3358   Or, as the swan said when he flew down from Olympus
         and landed in Greece, "Take me to your Leda."

3359   Little Miss Muffet accidentally got some fuzz-like material
         from her curds on a regal white bird and asked her father what it was.
         "That's whey down upon the swan," he ribbed her.

Swine

3360   What is a pig's favorite ballet?
         Swine Lake.

3361   What is a pig's favorite book?
         Swine Flu over the Cuckoo's Nest.

3362   What telephone number does
         a pig dial when it needs help?
         Swine-One-One.

3363   Did you hear about the squealing
         physicist, Albert Einswine?

3364   *Sign at a barbecue restaurant:* We
         Will Serve No Swine Before Its Time.

3365   Did you hear that pig farmers
         are now concerned that mad
         cow disease may be transmitted
         to pigs?
         *They are worried about the
         daze of swine neurosis.*

Swordfish

3366   What was the favorite food of King Arthur and his knights?
Swordfish.

3367   Why did the swordfish go to the psychiatrist?
Because he had a duel personality.

3368   *Patron:* "Waiter, how does the chef grill the swordfish?"
Waiter: "He asks it a lot of tough questions."

Tadpole

3369 Did you hear about the frog that hung a flag on a tadpole?

3370 Human father to son: When you were just a tadpole, you were as cute as a bug's ear.
Frog father to son: When you were just a tadpole, you were eating bugs' ears.

Tapir

3371 Did you hear about the overweight jungle animal with a long snout?
It decided to tapir off its eating.

Termite

3372 How do termites relax?
By taking a coffee table break.

3373 What did the pet termite eat?
Table scraps.

3374 Did you hear about the termites that invited themselves to dinner?
They ate a family out of house and home.

3375 Or, as the termite comedian said, "This one will bring the house down."

3376 *Termite No. 1:* "Let's go out for dinner tonight and eat a house."
Termite No. 2: "How about something different? Maybe a pagoda?"
Termite No. 1: "No way. You know how it is with Chinese food. An hour later and you're hungry again."

3377 Why did the termite prefer groups of hotel rooms?
He had a suite tooth.

3378 What happened to the family of termites that lived in poverty?
They got relief from the welfare board.

3379 Did you hear about the termite that was a conscientious objector?
He ate draft boards.

3380 What kind of life do termites lead?
Very boring.

3381 What was the pirate's downfall?
An attack of termites on his wooden leg.

3382   Speaking of wood reminds us of the termite
that was restricted to eating balsa wood. He was on a soft diet.

   3383   Young termites are babes in the wood.

      3384   Did you hear about the blockhead?
      He took out termite insurance on his brain.

         3385   Did you hear about the starving
         female Greek termite?
         She lunched a thousand ships.

3386   That raises an interesting question:
Where did Noah put the termites on the Ark?

   3387   Old termites never die. They just live happily ever rafter.

Tern

3388   The young gull was an only child. He was well-behaved
and a delight to his mother.
        The mother said to her infant, "Because you have been
so good, would you like a brother?"
        The small bird replied, "Oh, yes! One good tern deserves another."

   3389   Did you hear about the guy who throws small rocks at seagulls?
   He tries to leave no tern unstoned.

      3390   Why did the artist paint
      pictures of seagulls on rocks?
      He wanted to leave no stone unterned.

3391   *Bumpersticker:* Sunbathers leave no stern untoned.

      3392   *Sign posted at the Republican
      seagull convention:*
      No Left Terns.

   3393   What are the main traffic signs for seagulls?
   "Left Tern," "Right Tern," and "Tern for the Worse."

3394 Did you hear about the butcher who
bartered one of his sausages for a seagull?
He took a tern for the wurst.

3395 Why did the poet barter one of his poems for a seagull?
To take a tern for the verse.

3396 What kind of doctor might
make house calls to a seagull?
An in-tern-nest.

3397 Why do seagulls invest
in the stork market?
To tern a profit.

3398 A sailor being punished for a misdemeanor was ordered to take
a broom and sweep every link on the ship's anchor chain. As he started
sweeping, a seagull landed on the broom handle, which prevented him
from doing his chore. So he picked up the seabird and threw it into the
air. The bird returned to its newfound perch, once again impeding the navy
man's progress. Once again he flung the bird into the sea breeze.

This back-and-forth procedure continued all evening. The next morning
the chief petty officer observed that the job wasn't complete and irately asked,
"What have you been doing?"

The sailor replied, "I tossed a tern all night and couldn't sweep a link."

Thrush

3399 What's the busiest
time in a bird's day?
Thrush hour.

3400 Did you hear about the bird
that was very pleased with his singing ability?
He was thrushed with delight.

Tick

3401 What happened to the dog who swallowed a watch?
He ended up with a bunch of ticks.

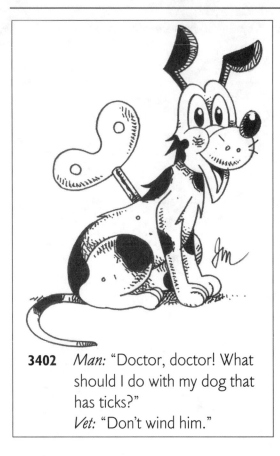

3402   *Man:* "Doctor, doctor! What should I do with my dog that has ticks?"
Vet: "Don't wind him."

3403   Why do we call it *politics?*
Because poly *means* many *and* ticks *refers to* blood-sucking parasites.

3404   Scientists have discovered tiny bloodsucking arachnids that infest the mouths of their prey.
They are lips ticks.

3405   And Wall Street traders are infested with other kinds.
Upticks and downticks.

3406   What arachnid is like the top of a house?
An attic.

3407   What do you call crazy arachnids?
Loony ticks.

3408   What crazy arachnids live on the moon?
Lunatics.

3409   Did you hear about the school for arachnids?
They learn reeling, writhing, and a rhythmic tick.

3410   What is a diplomatic arachnid?
One that is able to handle ticklish situations.

Tiger

3411   Did you hear about the Middle Eastern woman who dressed as a large cat for a costume party and waited impatiently for FedEx to pick up some packages?
When the driver arrived, it was the Tigress and "You Freight These."

3412 Why do tigers have stripes?
So they won't be spotted.

3413 Why do leopards have spotted coats?
Because the tigers bought all the striped ones.

3414 What marching song do you get when
you cross the ape man with a tiger?
"Tarzan Stripes Forever."

3415 What kind of fabric do you get when
you cross a tailor's pin and a tiger?
Pinstripes.

3416 What is a tiger's favorite book?
Revenge of the Tiger by Claude Ribbs.

3417 There was a young lady from Niger
Who smiled as she rode on a tiger.
They returned from the ride
With the lady inside,
And a smile on the face of the tiger.

3418 Did you hear about the craftsman from
India who created a mosaic floor?
He was a Bengal tiler.

3419 *Man No. 1:* "Would you rather have
a lion attack you or a tiger?"
Man No. 2: "I'd rather it attacked
the tiger."

3420 *Man to gas station attendant:*
"You know that tiger you put in my tank?
Well, it ate my muffler."

3421 What are the most popular
flowers in a zoo?
The dandelion and the tiger lily.

Toad

3422 What kind of shoe do amphibians prefer?
Open-toad sandals.

3423 What happened to the illegally parked amphibians?
They got toad away.

3424 Or, as we always say, "Show us a frog on a lily pad, and we'll show you a toadstool."

3425 What can you say about soup that's loaded with toadstools?
There's not mushroom for anything else.

3426 *Patron:* "Waiter, do you have frogs' legs?"
Waiter: "No, but we have toad stools."

3427 Where do amphibian teachers work?
At toad schools.

3428 Did you hear about the chef in Paris who cooked frogs in eggs and milk for breakfast?
He made French toads.

3429 What happened when the farmer tried raising frogs?
He found it was too rough a toad to hoe.

3430 How do amphibians get to the Land of Oz?
They follow the yellow brick toad.

3431 What children's song did country singer Willie Nelson write about riding on a giant frog?
"On the Toad Again."

3432 What do you call a big nuisance around a pond?
A toad hog.

3433 Did you hear about the angry amphibian on the highway?
He suffered from toad rage.

> **3434** What goes "dot-dit-dit-dot-croak"?
> *A Morse toad.*

> > **3435** What do you call Native Americans'
> > pet amphibians that sit one on top of another?
> > *A toadem pole.*

> > > **3436** What is a frogman's paid assistant?
> > > *A toady.*

3437 Or, as the frustrated father frog said to his daughter,
"If I toad you once, I toad you a thousand times . . ."

Tortoise

3438 Did we tell you about our favorite biology teacher?
She tortoise a real lesson.

> **3439** Speaking of teaching reminds us of the following limerick:
>
> > If there's one thing that nature has taught us,
> > It's the virtues of being a tortoise.
> > > They can slumber, we hear,
> > > More than half of the year,
> > In the depths of their snug winter quartoise.

Toucan

3440 Did you hear about the two brightly colored birds that got married?
They decided that toucan live as cheaply as one.

Trout

> **3441** Why can the rainbow trout be called a musical fish?
> *Because it has chromatic scales.*

3442 What do you call it when a government
is overthrown by militant fish?
A coup d'trout.

Tuna

3443   Isn't "tuna fish" redundant?

    3444   Why do some men prefer to go fishing alone?
Because they think tuna boat is one too many.

      3445   Did you hear about the fish
that knows notes in all scales?
It was a piano tuna.

       3446   Who is a favorite fish singer?
Tuna Turner.

3447   Why was the fisherman kicked out of the glee club?
Because he couldn't carry a tuna.

    3448   Did you hear about the new TV game show on which
contestants try to guess what's inside the mystery sandwich?
It's called Name That Tuna.

      3449   Then there was the man who parked his car near
the ocean's edge at low tide and forgetfully left the
windows down overnight. The next morning he
discovered tuna in his Mercury.

       3450   What did Julius Caesar say when he saw
his friend eat an entire can of fish?
"Et tuna, Brute?"

   3451   Where do fish earn graduate degrees?
At a tuna-versity.

Turkey

3452   Why did the turkey bolt down his food?
Because he was a gobbler.

    3453   Why are New England turkeys hard to understand?
Because they speak in gobbled English.

3454 Did you hear about the government officials who talked turkey?
They spoke gobbledygook.

3455 What makes a turkey similar to a ghost?
It's a-gobblin'.

3456 Thanksgiving is a time when turkeys turn from gobblers to gobblees.

3457 Did you hear about the farmer who kept big flocks of chickens and ducks but only a few turkeys?
His was The House of Seven Gobbles.

3458 Or, as the mother turkey said to her daughter who was eating so fast she didn't breathe, "Don't gobble your food."

3459 Did you hear about the one-legged turkey?
It went around saying "hobble-hobble."

3460 What sound does a space turkey make?
"Hubble, Hubble, Hubble."

3461 Why couldn't the turkey eat any more?
Because it was stuffed.

3462 How did the emcee introduce the after-dinner speaker at a Thanksgiving celebration?
"We have just enjoyed a turkey stuffed with sage. It is now my pleasure to introduce a sage stuffed with turkey."

3463 Did you hear about the X-rated turkey?
It's served with very little dressing.

3464 Why did the Pilgrim kill the turkey?
Because he was in a fowl mood.

3465 Or, as the turkey said to the Pilgrim, "You're a no-good baster."

3466 What shows that turkeys are good at arithmetic?
They count the number of chopping days until Thanksgiving.

3467 Did you hear about the young turkey who was on his way
to the big city for the first time?
A fellow passenger offered him some advice:
"You'll be all right as long as you don't lose your head."

3468 Did you hear about the conservative turkey?
It has two right wings.

3469 Why did they let the turkey join the band?
Because it had the drumsticks.

3470 Why did the bandleader save the drumsticks from thirty-eight turkeys?
Because he wanted seventy-six tom bones.

3471 As the father turkey said to his misbehaving daughter,
"If your mother could see you now, she'd turn over in her gravy."

3472 Did you hear about the waiter who dropped
a Thanksgiving dinner and feared he had created an
international incident?
It was the downfall of Turkey, the ruin of Greece,
and the breaking up of China.

3473 What is the traditional Thanksgiving menu?
Roast turkey, stuffing, candied yams, and pickled relatives.

3474 Why do turkeys have such a persecution complex?
Because they're cut to pieces, they have the stuffing
knocked out of them, and they're picked on for days.

3475 Is turkey soup good for your health?
Not if you're the turkey.

3476 As the leftover turkey said upon being wrapped
and refrigerated, "Curses. Foiled again."

3477 Or, as we always say, "Show us a man
who throws Thanksgiving leftovers in the
garbage, and we'll show you a man who
quits cold turkey."

3478   Why did the man quit smoking cold turkey?
Because the feathers made him cough.

3479   That reminds us of the hostess who served a delicious turkey dinner that tickled all of the guests. She forgot to remove the feathers.

3480   Said a farmer outside Albuquerque,
"Though Thanksgiving looms misty and murque,
        All may still turn out well,
        For I've managed to sell
Some chickens, a duck, and a turque."

3481   Why was the man afraid to talk turkey?
Because he was chicken.

3482   Why did the turkey cross the road?
To show he wasn't chicken.

3483   Have you seen a chicken jog?
No, but I've watched the turkey trot.

3484   How are a turkey, a donkey,
and a monkey the same?
They all have keys.

3485   Did you hear about the film executive who produced so many movies that turned out to be turkeys that he was made an honorary Pilgrim?

Turtle

3486   Did you hear about the tortoise with an excellent memory?
He had turtle recall.

3487   What do you call a tortoise that is an informer?
A turtle-tale.

3488   A truckload of tortoises crashed into a truckload of terrapins.
It was a turtle disaster.

3489 What is a vicious turtle?
A terror-pin.

3490 How is a turtle like a cautious investor?
*Neither makes progress until he sticks
his head out.*

3491 What's worse than a centipede with fallen arches?
A turtle with claustrophobia.

3492 Why did the turtle cross the road?
To get to the Shell station.

3493 Did you hear about the shy turtle?
*He asked a psychiatrist to get him out of
his shell. (He was really shell-shocked.)*

3494 How did the turtle pay for his meal?
By shelling out cash.

3495 How do turtles communicate
with each other?
With shell-phones.

3496 *Turtle teacher: "Will you please answer the question?"
Turtle student: "Yes, I shell."*

3497 Or, as one Shakespearian turtle said to another,
"All's shell that ends shell."

3498 What is a little crying turtle?
A young weeper-snapper.

3499 Did you hear about the turtle college graduate?
He was a Phi Beta Snappa.

3500 As the patron said to the waiter,
"I'd like some turtle soup. And make it snappy!"

3501 Turtles who argue with each other are at loggerheads.

3502   What do fashion-conscious turtles wear?
People-neck sweaters.

> **3503**   What was the turtle doing on the turnpike?
> *About four feet an hour.*

> > **3504**   *TV interviewer:* "How's business?"
> > *Turtle salesman:* "Slow."

3505   That reminds us of the waiter who liked watching the turtles at the zoo.

> **3506**   Did you hear about the near-sighted turtle?
> *He fell in love with an army helmet.*

> > **3507**   A turtle is a reptile with a mobile home.

> > > **3508**   As one turtle asked another,
> > > "Don't you love the sound of rain on your roof?"

Unicorn

3509 Why is a lisping unicorn always a female?
Because the unicorn is a myth.

    3510 As Confucius says, "It is risky business to play leapfrog with a unicorn."

        3511 How did the guards in *Tales of 1001 Nights* announce the arrival of the king?
With a unicorn.

            3512 Or, as one mythical creature said to another, "Unicorniest guy I ever met."

Viper

3513 What kind of snakes are part of
a car in the frozen tundra?
Wind-chilled vipers.

3514 Why didn't the British viper vipe 'er nose?
Because the adder 'ad 'er 'andkerchief.

Vixen

3515 As one vixen said to another,
"Hey, you're pretty foxy."

3516 Or, as one fox said to another,
"So, are you vixen to invite me over?"

Vulture

3517 Did you hear about the vultures who formed a club?
They wanted to go on scavenger hunts.

3518 As one vulture said to another,
"I feel sick. I think I ate something fresh."

3519 Or, as another vulture said to yet another, "I've got a bone to pick with you."

3520 What is a vulture's favorite meal?
Leftovers.

3521 Did you hear about the guy
who does bird imitations?
He eats like a vulture.

3522 After a period of religious fasting, a frustrated (and hungry) boy vulture
asked his father, "When and what can we eat?"
With infinite patience, the father replied, "Carrion, my wayward son."

Wallaby

3523   As one Australian kangaroo said to another, "Wallaby a son of a gun!"

3524   What jumps and collects pollen?
A wallabee.

Walrus

3525   What do you call a large seal in a hurry?
A walrush.

3526   How do walruses deal with difficult problems?
They appoint a tusk force.

3527 What sound does a disapproving walrus make?
Tusk-tusk.

Wasp

3528 What sweet can compete with honey?
Waspberry jam.

3529 Where do sick hornets go?
To the waspital.

3530 What is the difference between a fashion model
and an exterminated wasps' nest?
One is wasp-waisted and the other is wasted wasps.

Weasel

3531 What is the favorite song of certain
small, long-tailed mammals?
"Weasel While You Work."

3532 Did you hear about the train that
encountered a bunch of small mammals?
It had to make a weasel stop.

3533 What is a pig farmer's favorite nursery rhyme?
"Slop Goes the Weasel."

3534 There was an old woman of Ming
Who, when somebody asked her to sing,
Replied, "Ain't it odd?
I can never tell 'God
Save the Weasel' from 'Pop Goes the King.'"

3535 Or, as one baby weasel said to another, "My pop is bigger than yours."

Weevil

3536 Did you hear about the two boll weevil brothers?
One was very successful; the other was the lesser of two weevils.

3537   What road leads to a cotton field?
The route of all weevil.

> **3538**   Or, as the Egyptian undertaker said when he found bugs
> feasting on an embalmed body, "Mummy is the loot of all weevil."

> > **3539**   What is the menace of the bug world?
> > *The weevil empire.*

3540   Then there was the cotton farmer who saw his crop ravished by bugs,
who faced bankruptcy, but who remained hopeful and prayerfully stated:
"Though I walk through the valley of the shadow of debt, I shall fear no weevil."

> > **3541**   What insect can leap over
> > fourteen cans of bug spray?
> > *Weevil Knievel.*

> > > **3542**   What kind of insects are found
> > > in tenpins alleys?
> > > *Bowl weevils.*

3543   Or, as one cotton-eating bug said to another at the big dance,
"After the boll weevil all go home."

Whale

3544   Did you hear about the whales that had a people of a time?

> **3545**   What do the British call Moby Dick?
> *The Prince of Whales.*

3546   Or, as a humble Captain Ahab said after Moby Dick
chomped off the front end of his boat, "I'm not prowed."

> **3547**   What's at the end of Moby Dick?
> *A whale of a tail.*

> > **3548**   Or, as the old whale said when he was
> > overtaken by an iceberg, "My tale is told."

3549 Where do whales learn how to spell?
In a Moby dicktionary.

3550 Who was the strongest man in the Bible?
Jonah, because even the whale couldn't keep him down.

3551 Or you could say that Jonah's experience teaches us that you can't keep a good man down.

3552 How did Jonah feel after the whale swallowed him?
Down in the mouth.

3553 Why did the whale release Jonah?
Because he couldn't stomach him.

3554 That reminds us of the old Burma Shave roadside sign:
The whale put Jonah down the hatch,
But coughed him up because he scratched.

3555 What does Jonah have in common with a fire siren?
They both have big wails.

3556 Or, as Jonah once said, "All's whale that ends whale."

3557 What do whales chew?
Blubber gum.

3558 Do whales ever cry?
Yes. Haven't you ever seen whales blubber?

3559 Did you hear about the gossipy whale?
It was a blubber mouth.

3560 How does whale blubber prevent juvenile delinquency among Eskimos?
As soon as a kid misbehaves, his parents whale him till he blubbers.

3561   For many years a certain white whale and a tiny herring were inseparable friends. Wherever the white whale roamed in search of food, the herring was sure to be swimming right along beside him.

One fine spring day the herring turned up off the coast of Norway without his companion. Naturally all the other fish were curious, and an octopus finally asked the herring what happened to his whale friend.

"How should I know?" the herring replied. "Am I my blubber's kipper?"

3562   What do you call a timepiece for cetaceans?
A whale watch.

3563   Did you read the new autobiography of a whale?
It's titled *Weight and Sea.*

3564   Did you hear about the cetacean that begs for food from the visitors at the aquarium?
He's a real ne'er-do-whale.

3565   What's the favorite TV show of aquarium employees?
Whale of Fortune.

3566   Whales are mammals, and mammals have hair.
Thus, the slogan should be: Shave the Whales.

3567   Did you hear about the nearsighted whale that fell in love with a submarine?
Every time the boat fired a torpedo, the proud whale handed out cigars.

3568   How do you circumcise a whale?
You send down four skin divers.

3569   The young whale hadn't much of a spume.
He was only a little squirt.

3570   Or, as one whale complained to another,
"Why are you always spouting off?"

Whooping Crane

3571   What is a whooping crane?
A stork with pneumonia.

3572 What birds make a big noise?
Whooping cranes.

> **3573** What did the male crane say to the female?
> *"We either whoop it up or face extinction."*

> > **3574** Whooping cranes need cough drops.

Wolf

3575 To err is human; to howl about it, lupine.

> **3576** Did you hear about the wolf comedian?
> *He had his audience howling with laughter.*

> > **3577** Or, as one wolf said to another, "Howl-o there."

3578 Did you hear about the wolf businessman?
He was a howling success.

> **3579** What is a wolf's favorite song?
> *"Howl, Howl, the Gang's All Here."*

3580 Did you hear about the athletic wolf?
He was voted into the Howl of Fame.

3581 Where do wolves stay on vacation?
At the Howliday Inn.

3582 A decision to shoot more wolves met with howls of protest.

3583 How is a wolf like a powerful cleaning agent?
It works fast and leaves no ring.

3584 A wolf is a big dame hunter who knows all the ankles.

3585 A sailor is a wolf in ship's clothing.

3586 What would you call a sailor in a polyester leisure suit?
A wolf in cheap clothing.

3587 What was the big bad wolf's motto?
"I'm ready, villain, and able."

3588 Why are wolves like playing cards?
Because they belong to a pack.

3589 How did the hunter get his hands full of splinters?
He bare-handedly caught a timber wolf.

3590 How does a werewolf brush its hairy mouth?
With a fine tooth comb.

3591 What is a wolf gang?
An assemblage of wanna-be Mozarts.

Woodchuck

3592 Did you hear about the woodchuck that escaped
from the pet store in a shopping center?
The manager said that the chuck is in the mall.

3593 How much wood would a woodchuck chuck
If a woodchuck could chuck wood?
A woodchuck would chuck
All the wood that a woodchuck could chuck
If a woodchuck would chuck wood.

Woodpecker

3594 Why did the cockney owl 'owl?
Because the woodpecker would peck 'er.

3595 As one woodpecker said to another,
"Whoever said opportunity knocks only once?"

3596 Why did the homeowner get mad at the woodpecker?
He was sick and tired of saying, "Come in."

3597 How is a woodpecker like a successful businessman?
He uses his head and pecks away until a job is finished.

3598 A woodpecker in the woods took a powerful peck at the trunk of a huge oak tree, and at the very same instant a bolt of lightning struck and felled the tree. The amazed woodpecker commented to himself, "Wow! A guy just doesn't realize his own strength."

3599 Two former college roommates met at a reunion, and one asked, "How are things at work?"
The other replied, "I feel as if I'm in a hot-air balloon and just spotted a woodpecker."

3600 Did you hear about the poor fellow who was a real blockhead?
Woodpeckers followed him everywhere.

3601 What is green and pecks on trees?
Woody Woodpickle.

3602 Why didn't the baby woodpecker like bedtime stories?
Because they were boring.

3603 Did you hear about the unpopular woodpecker?
He was boring company.

3604 Or, as the tree said after being attacked all day by a woodpecker, "I'm getting bored."

Worm

3605 Did you hear about the worm who joined the marines?
He wanted to be in the apple corps.

3606 Did all of the animals enter Noah's ark in pairs?
No. The worms went in apples.

3607 What did Noah say to his sons who were fishing over the side of the ark?
"Take it easy on the bait, boys. After all, I have only two worms."

3608 As one worm said to another, "You're late for our meeting. Where in earth have you been?"

3609 Did you hear about the realistic and sensible worm?
He was very down-to-earth.

3610 Why is a worm like a naughty child?
Because it's always wriggling out of things.

3611 One day in his orchard, a farmer found in a shiny red apple a worm that made a whirring noise like an electric motor, so he adopted the worm as his pet, named it (obviously) Motor, and made a small fortune in the circus with this wriggling, squiggling freak of nature. Unfortunately, the wonderful worm disappeared one day, much to the chagrin of its owner.

To abate his dismay, the farmer spent much time in his orchard, examining one apple after another. One day, he retrieved an apple that fell far from a tree, broke it open, and, miraculously, out bored Motor.

3612 What happened to the worm in a cornfield?
It went in one ear and out the other.

3613 *Apple No. 1:* "What's the matter? What's eating you?"
Apple No. 2: "Worms."

3614 What's worse than biting into an apple and finding a worm?
Finding half a worm.

3615 As the bookworm said to the librarian,
"May I burrow this book?"

3616 *Bumper sticker:* Librarians Use Bookworms for Bait.

3617 Did you hear about the bird that flew into a library?
It was looking for bookworms.

3618 Two librarians were talking, and one asked, "Is your husband a bookworm?"
"No," replied the other, "just an ordinary one."

3619 How can you tell which end of a worm is its head?
Tickle it in the middle and see which end laughs.

3620 Two worms were waiting outside a psychiatrist's office. One commented, "I can't tell whether you're coming or going."
The other replied, "That's why I'm here."

3621 Did you hear about the two worms who met coming out of their holes in the ground?
"I think I'm in love with you," gushed the first.
"Don't be ridiculous," replied the second. "I'm your other end."

3622 Did you hear about the worms in the Hemingway family cemetery?
They worked in dead Ernest.

3623 Ooey Gooey was a worm,
A wondrous worm was he.
He stepped upon a railroad track;
A train he did not see:
Ooey Gooey.

3624 *Doctor:* "Do you like fishing, sir?"
Patient: "Yes."
Doctor: "That's good. Because you've got worms."

3625 Or, as we always say, "Every time we think of caterpillars, we get a worm fuzzy feeling."

3626 What made the alcoholic worm optimistic?
He knew he didn't have to worry about falling down.

3627 Did you hear about the nearsighted glowworm?
It fell in love with a cigarette.

3628 Two anglers began reviewing past fishing exploits and opened a can of worms.

3629   A family of worms was worming its way around a navy pier when the youngest offspring was frightened by the sight of a submarine.
"Don't worry," the mother worm said soothingly.
"It's just a can of people."

3630   What do you call a weight loss program, sponsored by the Lutheran Church, that is guaranteed to make one shed those extra pounds?
The Diet of Worms.

> **3631**   Did you hear about the two silkworms who had a fight?
> *Neither won because they ended up in a tie.*

> > **3632**   *Barefoot fisherman:* "How come these here night crawlers are so much more expensive than the other ones?"
> > *Bait shop owner:* "Them's fightin' worms."

Wren

3633   As one irritated bird said to another, "Wren are you going to leave?"

> **3634**   There was an old man un-sheared,
> Who said, "It is just as I feared:
> > Three hawks and a hen,
> > Four rooks and a wren
> Have all built their nests in my beard."

3635   A woman tried to thaw out a nearly frozen bird one winter with her hair dryer. Fearful that the bird might not survive, she commented to her husband, "I really shouldn't do this in front of the chilled wren."

Xiphiidae

3636 What is a Greek swordfish's favorite song?
"Zip a dee doo dah, xiphiidae ay."

Yak

3637   Did you hear about the talkative Tibetan ox?
He was a yackety-yak.

3638   What kind of Tibetan ox
can do many kinds of work?
A yak-of-all-trades.

3639   What's the favorite children's toy in Tibet?
A yak-in-the-box.

3640   What is the favorite children's story in Tibet?
"Yak the Giant Killer."

3641   What is the most vicious Tibetan animal?
Yak the Ripper.

3642   What's the favorite song in Tibet?
"Hit the Road, Yak."

3643   What song was written about the huge
yak in the zoo who woke up each morning with a long yawn?
"Mighty Yak Arose."

3644   Who was the infamous Tibetan vampire?
Count Yakula.

3645   What does a yak put ice cream in?
Cognac.

3646   What do you call a Tibetan ox with vertigo in Africa?
An Afro dizzy yak.

3647   There once was a man in Tibet
Who worked in the hills as a vet.
He treated the backs
Of overworked yaks;
How low (or how high) can one get?

3648   Or, as the Tibetan chef exclaimed when he
smelled something burning in his oven, "Oh, my baking yak!"

3649   What ox scene will never be seen?
A yak in a kayak.

Yellow Jacket

3650   What did one yellow jacket give another?
A coat hanger.

3651   Or, as Confucius says, "If the yellow jacket buzzes, don't wear it."

Zebra

3652 What's black and white and red all over?
An embarrassed zebra.

3653 What's black and white and blue all over?
A zebra in an icebox.

3654 Or, as the angry zebra said,
"I feel like a horse of a different choler."

3655 Why is the colorful zebra an appropriate national animal for South Africa?
Because it has op-art hide.

3656 What did the well-dressed zebra wear?
A pinstriped suit.

3657 Did you hear about the zebra in a hurricane?
He had to glue on his stripes.

3658 Why did the horse break into the jail?
He wanted to impersonate a zebra by standing behind bars.

3659 Then there was the drunk who saw a zebra behind bars
and asked the zookeeper, "What's he in for?"

3660 Did you hear about the zebra who fell in love
with a horse that had sat down on a freshly
painted park bench?

3661 Did you hear about the dumb
guy who bought a pet zebra?
He named it Spot.

3662 What did the male zebra like
about his girlfriend?
He thought she had nice lines.

3663 Did you hear about the striped animal
who was a movie starlet?
*Her dresses were so low-cut
that ze bra showed.*

3664 Did you hear the one about the horse
who fell in love with a zebra?
*Unfortunately, he spent the first night
with her just trying to take off her pajamas.*

3665 What has stars and stripes?
A movie about a zebra.

3666 If the alphabet goes from A to Z,
then what goes from Z to A?
Zebra.

3667 Speaking of the end of the alphabet reminds us of the
woman who always peeked at the ending of suspense novels.
Even when she was given a dictionary as a gift, the woman
immediately turned to the last page and exclaimed,
"Hah! The zebra did it!!"

Zebu

3668 As the Frenchman commented at the zoo,
"Asiatic oxen are zebu-tiful animals."

Zyzzyva

3669   Besides being a weevil, what is zyzzyva?
*The last word in our alphabetical animals, the last word in many
dictionaries, and the name of a literary publication. That's quite a distinction
for a skinny bug, wouldn't you say?*

Part

TWO

Animals in Other Modes:
From Bars to Zoos

Bar Puns:
The Best Bar Puns—Bar None

Puns occupy a central place in the oral (and aural) folklore of most societies. In Word Play, Peter Farb explains that "the majority of American children are strikingly punctual in acquiring a repertoire of riddles at about age six or seven."

Children grow up to be adults, and they keep collecting puns. Over the years, we have noticed a growing canon of jokes, most of them involving wordplay, about animals who walk into bars to order beers and other alcoholic treats. So here's a punny round of setups—on the house.

3670   A termite walks into a bar and asks, "Where's the bar tender?"

3671   A grasshopper hops into a bar, and the bartender says, "Hey, we have a drink named after you!"
        The grasshopper replies, "Really? You have a drink named Irving?"

3672   A duck waddles into a bar and orders a beer.
That'll be four dollars," says the bartender.
"Just put it on my bill."

3673   Another duck walks into the bar, and the bartender looks at him and says, "Hey, buddy, your pants are down."

3674   A small pig goes to a bar on a hot day and has many drinks to quench his thirst. The pig sitting next to him says, "You've been drinking all afternoon and haven't been to the bathroom once. How do you do it?" The first pig replies, "Oh, I'm the little pig who goes wee-wee wee-wee all the way home."

3675   A koala walks into a bar, sits down, and orders a sandwich. He eats the sandwich, pulls out a gun, and shoots the waiter dead. As the koala stands up to go, the bartender shouts, "Hey! Where are you going? You just shot my waiter, and you didn't pay for your sandwich!" The koala yells back at the bartender, "Hey, man, I'm a koala! Look it up!" The bartender opens his dictionary and sees the following definition for koala: "A tree-dwelling marsupial of Australian origin, characterized by a broad head, large hairy ears, dense gray fur, and sharp claws. Eats shoots and leaves."

3676   After winning first prize in a show, a dog celebrates by having a drink in a bar. When he leaves, however, he forgets that he has placed his prize on the counter. The dog realizes his mistake when he gets home, so he sends his son to retrieve it. When the puppy enters the tavern, the bartender asks, "What'll you have, boy?"
The puppy replies, "Pap's blue ribbon."

3677   A polar bear lumbers into a bar and says to the bartender,
"I'll have a gin . . . and tonic."
The bartender says, "What's with the big pause?"
Replies the bear, "I dunno. I've always had them."

3678   A horse trots into a bar in search of refreshment.
The bartender looks at him and asks, "Why the long face?"

3679   An anteater walks into a bar and says that he'd like a drink.
"Okay," says the bartender. "How about a beer?"
"No-o-o-o-o-o-o-o-o-o," replies the anteater.
"Then how about a gin and tonic?"
"No-o-o-o-o-o-o-o-o-o-o."
"A martini?"
"No-o-o-o-o-o-o-o-o-o-o."
Finally the bartender gets fed up and says, "Hey, listen, buddy, if you don't mind my asking, why the long *nos*?"

3680   A giraffe walks into a bar and announces, "The highballs are on me."

3681   Actually, bartenders don't enjoy having giraffes as their customers. That's because giraffes make one drink go a long way. And bartenders don't like serving customers who are already high.

3682 A snake slithers into a bar, and the bartender says,
"I'm sorry, but I can't serve you."
"Why not?" asks the snake.
The bartender says, "Because you can't hold your liquor."

3683 A dog limps into a bar on three legs and snarls,
"I'm looking for the man who shot my paw."

3684 A guy walks into a bar and sees a dog playing poker. The guy asks the
bartender, "Is that dog really playing poker?"
"Yep," the bartender replies.
"What can a dog do with his winnings?"
"I don't know—he never wins," smirks the bartender.
"Is he a rotten player?" the guy asks.
"No, but every time he has a good hand, he wags his tail."

3685 An elephant walks into a waterfront bar for a drink and notices
a gorgeous lady elephant sitting several seats away from him. He asks
the bartender to place a drink in front of every seat between him and
the female. He then begins to take a drink out of each glass, progressing
along the line a seat at a time. When asked what he is doing, the elephant
replies, "I'm going down to the she in sips."

3686 That same elephant walks into another bar, but he is informed that
they're not permitted to serve alcoholic beverages to elephants. "I don't
want a drink," the elephant replies. "I just came in for the peanuts."

3687 The very same elephant reappears in his favorite bar after an absence
of several months. When asked where he's been, the elephant answers,
"Oh, I've been on the circus wagon."

3688 A flea, after a few drinks in a saloon in the Old West, jumps out
over the swinging doors and lands in the middle of the street.
"All right," he shouts, "who moved my dog?"

3689 A tiny insect somehow managed to become a psychoanalyst.
To celebrate his new career, he went into the local saloon for a drink.
The bartender asked him, "Are you a medical bug?"
"No," was the reply, "I'm a Freud gnat."

3690   A salamander was paroled from prison and went to the local saloon for a drink. The bartender asked him, "Are you that salamander criminal?"

"No," came the reply, "I'm a freed newt."

3691   An old and arthritic dog was run over by a street-cleaning vehicle but somehow managed to drag himself into a nearby saloon. "Are you okay?" asked the bartender.

"No," replied the dog, "I'm a flayed mutt."

3692   A shrimp walks into a saloon, and the bartender says, "I'm sorry, but we don't serve food here."

3693   Now it's time to pay the check, so the bartender goes over to the animals at the end of the night.

The skunk says, "Don't look at me. I've only got a scent—and it's a bad one."

The duck says, "My bill is already too big."

The cow says, "You'll have to ask one of the udders."

Another cow says, "I'm out of moolah."

The beaver says, "You'll have to ask one of the otters. I'll be dammed if I'll pay."

The deer says, "I had a buck last week, and I'm expecting a little doe soon."

The frog says, "I've got just one greenback."

The vampire bat is thinking, "Which one can I stick for the drink today?"

The zebra says, "It's black and white—I haven't the money."

The rhinoceros says, "I'll just charge it."

The snake says, "If you think I'm paying that, you can kiss my asp."

Another snake says, "It's hiss turn to pay."

The amoeba says, "I've got to split now."

The paramecium says, "I'll split it with him."

The chicken says, "I'm too cheep to pay."

The Manx cat says, "I know you've heard this tail before, but I'm a little short."

The giraffe says, "That's too high for me."

The turtle and the snail say, "We can't shell out."

The trotters say, "Take fifty cents from two quarter horses."

The bumblebee says, "Buzz off."

But the lion says, "I'll pay—I've still got pride."

Classrooms:
School Daze with Teacher Qs and Student As

Many among us lament the decline in student achievement in the United States. Critics point to declining SAT and ACT scores and deplore that our young scholars no longer can distinguish a subject from a predicate or a radius from a diameter, nor can they identify the capitals of their own states and the members of Congress therefrom.

Fear no more, for as the transcripts below indicate, students are in full control of their knowledge of the animal kingdom.

3694 *Teacher:* "The animal kingdom is divided into what two classes?"
Student: "The aardvarks and the aaren'tvarks."

3695 *Teacher:* "What is an adder?"
Student: "Something that's slithery and good at counting."

3696 *Teacher:* "What is unique about an amoeba?"
Student: "It's a mathematically inclined organism that multiplies by dividing."

3697 *Teacher:* "What is *comeuppance*?"
Student: "It's what happens when you spread the food at a picnic."

3698 *Teacher:* "Under what circumstances can a pronghorn antelope jump 20 feet?"
Student: "When it's followed closely by a mountain lion."

3699 *Teacher:* "What is an apiary?"
Student: "A house for apes."

3700 *Teacher:* "Please define *aspire*."
Student: "It's how Cleopatra died."

3701 *Teacher:* "Have you ever hunted bear?"
Student: "No, but I've gone fishing in my shorts."

3702 *Teacher:* "How'd you get stung?"
Student: "By smelling a flowber."
Teacher: "There's no *b* in *flower*."
Student: "There was in this one."

3703 *Teacher:* "Please define *betray*."
Student: "It's where bees are placed for examination."

3704 *Student:* "My pet bird is dead."
Teacher: "That's too bad. How did it die?"
Student: "Flew—"
Teacher: "Bird flu? That's terrible."
Student: "—in front of a bus."

3705 *Teacher:* "Why was the bird punished in school?"
Student: "It was caught peeping during a test."

3706 *Teacher:* "What is it called when birds fly south for the winter?"
Student: "Migratious, I don't know."

3707 *Teacher:* "Do camels travel in herds or flocks?"
Student: "My father says they come in packs."

3708 *Teacher:* "Over a thousand camels are used each year to make paintbrushes."
Student: "Isn't it amazing what animals can be taught to do these days?"

3710 *Teacher:* "Have you ever seen the Catskill Mountains?"
Student: "No, but I've seen what they do to mice."

3711 *Teacher:* "What are four animals that belong to the cat family?"
Student: "The father cat, the mother cat, and two kittens."

3709 *Teacher:* "What are cat burglars?"
Student: "They are crooks who pussyfoot around your house."

3712 *Teacher:* "If there were nine cats in a box and two jumped out, how many would be left?"
Student: "None, if they were copycats."

3713 *Teacher:* "Please define three different kinds of cats."
Student: "Cats with deep feelings are Feline cats. Cats with bad tempers are Angorie cats. And cats that are intended for kids to maul are Maultese cats."

3714 *Teacher:* "If apples come from apple trees, where do chickens come from?"
Student: "Pole trees."

3715 *Teacher:* "Use *conscience-stricken* in a sentence."
Student: "Don't conscience strickens before they hatch."

3716 *Teacher:* "If you had twenty-seven cows and I gave you nineteen more, what would you have?"
Student: "A dairy farm."

3717 *Teacher:* "Why are cows kept in a pasture?"
Student: "So they'll give pasteurized milk."

3718 *Teacher:* "Please define *coward*."
Student: "It's the place bovines are kept."

3719 *Teacher:* "Analyze this sentence: 'It was getting to be milking time.' What mood?"
Student: "The cow."

3720 *Teacher:* "Please define *noticeable*."
Student: "To spot a male cow."

3721 *Teacher:* "What is apartheid?"
Student: "It's one portion of a cowhide."

3722 *Teacher:* "What is the cranium?"
Student: "That portion of the zoo where cranes are kept."

3723 *Teacher:* "What's the purpose of reindeer?"
Student: "It makes the grass grow."

3724 *Teacher:* "What were dinosaurs originally called?"
Student: "An endangering species."

3725 *Teacher:* "Petroleum comes from things such as decomposed dinosaurs."
Student: "That proves there's no fuel like an old fuel."

3726 *Teacher:* "What was the fastest dinosaur?"
Student: "The prontosaurus."

3727 *Teacher:* "What can you tell me about Dalmatians?"
Student: "The first one was spotted in 1876."

3728 *Teacher:* "Please define *doggerel*."
Student: "It's a little pooch."

3729 *Teacher:* "What is dogmatism?"
Student: "It's puppyism come to its full growth."

3730 *Teacher:* "What is an example of a collective noun?"
Student: "A pound of puppies."

3731 *Teacher:* "What is a comet?"
Student: "I don't know."
Teacher: "It's a star with a tail."
Student: "Oh, you mean like Lassie?"

3732 *Teacher:* "This essay you wrote, 'My Dog,' is the same as your brother's paper."
Student: "It's the same dog."

3733 *Teacher:* "Use *defeat, deduct, defense,* and *detail* in a sentence."
Brooklyn student: "De feet of de duck get under de fence before de tail."

3734 *Teacher:* "What was the first animal to circumnavigate the globe?"
Student: "That duck from Paris."
Teacher: "What duck from Paris?"
Student: "Sir France's drake."

3735 *Teacher:* "Use *paradox* in a sentence."
Student: "The farmer had four geese and a pair o' ducks."

3736 *Teacher:* "A thousand elephants a year are used to make ivory keys for pianos."
Student: "Isn't it amazing that big animals can be trained to do such fine work?"

3737 *Teacher:* "What do elephants have that no other animal has?"
Student: "Baby elephants."

3738 *Teacher:* "Where are elephants found?"
Student: "Elephants are so large that they're hardly ever lost."

3739 *Teacher:* "What's the difference between an Indian elephant and an African one?"
Student: "About three thousand miles."

3740 *Teacher:* "How do you spell *elephant?*"
Student: "E-L-E-F-A-N-T."
Teacher: "The dictionary spells it E-L-E-P-H-A-N-T."
Student: "You asked me how I spell it, not how the dictionary spells it."

3741 *Teacher:* "Name nine animals from Africa."
Student: "Eight elephants and a giraffe."

3742 *Teacher:* "What is an emu?"
Student: "The sound a cat makes."

3743 *Teacher:* "How do you spell *farm?*"
Student: "E-I-E-I-O."

3744 *Teacher:* "Do fish perspire?"
Student: "How do you think the ocean gets salty?"

3745 *Teacher:* "Here's an easy question. What is flypaper?"
Student: "There's a catch to it, isn't there?"

3746 *Teacher:* "Why will TV never replace the newspaper?"
Student: "You can't swat flies with a TV."

3747 *Teacher:* "A single fly has millions of offspring."
Student: "How many offspring does a married fly have?"

3748 *Teacher:* "In this computer age, what is downtime?"
Student: "Molting season for geese."

3749 *Teacher:* "Where does mohair come from?"
Student: "From a goat named Moe."

3750 *Teacher:* "What is the most common habitat of gnus?"
Student: "Crossword puzzles."

3751 *Teacher:* "What's a Hindu?"
Student: "It lays eggs."

3752 *Teacher:* "Use *gladiator* in a sentence."
Student: "The farmer's hen stopped laying eggs, so he was gladiator."

3753 *Teacher:* "What would Thanksgiving dinner be like if the Pilgrims had landed in Africa instead?"
Student: "I don't know, but I'd sure hate to try to stuff a hippopotamus."

3754 *Teacher:* "What is the principal part of a horse?"
Student: "The mane part."

3755 *Teacher:* "What is the opposite of *sorrow*?"
Student: "Joy."
Teacher: "That's right. Now what's the opposite of *misery*?"
Student: "Happiness."
Teacher: "Right again. Now what's the opposite of *woe*?"
Student: "Giddyup."

3756 *Teacher:* "Who was Eric the Red?"
Student: "He was a Norse of a different color."

3757 *Teacher:* "I asked you to draw a horse and cart, but you only drew a horse."
Student: "The horse will draw the cart."

3758 *Teacher:* "What is an ibex?"
Student: "It's a listing at the end of a book."

3759 *Teacher:* "Name the sexes."
Student: "Male sex, female sex, and insects."

3760 *Teacher:* "What fish kills other fish in the ocean?"
Student: "Jack the Kipper."

3761 *Teacher:* "What is the capital of Malaysia?"
Student: "Koala Lumpur."

3762 *Teacher:* "Why did you take my ornithology class?"
Student: "Just for a lark."

3763 *Teacher:* "What is the equator?"
Student: "It's a menagerie lion running around the middle of the earth."

3764 *Teacher:* "If you were a big-game hunter and suddenly met an alligator, a lion, and a rhinoceros, which animal would you get fur from?"
Student: "I'd get as fur from all of them as I could."

3765 *Teacher:* "If you were in Africa and saw a lion coming, what steps would you take?"
Student: "The longest steps I could."

3766 *Teacher (holding a picture of a deer):* "What is this a picture of?"
Student: "I have no idea. Give me a hint."
Teacher: "What does your mother call your father?"
Student: "Oh, so that's what a louse looks like."

3767 *Teacher:* "What is a myth?"
Student: "A female moth."

3768 *Teacher:* "Taurus the bull, Pisces the fish, and Cancer the crab are all animal signs of the zodiac. What is another one?"
Student: "Mickey the mouse."

3769 *Teacher:* "Please spell *mouse*."
Student: "M-O-U-S."
Teacher: "But what's at the end of it?"
Student: "A tail."

3770 *Teacher:* "Please use *minute* in a sentence."
Student: "My newt is very small."

3771 *Teacher:* "What's an ocelot?"
Student: "Sir Ocelot was a knight."

3772 *Teacher:* "What is an octopus?"
Student: "A cat with only eight lives."

3773 *Student:* "May I bring my pet keet to school?"
Teacher: "Do you mean a parakeet?"
Student: "No, I only have the one."

3774 *Teacher:* "What is pigskin used for?"
Student: "It's for holding pigs together."

3775 *Teacher:* "If the statue of George Washington in front of City Hall could speak, what do you think he would say today?"
Student: "He'd say, 'I'm going to shoot about ten thousand pigeons.'"

3776 *Teacher:* "What are two animals from the Arctic region?"
Student: "Two polar bears."

3777 *Teacher:* "What is a Trojan horse?"
Student: "A phony pony."

3778 *Teacher:* "Please define *ramparts*."
Student: "They're things like hooves, horns, and wool."

3779 *Teacher:* "Do you know Edgar Allan Poe's 'Raven?'"
Student: "No. What's he mad about?"

3780 *Teacher:* "The title of the former ruler of Russia was *czar*, and the title of his wife was *czarina*. What were the children called?"
Student: "Sardines."

3781 *Teacher:* "Can you write a poem about a lamb that has just been sheared?"
Student: "Bare, bare back sheep."

3782 *Teacher:* "Please define *delamination*."
Student: "It's an aborted baby sheep."

3783 *Teacher:* "Use the word *distinct* in a sentence."
Student: "Distinct a skunk makes is terrible."

3784 *Teacher:* "Can you get fur from a skunk?"
Student: "Yes, as fur as I can."

3785 *Teacher:* "What is unique about the sole?"
Student: "It's the only fish that leaves footprints on the ocean floor."

3786 *Teacher:* "Please use *termite* in a sentence."
Student: "Unless I get better grades, this termite be my last one."

3787 *Teacher:* "What is a goblet?"
Student: "A baby turkey."

3788 *Teacher:* "Why did the Pilgrims roast wild turkeys?"
Student: "You'd be wild, too, if you found out what the Pilgrims had in mind."

3789 *Teacher (before Thanksgiving):* "What are you thankful for?"
Student: "I'm thankful that I'm not a turkey."

3790 *Teacher:* "What is a vegetarian?"
Student: "It's a horse doctor."
Teacher: "No. You're thinking of a veterinarian."
Student: "I thought a veterinarian was a former member of the armed forces."

3791 *Teacher:* "Please define *valorous*."
Student: "A valorous is a huge animal vit tusks that lives in the vater."

3792 *Teacher:* "Swimming is an ideal exercise for losing weight."
Student: "Try telling that to a whale!"

3793 *Teacher:* "Eskimos eat whale meat and blubber."
Student: "I'd blubber, too, if all I had to eat was whale meat."

3794 *Teacher:* "Evolution claims that man descended from apes."
Student: "What about Welshmen? I thought they came from whales."

3795 *Teacher:* "What is a wombat for?"
Student: "For playing wom?"

3796 *Teacher:* "It takes a hundred silk worms to make a single tie."
Student: "Isn't it amazing what a bunch of worms can be trained to do?"

3797 *Teacher:* "What do worms live on?"
Student: "What difference does it make? I've never seen a worm that couldn't make both ends meet."

3798 *Teacher:* "Please define *rebate*."
Student: "To put another worm on your fishhook."

3799 *Teacher:* "What does *unabated* mean*?*"
Student: "A fishhook without a worm."

3800 *Teacher:* "If a two-legged animal is a biped, and a four-legged one is a quadruped, what is a zebra?"
Student: "A stri-ped."

3801 *Teacher:* "For the species to survive, animals must breed."
Student: "Yeah, if they didn't breed, they'd suffocate."

3802 *Teacher:* "How many animals did Moses take on the ark?"
Student: "Moses didn't take any on the ark. Noah did."

3803 *Teacher:* "Please define *archives*."
Student: "It's Noah's skin allergy to animals."

3804 *Teacher:* "What animal was first out of the ark?"
Student: "I don't know. But Noah came fourth."

Contrasts:
What's the Difference between _____ and _____?

Many English-speaking children cut their punning eyeteeth by hearing and posing a special kind of riddle. Each question begins with the formula "What's the difference between _____ and _____?" The answer may be built on both items or only one. For example:

What's the difference between a tube and a crazy Dutchman?
One is a hollow cylinder; the other is a silly Hollander.

What's the difference between a film and a witch's cauldron?
One is a motion picture. The other is a potion mixture.

Some of the best of these "difference" riddles are animalistic.
What's the difference between an ornithologist and a stutterer?
One is a bird watcher, and the other is a word botcher.

One doesn't have to be a word botcher to enjoy these zoological switcheroos:

What's the difference between . . .

3805   . . . a healthy rabbit and the authors of this book?
One is a fit bunny, and the others are a bit funny.

3806   . . . a hymn and an angry seabird?
One is the Rock of Ages, and the other is an auk of rages.

3807   . . . big embraces and lice?
The first are bear hugs, and the second are hair bugs.

3808   . . . Goldilocks and a genealogist?
A genealogist is interested in forebears.

What's the difference between . . .

3809   . . . a run-down hotel and a banner for a hive?
One is a flea bag, and the other is a bee flag.

3810   . . . a mangy dog and a dead stinging insect?
One is a seedy beast, and the other is a bee deceased.

3811   . . . a bird with one wing and a bird with two wings?
It's a matter of a pinion.

3812   . . . an American buffalo and an Australian bison?
You can't wash your hands in a buffalo.

3813   . . . a counterfeit coin and a crazy rabbit?
One is bad money, and the other is a mad bunny.

3814   . . . a sensitive spot in your elbow and a rabbit's conversation piece?
One is a funny bone, and the other is a bunny phone.

3815   . . . sacks of dough and rabbit periodicals?
One is money bags, and the other is bunny mags.

3816   . . . a unicorn and lettuce?
One is a funny beast, and the other is a bunny feast.

3817   . . . a miser and a canary?
One's a little cheap, and the other a little cheeper.

3818   . . . a pet canary and one from Louisiana?
One's a canary encaged, and the other's a Cajun canary.

3819   . . . a fisherman and a farmer?
A fisherman puts the carp before the horse.

3820   . . . a cat and a comma?
A cat has claws at the end of its paws, while a comma is a pause at the end of a clause.

3821   . . . a cat and a puss?
Your cat is likable, but not your puss.

What's the difference between . . .

3822   . . . a frog and a cat?
A frog croaks all the time, a cat only nine times.

3823   . . . a manufacturer of expensive floor coverings and contented cats?
The first produces Persian rugs, and the second produces purrs on rugs.

3824   . . . a cat and a match?
One's light on its feet, and the other lights on its head.

3825   . . . muddy cows and a royal war?
One is brown cattle, and the other is a crown battle.

3826   . . . an angry crowd and a cow with a sore throat?
One boos madly, and the other moos badly.

3827   . . . a coyote and a flea?
One howls on the prairie, and the other prowls on the hairy.

3828   . . . a deer and a small witch?
One is a hunted stag, and the other is a stunted hag.

3829   . . . a world without any prehistoric animals and a room with no exit?
One has no dinosaurs, and the other has no sign o' doors.

3830   . . . a good dog and a poor student?
One rarely bites, and the other barely writes.

3831   . . . a high-class dog and one that never argues?
One has pedigrees, and the other pet agrees.

3832   . . . a flea-infested dog and a bored houseguest?
One is going to itch, and the other is itching to go.

3833   . . . a Rodin statue and a starving dog?
One's a Thinker, and the other's a thin cur.

3834   . . . a hairy dog and a painter?
One sheds his coat, and the other coats his shed.

What's the difference between . . .

3835   . . . a well-dressed man and a tired dog?
The man wears a suit, and the dog just pants.

3836   . . . a bombastic punster and a car-chasing canine on a hot day?
One puns and rants, and the other runs and pants.

3837   . . . a bee and a stubborn donkey?
One gets all the honey, and the other gets all the whacks.

3838   . . . a stubborn donkey and a stamp?
One you lick with a stick, and the other you stick with a lick.

3839   . . . St. George and Rudolph the red-nosed reindeer?
One slays the dragon, and the other's draggin' the sleigh.

3840   . . . a racehorse and a duck?
One goes quick on its legs, and the other goes quack on its eggs.

3841   . . . an elephant and a flea?
An elephant can have fleas, but a flea can't have elephants.

3842   . . . an aching vulpine and two pair of stockings?
The first is a sore fox, and the others are four socks.

3843   . . . a dog and a fox?
About five drinks.

3844   . . . a father gorilla, a bald-headed man, an orphan, and a crown prince?
One is a hairy parent, one has no hair apparent, one has ne'er a parent, and one is an heir apparent.

3845   . . . a barn and a fast dog?
One is a hay ground, and the other a greyhound.

3846   . . . fast lectures and a groomed pony?
One is a hurried course, and the other is a curried horse.

3847   . . . a horse race and a political race?
In a horse race the whole horse wins.

What's the difference between . . .

3848 . . . a tailor and a horse trainer?
One mends a tear, and the other tends a mare.

3849 . . . a long-winded political speech and a cowboy?
One is a filibuster, and the other is a filly buster.

3850 . . . a kangaroo and a logger?
One hops and chews, and the other chops and hews.

3851 . . . an awestruck man and a leopard's tail?
One is rooted to the spot, and the other is spotted to the root.

3852 . . . a jungle and a grocery store?
Checkout lions.

3853 . . . a tiger and a lion?
A tiger has the mane part missing.

3854 . . . a soaking wet day and a lion with a toothache?
One is pouring with rain, and the other is roaring with pain.

3855 . . . a jumping magician and a crying gecko?
One is a leaping wizard, and the other is a weeping lizard.

3856 . . . a one-*L* lama, a two-*L* llama, and a three-*L* lllama?
*The first is a Tibetan monk, the second is a South American animal,
and the third is a huge fire.*

3857 . . . a New England fisherman and a Mafia network?
One is a lobster man, and the other is a mobster LAN.

3858 . . . fly and a mosquito?
You can't sew a zipper on a mosquito.

3859 . . . a movie starlet and a mouse?
One charms he's, and the other harms cheese.

3860 . . . playing solitaire and a dining mouse?
One has ease to cheat, and the other has cheese to eat.

What's the difference between . . .

3861   . . . a butcher and a night owl?
One weighs a steak, and the other stays awake.

3862   . . . a girl who likes Irishmen and a spinster?
One loves a Pat and carrots, and the other loves a cat and parrots.

3863   . . . a pigeon and a poor farmer?
The pigeon can still make a deposit on a new tractor.

3864   . . . a mean French dog and a piece of linguine?
One's a nasty poodle, and the other's a pasta noodle.

3865   . . . a ship's mast and a baby dog in a refrigerator?
One's perpendicular, and the other's pup in de cooler.

3866   . . . a tough little dog and a small cute minnow?
One's a gritty puppy, and the other's a pretty guppy.

3867   . . . a puppy for sale and one at home?
In the pet shop, you choose the pup. At home, it's the pup that chews.

3868   . . . a rooster, a patriot, and an old maid?
*A rooster says, "Cock-a-doodle-do," a patriot says, "Yankee-doodle-do,"
and an old maid says, "Any old dude'll do."*

3869   . . . yachtsmen and shad?
Yachtsmen sail, but shad roe.

3870   . . . cash borrowed from your mother and the price of a skunk?
One is money owed her, and the other is odor money.

3871   . . . a dead snake and a dead lawyer lying in the street?
There are skid marks in front of the snake.

3872   . . . a stoic and a cynic?
A stoic brings the baby, and then you wash it in the cynic.

3873   . . . a baby frog and the month's rent?
One's a tadpole, and the other's a pad toll.

What's the difference between . . .

3874   . . . a fish and a piano?
You can't tuna fish.

3875   . . . a lawyer and a vulture?
A vulture waits until you're dead to eat your heart out.

3876   . . . a dog and a marine biologist?
One wags a tail, and the other tags a whale.

Crosses:
What Do You Get When You Cross ____ with ____?

In these days of genetic miracles, you never can tell what you'll get when you combine an animal with another animal or with something else. For example:
What do you get when you cross two punsters with a hen?
Two comedians who lay eggs with a lot of bad yolks.
What do you get if you cross a hyena with the authors of this book?
An animal that laughs at its own jokes.

Here is a collection for your genetic imagination to play with. Maybe you'll find funny crosses of your own.

What do you get when you cross . . .

3877 . . . an abalone with a crocodilian?
A crocabolone.

3878 . . . a stray cat with a crocodilian?
An alleygator.

3879 . . . a detective with a crocodilian?
A private investigator.

3880 . . . an amoeba with a bunny?
A rabbit that can multiply and divide itself.

3881 . . . an armadillo with a chicken?
A peccadillo.

3882 . . . a donkey with an owl?
A smart ass that knows it all.

3883 . . . a donkey with an earthquake?
Asphalt.

3884 . . . a telephone with a monkey?
A ring-tailed baboon.

3885 . . . a sheep with a gorilla?
A baaa-boon.

3886 . . . bats with a lonely-hearts club?
Lots of blind dates.

3887 . . . a bee with chopped beef?
A humburger.

3888 . . . a bee with a doorbell?
A humdinger.

What do you get when you cross . . .

3889 . . . a hummingbird with a doorbell?
A humdinger of a different tune.

3890 . . . a robin's leg, a haddock, with a hand?
Bird's-thigh fish fingers.

3891 . . . a bird with a zero?
A flying none.

3892 . . . a bird with a magician?
A flying sorcerer.

3893 . . . a sparrow with a mole?
A miner bird.

3894 . . . a singing bird with a seamstress?
A hemmingbird.

3895 . . . a doctor with a bloodhound?
A medical scenter.

3896 . . . a basketball, an infant, with a snake?
A bouncing baby boa.

3897 . . . pasta with a boa?
Spaghetti that winds itself around a fork.

3898 . . . an Eskimo with a pig?
A polar boar.

3899 . . . a rodeo bronco with a cornfield?
Buckin' ears.

3900 . . . a flea with a rabbit?
A bug's bunny.

3901 . . . a garbage collector with an insect?
A litterbug.

3902 . . . a steer with a toad?
A bullfrog.

3903 . . . a mean person with a toad?
A bully frog.

3904 . . . a bull with a lion?
Bullion.

3905 . . . a rabbit with a leek?
A bunion.

3906 . . . a rabbit with a grasshopper?
A bunny hop.

3907 . . . a camel with a cow?
Lumpy milk shakes.

3908 . . . another camel with another cow?
A dromedairy.

3909 . . . a potato with a canary?
A potato chirp.

3910 . . . a canary with a small ape?
A chirpmonk.

3911 . . . a canary with a cat?
A Peeping Tom.

3912 . . . a sheep dog with a baby fish?
A shag carp-ette.

3913 . . . a cat with a lemon?
A sourpuss.

What do you get when you cross . . .

3914 . . . a cat with a cobbler?
Puss 'n' boots.

3915 . . . a cat with an oyster?
A purrl.

3916 . . . a kitten with a tomato?
Catsup.

3917 . . . a duplicating machine
with a feline?
A copycat.

3918 . . . Evel Knievel with a cat?
*Someone who makes his jumps by
a whisker.*

3919 . . . a feline with a post?
A caterpillar.

3920 . . . a worm with a fur coat?
A caterpillar.

3921 . . . a horse with a soccer player?
A centaur forward.

3922 . . . a hyena with a chameleon?
Dr. Chuckle and Mr. Hide.

3923 . . . a pig with a centipede?
Bacon and legs.

3924 . . . an electronic organ with
a chicken?
Hammond eggs.

3925 . . . a dog with a chicken?
Barkin' and eggs.

3926 . . . a lighthouse with a chicken?
Beacon and eggs.

3927 . . . a hen with gunpowder?
An eggsplosion.

3928 . . . a chicken with a bell?
An alarm cluck.

3929 . . . a cement mixer with a chicken?
A brick layer.

3930 . . . a chicken with a racehorse?
A hen that lays odds.

3931 . . . a chicken with an alligator?
A henbag.

3932 . . . a chicken with a banjo?
A self-plucking hen.

3933 . . . a chicken with a dictionary?
Fowl language.

3934 . . . a chicken with a ghost?
A poultrygeist.

3935 . . . a chicken with a steer?
Roost beef.

3936 . . . a shellfish with a sheep?
A clam chop.

3937 . . . a cobra with a cornet?
A snake in the brass.

3938 . . . Dracula with a fish?
Cape Cod.

What do you get when you cross . . .

3939   . . . Lassie with a lilac?
A collie flower.

3940   . . . A cantaloupe, Lassie, and
an infant?
A melon collie baby.

3941   . . . a collie with a malamute?
*A commute, which is a dog that
likes to travel.*

3942   . . . a collie with a Lhasa Apso?
*A collapso, which is a dog that
folds up for easy transport.*

3943   . . . grass seed with a cow?
A lawn mooer.

3944   . . . a cow with a belly dancer?
A milk shake.

3945   . . . a Hershey bar, a cow, and
an Arab?
A chocolate milk sheik.

3946   . . . a cow with a tavern from
outer space?
A Milky Way bar.

3947   . . . a lemon with a cow?
Sour cream.

3948   . . . a steer with a channel marker?
A cowbuoy.

3949   . . . a coyote with an ass?
*A Doncoyote—an ass that brays
at windmills and tilts at the moon.*

3950   . . . a crocodile with a camera?
A snapshot.

3951   . . . a garden hose with
a crocodilian?
An irrigator.

3952   . . . a dinosaur with a chicken?
Tyrannosaurus Pecks.

3953   . . . the modern world's tallest
animal with a dinosaur?
Giraffic Park.

3954   . . . an Australian dog with
a drummer?
Dingo Starr.

3955   . . . Dracula with a dog?
*A beast whose bite is worse
than its bark.*

3956   . . . chili pepper, a shovel, and
a collie?
A hot diggety dog.

3957   . . . a jeep with a dog?
A Land Rover.

3958   . . . a grouch with a dog?
An unwelcome waggin'.

3959   . . . a timepiece with a puppy?
A watchdog.

3960   . . . a leopard with a watchdog?
A terrified letter carrier.

What do you get when you cross . . .

3961 . . . an amnesiac, an insomniac, an agnostic, and a dyslexic?
Someone who forgets why he stays awake all night wondering whether there is a dog.

3962 . . . a kennel with a coffee shop?
Chock Full O' Mutts.

3963 . . . a bassett hound with a Newfoundland?
A newfound asset hound—a dog for financial advisers.

3964 . . . a yule log with a duck?
A fire quacker.

3965 . . . an electric eel with a sponge?
A shock absorber.

3966 . . . a lamprey eel with a baboon who attended a famous American college?
The Harvard Lampoon.

3967 . . . an eel with a jellyfish?
Current jelly.

3968 . . . bacteria with an electric eel?
Culture shock.

3969 . . . a fish with two elephants?
Swimming trunks.

3970 . . . a parrot with an elephant?
A creature that tells you everything it remembers.

3971 . . . a computer with an elephant?
A machine with lots of memory.

3972 . . . a contortionist with an elephant?
Someone who can tickle his own ivories.

3973 . . . an elephant with a conceited genius?
A big know-it-all.

3974 . . . an elephant with a shag carpet?
A great big pile in your living room.

3975 . . . an elephant with a rhinoceros?
Elephino!

3976 . . . an elephant with a skin doctor?
A pachydermatologist.

3977 . . . a fawn with a ghost?
Bamboo.

3978 . . . a trumpet with a fisherman's trap?
A hornet.

3979 . . . a seafood eatery with antique furniture?
Fish and Chippendale.

3980 . . . a bug in spats with a baker?
A shoe-fly pie.

3981 . . . a frog with a soft drink?
Croaka-Cola.

What do you get when you cross . . .

3982 . . . a frog with a dog?
A croaker spaniel.

3983 . . . a coward with a frog?
A chicken croakette.

3984 . . . a rabbit with a frog?
A bunny ribbit.

3985 . . . a Muppet with some mist?
Kermit the Fog.

3986 . . . a toad with a trumpet?
A frog horn.

3987 . . . a giraffe with Santa Claus?
St. Neck.

3988 . . . a giraffe with an ostrich?
We don't know, but you'll really be sticking your neck out.

3989 . . . a giraffe with a swordfish?
The wildest-looking tree surgeon you ever saw.

3990 . . . a giraffe with a rooster?
An animal that wakes you up on the top floor.

3991 . . . an amnesiac with an insect?
A forget-me-gnat.

3992 . . . an African antelope with underwear?
A gnu's brief.

3993 . . . a mother-in-law with a goat?
Someone's who's always butting into other people's affairs.

3994 . . . a goat with a sheep?
An animal that eats tin cans and gives back steel wool.

3995 . . . a goose with a Boston taxi?
Something that honks before it runs you over.

3996 . . . a groundhog with a comedian?
Six more weeks of jokes.

3997 . . . a woodchuck with a brave person?
A groundhog that's not afraid of his shadow.

What do you get when you cross . . .

3998 . . . a fish with a fowl?
A hadduck.

3999 . . . a rabbit with a sprinkler?
Hare spray.

4000 . . . a rabbit with a spider?
A hare net.

4001 . . . shrubbery with a pig?
A hedgehog.

4002 . . . a rodent with a large river beast?
A hippopotamouse.

4003 . . . a tuber with a large river beast?
A hippotatomus.

4004 . . . a hippopotamus with a tube of glue?
A stick-in-the-mud.

4005 . . . an oil container with a hyena?
A barrel of laughs.

4006 . . . an Eskimo with a lizard?
An igluana.

4007 . . . an Irish wolfhound with an English springer spaniel?
An Irish springer—a dog that's fresh and clean as a whistle.

4008 . . . jam with a herring?
Jellyfish.

4009 . . . an automobile with a kangaroo?
A car that jump-starts itself.

4010 . . . a dog with a kangaroo?
A pooch with a pouch.

4011 . . . a kangaroo with a mink?
A fur coat with pockets.

4012 . . . a young goat with a blender?
A mixed-up kid.

4013 . . . a cat with a wrench, hammer, and saw?
A tool kitty.

4014 . . . a kitten with a sapling?
A pussy willow.

4015 . . . an animal in a Scandinavian zoo with the end of a marathon?
A Finnish lion.

4016 . . . a lion with a monastery in the winter?
A roaring friar place.

4017 . . . a trampoline with an iguana?
Leaping lizards!

4018 . . . a shellfish with a crook?
A lobster mobster.

4019 . . . a lobster with a baseball player?
A pinch hitter.

What do you get when you cross . . .

4020 . . . insect repellant with a bottle of aspirin?
A cure for a lousy headache.

4021 . . . hot dogs with bobcats?
Sausage lynx.

4022 . . . men's jewelry with bobcats?
Cuff lynx.

4023 . . . a horse with Sir Lancelot?
A knight-mare.

4024 . . . a mink with an ape?
A fur coat with sleeves that are too long.

4025 . . . a mockingbird with a turkey?
A stupid bird that makes the same mistake over and over.

4026 . . . a mole with a porcupine?
A tunnel that leaks.

4027 . . . a can of oil with an ape?
A grease monkey.

4028 . . . a comedian, a keg, and some chimpanzees?
More fun than a barrel of monkeys.

4029 . . . a monkey with several beaten egg whites?
Meringue-tan.

4030 . . . an Indian monkey, a vine of the legume family, and a plant with yellow cup-shaped flowers?
Rhesus Peanut Buttercup.

4031 . . . an abbot with a trout?
A monkfish.

4032 . . . a key maker, a mother bird, and Frankenstein?
A lock-nest monster.

4033 . . . cocoa with a big elk?
Chocolate moose.

4034 . . . a large elk with an insect?
A moosequito.

4035 . . . a computer with a million mosquitoes?
A megabite.

4036 . . . a cow with a mule?
Milk with a real kick to it.

4037 . . . a calculator with a mule?
A computer that gives you a boot when you turn it on.

4038 . . . coffee with salamanders?
A cup chock full o' newts.

4039 . . . an octopus with a centipede?
A pet that costs an arm and a leg.

4040 . . . an octopus with a cow?
An animal that can milk itself.

4041 . . . a mink with an octopus?
A coat of arms—or a coat with too many sleeves.

4042 . . . an octopus with a farm worker?
We don't know, but it can sure pick lettuce.

What do you get when you cross . . .

4043 . . . a squid with a cat?
An octopussy with eight legs and nine lives.

4044 . . . a pig with an octopus?
A football that throws itself.

4045 . . . a squid with a grizzly?
Octobear.

4046 . . . a policeman with an octopus?
A cop with eight long arms of the law.

4047 . . . a clock with an octopus?
Either a timepiece with eight hands or an octopus that's really ticked off.

4048 . . . an octopus with a dragon?
An octagon.

4049 . . . an ostrich with a turkey?
A bird that buries its head in the mashed potatoes.

4050 . . . an owl with a canine?
A hoot dog.

4051 . . . a beast of burden with a village idiot?
An oxymoron.

4052 . . . a horse with a bovine beast of burden?
An equinox.

4053 . . . an oyster with an owl?
Pearls of wisdom.

4054 . . . a parrot with a centipede?
A walkie-talkie.

4055 . . . a softball pitcher, a parrot, and a clock?
Underhanded polly-ticks.

4056 . . . a parrot with a canary?
A bird that knows the words and the tune.

4057 . . . a parrot with a gorilla?
We don't know, but when it talks, everyone listens.

4058 . . . a parrot with a lion?
An animal that says, "Polly wants a cracker—now!"

4059 . . . a parrot with an eagle?
A paralegal.

4060 . . . a parrot with a shark?
An animal that can talk your ear off.

4061 . . . an icicle and a shark?
Frostbite.

4062 . . . a stream of water, a writing object, and a short seabird?
A fountain penguin.

4063 . . . a pig with a parrot?
Something that hogs the entire conversation.

4064 . . . a pig with a fir tree?
A porkerpine.

What do you get when you cross . . .

4065 . . . a hog, a billiards stick, and a fir tree?
A pork-cue-pine.

4066 . . . a pigeon with an army general?
A military coo.

4067 . . . a pigeon with a chicken?
The Coo Clucks Klan.

4068 . . . a dove with a high chair?
A stool pigeon.

4069 . . . a pigeon with a parrot?
A bird that apologizes for the mess it makes.

4070 . . . a literary character with an unkempt football player?
Rumple pigskin.

4071 . . . a pig with a karate expert?
A pork chop.

4072 . . . a motorized bicycle with a freshwater fish?
A motorpike.

4073 . . . a freshwater fish with a Boston church service?
The Mass Pike.

4074 . . . a mallard, a disk jockey, and a cat?
A duck-billed platter puss.

4075 . . . a pointer with a setter?
A poinsettia.

4076 . . . another pointer with another setter?
An upsetter and a disappointer.

4077 . . . an Arctic bear with a camera?
A Polaroid.

4078 . . . a spaniel, a French dog, and a ghost?
A cocker-poodle-boo.

4079 . . . a bear with a dog?
Winnie the Poodle.

4080 . . . a porcupine with an alarm clock?
A stickler for punctuality.

4081 . . . a porcupine with corn on the cob?
Something that tastes good and lets you pick your teeth at the same time.

4082 . . . a porcupine with a sheep?
An animal that knits its own sweaters.

4083 . . . a turtle with a porcupine?
A slowpoke.

4084 . . . a porcupine with a goat?
A stuck-up kid that's hard to handle.

4085 . . . a mink with a porcupine?
A fur coat that is safe from pickpockets.

What do you get when you cross . . .

4086 . . . a praying mantis with a bee?
*An insect that says grace
before it stings you.*

4087 . . . a clam with a pig?
A quahog.

4088 . . . a pony with two dimes
and a nickel?
A quarter horse.

4089 . . . a rabbit's foot with poison ivy?
A rash of good luck.

4090 . . . a rabbit with a kilt?
Hopscotch.

4091 . . . a rabbit with a computer?
Floppy disks.

4092 . . . a large rodent with
a machine gun?
*A creature that goes
rat-a-tat-tat-tat.*

4093 . . . a rattlesnake with a muffin?
A snake that rattles and rolls.

4094 . . . a rattlesnake with a horse?
*We don't know, but if it bites you,
you can ride it to the hospital.*

4095 . . . a shellfish with a rooster?
A cockle-doodle-do.

4096 . . . a rooster with a steer?
A cock-and-bull story.

4097 . . . a salamander with
a comedian?
A shtick–in-the-mud.

4098 . . . a salmon with a feather?
A fish that's tickled pink.

4099 . . . a sheep and rain?
A wet blanket.

4100 . . . a sheep with a kangaroo?
A woolly jumper.

4101 . . . a sheep with
an ancient elephant?
A woolly mammoth.

4102 . . . a lion with a lamb?
Something that's wild and woolly.

4103 . . . a sheep with a sauna?
A woolly sweater.

4104 . . . a boa with a sheep?
A wraparound sweater.

4105 . . . a sheep with Scrooge?
Baaa humbug.

4106 . . . a peanut with a perch?
A shellfish.

4107 . . . a skunk with
a brandy-toting dog?
A Scent Bernard.

4108 . . . a giant with a skunk?
A big stink.

4109 . . . a bear with a skunk?
Winnie the Phew.

4110 . . . a skunk with a boomerang?
*A disgusting smell that you can't
get rid of.*

What do you get when you cross . . .

4111 . . . a skunk with an owl?
*An animal that stinks but
doesn't give a hoot.*

4112 . . . a skunk with a mouse?
Dirty looks from the mouse.

4113 . . . a porcupine with a skunk?
A pretty lonely animal.

4114 . . . a silkworm with a harmless
garden snake?
Silk garters.

4115 . . . a chocolate bar with a snake
that sheds its skin?
*Something that molts in
your mouth.*

4116 . . . a snake with a cow?
A puff udder.

4117 . . . a snake with a funeral vehicle?
Hiss and hearse.

4118 . . . a young smart aleck
with a red fish?
A whippersnapper.

4119 . . . a flatfish with an African
American?
A filet of soul brother.

4120 . . . a minister with a fisherman?
*Someone interested
in saving soles.*

4121 . . . a starfish with a monkey's
favorite snack?
A star-spangled banana.

4122 . . . a lazy bull with some
bad directions?
A bum steer.

4123 . . . a saber with a salmon?
A swordfish.

4124 . . . a terrier with a bulldog?
*A terribull—a dog prone
to awful mistakes.*

4125 . . . Hollywood celebrities
with a tiger?
Stars and stripes.

4126 . . . a cowardly Communist admiral
with Charlie the Tuna?
Chicken of the Red Sea.

4127 . . . a turkey with a kangaroo?
*An animal that you can stuff
on the outside.*

4128 . . . a turkey with a bell?
*A bird that has to wring
its own neck.*

4129 . . . a turkey with a centipede?
Drumsticks for everyone.

4130 . . . a turtle with a teacher?
Snappy answers.

4131 . . . a turtle with a boomerang?
Snappy comebacks.

4132 . . . a tortoise with a sheep?
A turtleneck sweater.

What do you get when you cross . . .

4133   . . . a dog with a turtle?
*An animal that brings you
yesterday's newspaper.*

4134   . . . a vampire with a moose?
Vamoose!

4135   . . . a vulture with a small
grass shack?
A scavenger hut.

4136   . . . a frog with a pig?
A warthog.

4137   . . . a container of cold cereal
with a bug?
A bowl weevil.

4138   . . . a truck with a submarine?
A jeep with four-whale dive.

4139   . . . a cabbage with a whale?
Brussels spouts.

4140   . . . a tree with a wild dog?
A timber wolf.

4141   . . . a wolf with a rooster?
*An animal that howls when
the sun rises.*

4142   . . . a woodpecker with a marine?
A drill sergeant.

4143   . . . a bird with a ballpoint pen?
*A woodpecker with
a retractable beak.*

4144   . . . a woodpecker with
a homing pigeon?
*A bird that knocks on your door
before delivering a message.*

4145   . . . a parrot with a woodpecker?
A bird that talks in Morse code.

4146   . . . a chicken with a zebra?
*A four-legged dinner with
its own bar code.*

4147   . . . a penguin with a zebra?
*A climate-confused animal in
a striped tuxedo.*

Daffynitions:
A Beastly Fictionary

Some waggish genius once defined beatnik as "Santa Claus at the end of his Christmas run," and another verbathlete defined buccaneer as "the cost of a two-dollar pair of earrings."

Such punderful de-fun-itions take a fresh approach to the sounds of familiar words. You won't find such entries in dictionaries, only in fictionaries, but they have a name—daffynitions. Some of the daffiest can be found in the animal kingdom.

4148 *Aardvark:* How to succeed in Sveden.

4149 *Acrostic:* One angry bug.

4150 *Alarms:* What an octopus is.

4151 *Anatomy:* An insect's abdomen.

4152 *Annoyance:* What diluted bug spray does.

4153 *Antacid:* Hallucinogen used by insects.

4154 *Antelope:* What happens when your mother's sister runs off to get married.

4155 *Aqueduct:* A waterfowl.

4156 *Arctic:* A bug aboard Noah's ark.

4157 *Ascent:* What a hunting dog follows.

4158 *Aspersion:* A donkey from Iran.

4159 *Assess:* A female donkey.

4160 *Asset:* A small donkey.

4161 *Aviary:* A house of trill repute.

4162 *Avoidable:* What cowardly matadors try to do.

4163 *Awkward:* A bird sanctuary.

4164 *Bar stool:* What Davy Crockett stepped in.

4165 *Bambino:* A negative response from a mother deer.

4166 *Bassinet:* What a fisherman wants.

4167 *Bearskins:* What Adam and Eve wore in the Garden of Eden.

4168 *Bedbug:* An undercover agent.

4169 *Bee:* A honey musterer; a little stinger.

4170 *Beehive:* What an Australian school teacher tells an unruly child.

4171 *Behold:* What bee wrestlers use in matches.

4172 *Billy club:* A night spot for goats.

4173 *Bi-polar disorder:* Being attracted to both male and female white bears.

4174 *Bird dog:* A wolf in cheap clothing.

4175 *Braid:* How the donkey made noise.

4176 *Buffalo:* A greeting between two nudists.

4177 *Bugaboo:* Sneaking up behind an insect and frightening it.

4178 *Bulldozer:* A sleeping steer.

4179 *Bumblebee:* A clumsy insect.

4180 *Butterflies:* What happens when a waiter trips.

4181 *Butterfly:* What a goat has on the front of its trousers.

4182 *Castigate:* Bass-fishing tournament scandal.

4183 *Cat:* A beast of birdin'.

4184 *Catacomb:* An implement for grooming felines.

4185 *Catalog:* A record kept on cows and bulls; a catalyst.

4186 *Catatonic:* The favorite feline drink.

4187 *Category:* A bloody feline.

4188 *Caterpillar:* A soft scratching post for a cat.

4189 *Celtics:* What bug vendors do.

4190 *Chicken croquette:* A flirtatious hen.

4191 *Chicken farmer:* Brooder's keeper.

4192 *Cobra:* A brassiere for Siamese twins.

4193 *Codger:* A cranky fish.

4194 *Crocodile:* A jar of soap.

4195 *Crowbar:* A saloon for birds.

4196 *Curtail:* What the dog wags.

4197 *Debate:* What you use to catch de fish.

4198 *Déja`ewe:* The feeling you've sheared this sheep before.

4199 *Derange:* Where de deer and de antelope play.

4200 *Dog:* A creature who wears his heart in his tail.

4201 *Dogcatcher's truck:* Rabid transit.

4202 *Dogma:* A puppy's mother.

4203 *Dog pound:* A used-cur lot.

4204 *Donkey:* An object that unlocks a door to the godfather's house.

4205 *Doubloon:* Two water fowl.

4206 *Dreadlocks:* Fear of smoked salmon.

4207 *Eagle:* An electronic gull.

4208 *Earwig:* Something to keep your head warm on cold nights.

4209 *Elk:* A lodge animal.

4210 *Extinct:* A dead skunk.

4211 *Flea:* An insect that starts from scratch.

4212 *Fly ball:* A dance for bugs.

4213 *Fly swatter:* A baseball bat.

4214 *Flying buttress:* A flying nanny goat.

4215 *Furlong:* Desire for a mink coat.

4216 *Gable:* An effeminate male bovine.

4217 *Gatorade:* Welfare for alligators.

4218 *Grammatical:* Pertaining to the matriarch of the tick family.

4219 *Harem:* What a rabbit with many wives has.

4220 *Hen:* Mother clucker.

4221 *Hogwash:* A facility for cleaning pigs.

4222 *Horse sense:* Something a horse has that keeps it from betting on people.

4223 *Humbug:* A singing beetle.

4224 *Illegal:* A sick bird.

4225 *Impeccable:* Something a chicken can't eat.

4226 *Information:* How geese fly.

4227 *Insecticide:* A bug's method for killing itself.

4228 *Insects:* How people with unconventional beliefs congregate.

4229 *Jitterbug:* A nervous insect.

4230 *Lame duck session:* When politicians sing their swan songs.

4231 *Laughing stock:* Cattle with a sense of humor.

4232 *Leotard:* A feeble-minded lion.

4233 *Lion:* Predator in chief.

4234 *Meter Maid:* Windshield viper.

4235 *Microfiche:* One-millionth of a fish.

4236 *Microwave:* What an amoeba surfs on.

4237 *Moleskin:* The family of a burrowing rodent.

4238 *Monkey:* What unlocks doors in monasteries.

4239 *Moon:* What cows are always doin'.

4240 *Mushroom:* A place where Eskimos train their dogs.

4241 *Mutilate:* What cats do at night.

4242 *Mynah:* An animal that never becomes an adult.

4243 *Nag:* A woman who lacks horse sense.

4244 *Nighthawk:* A cough in bed.

4245 *Obstetrician:* A bird who delivers with a big bill.

4246 *Occidental:* Relating to the teeth of a male bovine.

4247 *Octagon:* A departed octopus.

4248 *Octopus:* An eight-sided cat.

4249 *Oxymoron:* A big dumb bull.

4250 *Palomino:* A friendly Italian horse.

4251 *Pandemonium:* A condo for pandas.

4252 *Paradox:* Two dachshunds.

4253 *Paraffin:* What's on the sides of a fish.

4254 *Parakeets:* Two Romantic poets.

4255 *Parapets:* Two cats.

4256 *Perjury:* A group of 12 cats in a courtroom.

4257 *Pet peeve:* Complaint from a cat or dog.

4258 *Plutocracy:* A Mickey Mouse form of government that's gone to the dogs.

4259 *Polarize:* What penguins see with.

4260 *Polecat:* A feline from Warsaw.

4261 *Politburo:* A well-mannered jackass.

4262 *Polydent:* A parrot with clean teeth.

4263 *Polygamy:* Marrying several parrots.

4264 *Polygon:* A dead parrot.

4265 *Polynesia:* Memory loss in parrots.

4266 *Polyphony:* A fake parrot.

4267 *Polyunsaturated:* A dry bird.

4268 *Posture:* An area where veddy, veddy British cows graze.

4269 *Propaganda:* A politically correct male goose.

4270 *Protestants:* Worker ants out to overthrow the Queen.

4271 *Psychologist:* One who pulls habits out of rats.

4272 *Puff adder:* A smoking mathematician.

4273 *Pursuit:* The cat's pajamas.

4274 *Quack doctor:* Physicians for curing lame ducks.

4275 *Questionable:* What to do upon discovery of a dead matador.

4276 *Racetrack:* Where the windows clean the people.

4277 *Raconteur:* A nocturnal mammal's road trip.

4278 *Rampage:* The leaf in an encyclopedia about male sheep.

4279 *Rampant:* Clothing line for sheep.

4280 *Ramshackle:* A chain used for tying up a male sheep.

4281 *Rattan:* What a rodent gets while sunbathing.

4282 *Satellite:* What you put on your horse when you go riding after dark.

4283 *Scratch pad:* A cat's home.

4284 *Shampoo:* A fake bear.

4285 *Shark:* A thing of beauty and a jaw forever.

4286 *Silver nitrate:* A rental fee for the Lone Ranger's horse after dark.

4287 *Skin flick:* How you get rid of a mosquito.

4288 *Stagnation:* A country of male deer.

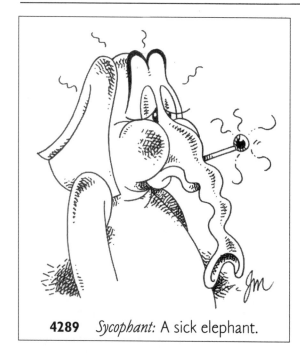

4289   *Sycophant:* A sick elephant.

4290   *Tadpole:* A kids' survey.

4291   *Terrapin:* A wrestling hold that induces extreme fright.

4292   *Toad:* Dragged.

4293   *Twain:* What a wabbit takes a twip on.

4294   *Wallaby:* An Australian cradle song.

4295   *Washable:* What a cattle rancher should do very carefully.

4296   *Weasel:* Something that blows on a tugboat.

4297   *Wholesale:* Where a gopher goes to buy a new home.

4298   *Wolf:* A man who believes in life, liberty, and the happiness of pursuit.

4299   *Woodpecker:* A knocking bird.

4300   *Worrywart:* A skittish frog.

4301   *Zebra:* A horse of a different stripe or color; a horse with venetian blinds.

In the Jungle:
Not the Jingle, Not the Jangle, Just the Jungle

We don't know who first spoke or wrote the catchy phrase Jingle Jangle Jungle (it's been used as a title for or line in books, songs, poems), but it's so delightful to say that—even though it might not fit as the title for this section—we used it as *not* the title. There are jungle jokes in other sections, which are mostly about certain animals in the jungle, but here before you we dangle a jangle of jokes that play a jingle on *jungle* before you.

4302   What do wild animals sing on Christmas?
"Jungle Bells."

4303   Jane complained about Tarzan's lack of innovation in hunting. To prove her wrong, Tarzan stormed into the jungle in search of dinner. Luck was with him, and he soon killed a bird and two monkeys. Pleased with his catch, Tarzan returned and proudly showed the game to Jane.
        Not at all impressed, she said, "Is that the best you can do? Finch and chimps!"

4304   What was Tarzan's favorite place to play?
The jungle gym.

4305   What did Tarzan say to Jane after getting home
from a hard day at the branch office?
"It's a jungle out there."

4306   A more modern husband told his wife,
"It's a jungle out there," and she replied, "Get lost in it."

4307 A hunter's false teeth fell out just as he was about to shoot a tiger in the jungles of the country formerly known as Ceylon. To this day, he is still looking for his bridge on the River Kwai.

4308 Three hunters in the jungles of Africa were preparing breakfast one morning when one of them decided he'd take a little walk to work up an appetite. When he didn't return after an hour, one of the others mused, "I wonder what's eating old Henry?"

4309 Did you hear about the new book titled *Jungle Flowers*? *It's by Dan D. Lyon and Chris-Anne Themum.*

4310 *Reporter:* "How is your jungle trip going?" *Traveler:* "Safari so good."

4311 *Boy No. 1:* "Did your uncle really disappear on a jungle safari?" *Boy No. 2:* "Yes. Something he disagreed with ate him."

4312 *Hunter No. 1:* "Did you really kill four lions with one club?" *Hunter No. 2:* "Yes. But there were fifty of us in the safari club."

4313 A famous trumpeter was on safari in the jungles of Africa and spent his evenings serenading the wild animals. The way he was able to tame the hungry beasts with his mellifluous tones was uncanny. One evening, however, a lone lion leaped out of the brush and devoured the horn player. The other animals severely criticized him and asked how he could destroy the creator of such melodious music.

The killer lion turned his head, held a paw to his ear, and said, "You'll have to shout. I'm hard of hearing."

Knock-Knock Jokes:
Puns upon Knockers' Names

Knock, knock.
Who's there?
Amos.
Amos who?
A mosquito just bit me.

Knock, knock.
Who's there?
Andy.
Andy who?
And he bit me again.

For decades, America has been bitten by the knock-knock fad, and knock-knock jokes have become an integral part of American folk culture. Most of us played the game as children, and many of us continue knock-knocking as adults.

The jokester says, "Knock, knock." The second person replies, "Who's there?" The knock-knocker comes back with something like "Amoeba." "Amoeba who?" is the ritual response. Then comes the punch line, such as "Amoeba dumb, but I'm not crazy."

Let's go knock-knocking on the door of the language zoo.

Knock-knock.
Who's there?

4314   Big horse.
       Big horse who?
       Big horse of you, we're two
       happy authors.

4315   Aardvark.
       Aardvark who?
       Aardvark a million miles
       for one of your smiles.

Knock-knock.
Who's there?

4316 Adam.
Adam who?
Adam fly is in my soup.

4317 Althea.
Althea who?
Althea later, alligator.

4318 Ammonia.
Ammonia who?
Ammonia bird in a gilded cage.

4319 Anna.
Anna who?
Anna partridge in a pear tree.

4320 Badger.
Badger who?
Too badger got a chip on
your shoulder.

4321 Barbie.
Barbie who?
Barbie Q. Chicken.

4322 Beryl.
Beryl who?
Beryl of monkeys.

4323 A burden.
A burden who?
A burden the hand is worth
two in the bush.

4324 A Cadillac.
A Cadillac who?
A Cadillac mean if you pull its tail.

4325 Catgut.
Catgut who?
Catgut your tongue?

4326 Cattle.
Cattle who?
Cattle always purr when you stroke it.

4327 Centipede.
Centipede who?
Centipede on the Christmas tree.

4328 Chesterfield.
Chesterfield who?
Chesterfield of grazing cows.

4329 Cook.
Cook who?
Cuckoo to you, too.

4330 Deduct.
Deduct who?
Deduct named Donald.

4331 Descartes.
Descartes who?
Don't put Descartes before
the horse.

4332 Domino.
Domino who?
Domino cowhand.

4333 Doughnut.
Doughnut who?
Doughnut count your chickens
before they're hatched.

Knock-knock.
Who's there?

4334 Ether.
Ether who?
Ether bunny.

4335 Samoa.
Samoa who?
Samoa ether bunnies.

4336 Estelle.
Estelle who?
Estelle samoa ether bunnies.

4337 Consumption.
Consumption who?
Consumption be done about all
those ether bunnies?

4338 Gibbon.
Gibbon who?
Gibbon take is an honest
way of life.

4339 Gillette.
Gillette who?
Gillette the cat out?

4340 Goat.
Goat who?
Goat to your room!

4341 Goose.
Goose who?
Goose who's coming for dinner?

4342 Gopher.
Gopher who?
Gopher a walk off a cliff.

4343 Gorilla.
Gorilla who?
Gorilla cheese sandwich
for me, please.

4344 Gretel.
Gretel who?
Gretel long little doggie.

4345 Hence.
Hence who?
Hence lay eggs.

4346 Hyena.
Hyena who?
Hyena tree sat a vulture.

4347 Iguana.
Iguana who?
Iguana hold your hand.

4348 Isaac.
Isaac who?
Isaac my dog on you.

4349 Jaguar.
Jaguar who?
Jaguar nimble, Jaguar quick.

4350 Jupiter.
Jupiter who?
Jupiter fly in my soup?

4351 Lion.
Lion who?
Lion to your parents will get you
in trouble.

Knock-knock.
Who's there?

4352   Lionel.
Lionel who?
Lionel roar if it's not fed.

4353   Knock, knock.
Who's there?
Llama.
Llama who?
Llama Yankee Doodle Dandy.

4354   Manor.
Manor who?
Manor a mouse—which are you?

4355   Marmalade.
Marmalade who?
"Marmalade me," said
the baby chicken.

4356   Megan, Elise, and Chicken.
Megan, Elise, and Chicken who?
He's Megan Elise and Chicken it
twice, gonna find out who's
naughty and nice.

4357   Noel.
Noel who?
Noel E. Phant is going to stick his
trunk in my business.

4358   Ocelot.
Ocelot who?
You ocelot of questions.

4359   Oily.
Oily who?
The oily bird catches the worm.

4360   Orangutan.
Orangutan who?
Orangutan times, but you didn't
answer the bell.

4361   Who.
Who who?
An owl like you.

4362   Owl.
Owl who?
Owl you know if you don't
open the door?

4363   Panther.
Panther who?
My panther too short.

4364   Plato.
Plato who?
Plato fish and chips, please.

4365   Possum.
Possum who?
Possum the potatoes, please.

Knock-knock.
Who's there?

4366 Ramsay.
Ramsay who?
Rams say "baaa."

4367 Rhoda.
Rhoda who?
Rhoda horse and now I'm sore.

4368 Rude and interrupting cow.
Rude and inter—
Moo!

4369 Toledo.
Toledo who?
It's easy Toledo horse to water,
but it's hard to make it drink.

4370 Veal chop.
Veal chop who?
Veal chop around for
some bargains.

4371 Walrus.
Walrus who?
Do you walrus ask that
same question?

4372 Wendy.
Wendy who?
Wendy red, red robin comes bob,
bob, bobbin' along.

4373 Willoughby.
Willoughby who?
Willoughby a monkey's uncle.

4374 Yukon.
Yukon who?
Yukon lead a horse to water, but
you can't make it drink.

A Miscellany:
Where Categories Don't Count

It's easy to herd animals into the Miscellaneous Pen (which could get full fast), but a closer look at the turn of a term drives most of the creatures into particular pens. On the other hand, we could justify putting some from this pen into other pens—but, by our rigorous, scientific tests, the ones here are less specific to species.

4375   There's a little known animal that begins with the letter x. It's actually a Greek swordfish, spelled *x-i-p-h-i-i-d-a-e,* and it's pronounced "*ziff-EYE-ih-dee*." With that in mind, let's let the punster talk us through animals A-Z.

Aardvark a million miles to put 26 animal puns in alphabetical order. I'd *badger* you and I'd keep *carp*ing on the subject, until I have no i*deers* left. I'd have no *egrets*, however, as I *ferret* out more animal puns. If necessary, I'd even *gopher* broke. Some may say it's a *hare*-brained attempt, but, *iguana* tell you, I'm no *jackass*—and I *kid* you not. I'm not doing this for a *lark* (although maybe just a *mite*). So don't *nag* me. In fact, you *otter* try to *parrot* me. But don't *quail* from the challenge. After all, you don't have to be a *raccoon*teur. So just *salmon* up some courage before you take a *tern* for the worse. Don't be afraid of people saying to you, "*unicorn*iest person I know." Stop crying and *viper* nose. Then say, "*wallaby* a son-of-a-gun," and start singing, "Zip-a-dee doo-dah, *xiphiidae* ay." Soon you'll be a *yak*-of-all-trades, and can put all of these animal puns in a book called "Who's *Zoo*."

4376   A former emperor of Persia loved wild animals and let them run loose throughout his domain. The people became so upset with the rampant animals that they revolted and overthrew their leader. That was the first time in history that the reign was called on account of game.

4377   Stalking game is a prey amble.

4378   It's good to know that the animals on Noah's
Ark were prepaired for the Great Flood.

4379   As Noah said while the animals were boarding
the ark, "Now I've herd everything."

4380   How could Noah see the animals in the dark?
The ark had floodlighting.

4381   Why couldn't Noah play cards in the ark?
Because some animal was standing on the deck.

4382   Many of the animals in the ark had offspring by
the end of the trip. Which means that Noah
became the first man to have bred his cast
upon the waters.

4383   Why were the animals in the ark so angry?
Because the captain acted like a Noah-it-all.

4384   Did you know that the Los Angeles freeways are mentioned
in the Bible? It states that God created every creeping thing.

4385   What's worse than a turtle with claustrophobia?
An elephant with hay fever.

4386   What animals are poor dancers?
Four-legged ones—because they have two left feet.

4387   Speaking of four-legged animals reminds us of the oldest known riddle
in the world. It was posed by the Sphinx in ancient Greek mythology and was
answered by Oedipus: What animal walks on four feet in the morning, two at
noon, and three in the evening? The answer: Man. He goes on all fours as a
baby, on two feet when he is grown, and uses a cane in old age.

4388   What did the man who quit the SPCA and PETA say to the mischievous gorilla?
"U R N N M L."

4389   As one animal-rights activist said to another, "They expect us to flea,
but weevil not be moved. Their propaganda is all lice, and mite makes right."

4390   The BBC Symphony Orchestra had a live concert at the Albert Hall one Friday night. There was a long queue. Eventually two dogs and a cat reached the pay point. The cat asked for three tickets, but the person in the sales booth refused, saying animals could not be admitted to the Albert Hall. The three protested that they were not animals, but in fact famous musicians. The first dog said, "I Bach." The second dog said, "I Offenbach." The cat said, "I Debussy."

4391   What makes farming a hard life?
A farmer goes to sleep with the chickens, gets up with the roosters, works like a horse, eats like a pig, and gets treated like a dog.

4392   A farmer proposed to a neighbor woman, who replied, "I have a dog that growls in the morning, a parrot that swears in the afternoon, and a cat that comes home late at night. What do I need with a husband?"

4393 *Holiday greeting sign at an animal shelter:* We Fish Ewe a Meowy Christmas (or Mare Egrets Moose) Panda Hippo Gnu Deer.

4394   What do you call a lion, a tiger, and a leopard in the same cage?
A menagerie à trois.

4395   A lion was prancing through the jungle one day, roaring at the top of his voice for all to hear, "I am king of the jungle, for my mighty strength and great prowess strike fear into all other creatures!"

An eagle landed on a nearby tree branch and boasted, "Not so fast, Leo, buddy! It is I who am the rightful king of the jungle, for my wings enable me to attack from above, and my beak and talons rip my victims to shreds!"

Whereupon a skunk walked calmly out of the trees. Approaching the ferocious feline and the fearsome flighted one, he meekly said, "You're both wrong. Needing neither fight nor flight, I disable my would-be opponents most skillfully! Wanna sniff?"

As the three animals, oblivious to their surroundings, busily engaged in a heated argument over who was the rightful king of the jungle, a huge grizzly bear walked up and ate them all—hawk, lion, and stinker.

4396 *Sign at the entrance to the wild-animal enclosure at a circus:*
No Trespassing. Survivors Will Be Prosecuted.

4397 Animals aren't as dumb as people think. After all, they have no lawyers.

4398 An animal trainer who works part-time putting his head inside a lion's mouth and part-time wrestling alligators under water was asked how he manages to stay alive.
He replied, "Well, I moonlight as a carpenter."

4399 When former vice president Hubert Humphrey first entered politics in Minnesota, it was the custom to raise funds by organizing afternoon gatherings or teas. To liven up one of these proceedings, Humphrey invited the actor Alan Alda, who in his spare time managed two singing groups, namely, the Kingsmen (of "Louie, Louie" fame) and an overly amorous group of ladies from Norway.

Unfortunately, the party did not succeed. And the article in the newspaper the next day reported: "Alda's cling Norses and Alda's Kingsmen couldn't put Humphrey's dumb teas back to gather again."

4400 Why is Tolkien's *Lord of the Rings* such compulsive reading?
Because it's hobbit-forming.

4401 Knock, knock.
Who's there?
Hobbit.
Hobbit who?
Hobbit letting me in the door?

4402 Did you hear about the two love-starved roosters that got caught in the rain?
One made it to the hen house, and the other made a duck under the porch.

4403 A Chinese chicken farmer was chagrined to discover that his animals were losing their feathers and dying from the cold. He sought the counsel of two consultants: Dr. Hing, who was a scientist, and Mr. Ming, who was a sorcerer.

Dr. Hing had taken many advanced courses in poultry science, while Mr. Ming specialized in meditation and reading tarot cards. The two wise men came to a unanimous conclusion: an infusion of gum tree leaves would alleviate feather loss in chickens. Unfortunately, their recommendation did not succeed. And the headlines in the newspaper the next day heralded: "All of Hing's Courses and All of Ming's Ken Couldn't Get Gum Tree to Feather a Hen."

4404   Recently, Chinese archeologists discovered a large cache of eggs that were buried in a deep cave for over a thousand years. People could not believe the eggs were that old. Scientists presented the evidence, showing that it was clearly a case of mined ova matter.

4405   Then there was the touching scene when a young woodland resident bade his mother a fawn farewell because she was so deer to his hart.

4406   What tragedy occurred when the discoverer of radium served her pet a caffeinated beverage meant for equines?
Curie horse-tea killed the cat.

4407 *Sign in a toy store next to its animal display:*
Don't Feed the Animals. They're Already Stuffed.

4408 What does a creature do when he loses a hand?
He goes to a secondhand store.

4409   A young couple received a wedding present from friends in Australia. It was a rare animal called a rary, which is a pet not unlike a small kangaroo and which, they were told, would talk if well fed. The pet ate more and better than the couple but never spoke. It grew to 500 pounds, and the couple went into debt. Reluctantly, they decided to get rid of the rary.
      The couple rented a dump truck, got help to load the heavy creature, drove into the hills, backed up to the edge of a steep cliff, and raised the bed of the truck. As the pesky pest plummeted off the precipice, it observed, "It's a long way to tip a rary."

4410 Did you hear about the accident involving a truckload of cats and dogs?
It was a doggone catastrophe.

4411 What historic Virginia town once had a huge pile of dead insects?
Mount Vermin.

4412 Authorities are seeking a six-foot octopus for the robbery of a convenience store. He is described as "heavily armed." His accomplice is a large porcupine described as "tall, dark, and prickly." Police have issued an "all points" bulletin.

4413   What kind of cheese is favored in Scotland?
Loch Ness Muenster.

4414   Did you hear about the woman who refuses to eat
calamari, crabs, clams, chicken, corn, cabbage, and cake?
She says firmly, "I do not like c-food."

4415   Did you hear about the other woman who's on a seafood diet?
She says flatly, "Whenever I see food, I eat it."

4416   When the first spaceship from Earth landed on Mars, it was met by
a giant creature with long black fur. "Are you the leader?" asked an incredulous
astronaut. "No," replied the Martian; "I'm just an ordinary Furry, so named
because of all my fur. But I'll take you to our leader." The visitors were then
ushered into a mammoth cave where they saw another huge creature, but this
one had an oversized hypodermic needle protruding from the top of his head.
"Are you the leader?" repeated the astronaut. "Yes," answered the
creature. "I'm the Furry with the syringe on top."

It's not the furry ones that bother us so much as the creepy crawlies that get
under our skins when they get on our skins. For example:

4417   *Patient:* "Doctor, doctor! What's the best way
to prevent diseases caused by biting insects?"
Doctor: "Don't bite any."

4419   Did you hear about the
dejected bug?
It committed insecticide.

4418   Two psychiatrists met on a street
corner, one of whom kept brushing
his jacket.
"What's wrong?" asked the other.
"I have these invisible insects
crawling all over me."
"Well, don't brush them off on me!"

4420   What kind of sex can spoil a picnic?
Insects.

4421   Speaking of picnics reminds us of
the couple who spread a blanket in
the woods. The lady commented,
"What a lovely place for a picnic."
"It must be," replied the man. "Ten
million insects can't be wrong."

4422 What happened when insects attacked a potato crop?
The farmer kept his eyes peeled.

    4423 How were insects transported to the Wild West?
    By Buffalo Bill Cootie.

        4424 What did the movie producer get when he
        crossed an insect with long feelers and a beetle?
        Antennae and Coleoptera.

4425 Did you hear about the flea that died of alcohol poisoning after
drinking the blood of a beer-guzzling dog?
This just goes to show that chiggers can't be boozers.

And there are some that are peticularly pettish—but not petty. For example:

4426 What did the dog have when
he finished obedience school?
A pet-degree.

    4427 What did the cat have
    done to its nails?
    A pet-icure.

        4428 What's furry, barks, and loves school?
        A teacher's pet.

            4429 Did you hear about the kid in
            school who was the teacher's pet?
            The teacher couldn't afford a cat.

                4430 Why is a dog in an
                auto like a rug?
                It's a carpet.

4431 What is a scaredy cat?
Something that's petrified.

    4432 Did you hear about the man who broke into an animal store?
    He was charged with petty theft.

4433   A young boy prepared a backyard grave for his deceased pet. He then bowed his head and said, "I do this in the name of the Father, the Son, and in the hole he goes."

Even though it's a jungle out there, beastly puns may help you succeed in a workaday world that depends on survival of the fittest. For example:

4434   A turtle makes progress when it sticks its neck out.

4435   Birds have bills, too, but they keep on singing.

4436   Behave like a duck. Keep calm and unruffled on the surface, but paddle like crazy underneath.

4437   Be like the woodpecker. Just keep pecking away until you finish the job. You'll succeed by using your head.

Tom Swifties:
"This is a horsey category," Tom said jocularly.

During the early part of the twentieth century, boys and girls grew up devouring fourteen million copies of the adventures of Tom Swift. Tom was a sterling young hero who survived one harrowing experience after another. In the course of the heroic action, Tom and his friends and enemies never just said something. They always said it *excitedly* or *sadly* or *hurriedly*.

Tom Swift and his wonderful electric aeroplane have been mothballed, but the adverbial pun game known as Tom Swifties still flies. The object is to match the adverb with the quotation to produce, in each case, a high-flying pun, such as:

"I love pancakes," said Tom flippantly.

"I hate pineapples," said Tom dolefully.

"I lost my flower," said Tom lackadaisically.

"What I do best on camping trips is sleep," said Tom intently.

For our purposes, many a Tom Swifty is beastly in nature.

"I love pancakes," said Tom flippantly.

4438 "I'm trying to make insects fly," Tom said flippantly.

4439 "Has an insect crawled under your fig leaf?" Eve asked adamantly.

4440 "I'm just an amoeba," said Tom divisively.

4441 "This may be a famous fish restaurant, but never before have I eaten such a foul, gritty dinner," said Tom carpingly.

4442   "I used to command a battalion of German ants," said Tom exuberantly.

4443   "I love one in nine donkeys," said Tom asininely.

4444   "That grizzly lives in the saloon," said Tom barbarically.

4445   "I just shot a quartet of grizzlies," Tom said forebearingly.

4446   "I hate milking cows," Tom said moodily.

4447   "I like to pretend I'm a sled dog," Tom said huskily.

4448   "Rover needs something to sleep on," said Tom dogmatically.

4449   "I'm out to capture Moby Dick," said Tom superficially.

4450   "There's a fly on my cheese," said Tom briefly.

4451   "There seems to be at least one annoying insect
        in every outhouse," said Tom aloofly.

4452   "Look out for the bear!" Tom yelled in a grizzly voice.

4453   "What an ugly hippopotamus," said Tom hypocritically.

4454   "How about a day at the racetrack?" Tom asked hoarsely.

4455   "Look at those new kittens," Tom said literally.

4456   "I won't stick my arm in a lion's mouth again," Tom said offhandedly.

4457   "The lion has its head caught in the top tree branches," said Tom uproariously.

4458   "I like hunting lions," said Tom pridefully.

4459   "I just married a lioness; look at my wedding ring!" roared Leo, with wild abandon.

4460   "What a friend we have in cheeses," Tom the mouse sang Kraftily.

4461   "Help! I'm being suffocated by a python," said Tom coyly.

4462   "I'd like to make you eat crow," Tom said ravenously.

4463   "I'd like a lambs wool sweater," said Tom sheepishly.

4464   "The Greek God of Shepherds died after tending his flock,"
Tom deadpanned sheepishly.

4465   "What's that bird with the long beak?" Tom asked stoically.

4466   "This is imitation turtle soup," Tom said mockingly.

4467   "Jonah was very unhappy," Tom wailed.

4468   "The French expression for 'There's a green worm in my glass' is
Il y a un ver vert dans mon verre," said Tom reverently.

A close cousin to the Tom Swifty is the Croaker, invented by Roy Bongartz.
Croakers are like Swifties except that the verb, rather than the adverb, supplies the pun.

4469   "That is the finest donkey I've owned," Farmer Tom asserted.

4470   "Watch out for that beehive in the tree," Tom droned.

4471   "You have very noisy cats," Tom mused.

4472   "The cattle must move faster," Tom prodded.

4473   "I'll have another dozen on the half shell," Tom clamored.

4474   "I'm going to stay away from the bull," Tom cowered.

4475   "I feel like milking a cow," Tom uttered.

4476   "Look at the blackbird," Tom crowed.

4477   "I love beagles," Tom dogmatized.

4478   "That's no beagle; that's a mongrel," Tom muttered.

4479   "Lined gloves are best for skiing," Tom inferred.

4480   "I resolve to teach my goose manners," Tom propaganderized.

4481   "This is for the birds," Tom groused.

4482   "The horse jumped, and I fell right off," Tom derided.

4483   "The male sheep was cut badly," Tom rambled.

4484   "I want a pet turtle," Tom snapped.

4485   "We're going to have leftover cutlets," Tom revealed.

4486   "The whale in the aquarium died," Tom blubbered.

Most pyrotechnic of all forms is the Double Croaker, in which both the verb and the adverb unite to ignite the statement.

4487   "I raise huge cats," Tom lionized categorically.

4488   "I couldn't begin the milking because only twelve of our twenty cows were in the barn. We still lacked eight," Tom uttered moodily.

4489   "You're a mangy cur," Tom barked doggedly.

4490   "I'm out to capture Moby Dick," Tom wailed superficially.

4491   "Get me off this horse!" Tom derided woefully.

4492   "Where did you get that meat?" Tom bridled hoarsely.

4493   "If I get a pet, I want a shaggy-haired bovine from Tibet," said Tom, yakking furiously.

The Vet's Clinic:
Where Animals Are, There the Vet May Be Also

Time now to vet the vet. There are vets aplenty in earlier entries, but those jokes generally turned on the animal; now, they turn on the vet.

4494   Did you hear about the obnoxious veterinarian?
He treats his patients like dogs.

4495   A veterinarian who was also a taxidermist put this sign on his office door: Either Way, You Get Your Dog Back.

4496   Another vet posted this sign: Your cat got a hairball problem? We can lick it.

4497   *Patron:* "Waiter, what's wrong with this hot dog?"
Waiter: "What do I look like? A veterinarian?"

4498   *Lion owner:* "Doctor, how do you treat lions?"
Veterinarian: "With utmost respect."

4499   A vet examined a limp parrot and said to the owner, "I'm sorry, but your parrot has died." The distressed owner wanted more tests. The vet's assistant brought in a black Labrador, which put its paws on the examination table, sniffed the parrot from head to toe, then looked at the vet sadly and shook its head. The assistant brought in a cat, which walked around the bird, sniffing carefully. The cat sat back and shook its head. The vet said, "I'm sorry, but your parrot is definitely dead." The resigned woman asked for a bill, looked at it, and said, "What! $500 just to tell me Polly is dead?" The vet sighed. "If you'd taken my word for it, the bill would have been $50, but with the Lab Report and the Cat Scan . . ."

4500   *Bumper sticker:* Veterinarians Make Horse Calls.

4501   *Sign in veterinarian's waiting room:* Be Back in Five Minutes. Sit! Stay!

In the Zoo:
Where Whose Zoo (or Zoo's Who) Is the Question

As with the vets, there are zoo jokes above. There the focus was on the animal; now, we're looking at the zoo.

4502 Did you hear about the book of famous animals?
It's called Zoo's Who.

4503 Why are so many zoo animals alcoholics?
Because they spend their lives behind bars.

4504 Or, as Confucius says, "A zoo is where
people visit and animals are barred."

4505 *Bumper sticker:* Zoos Protect Animals from People.

4506 Did you hear about the ex-marine who opened an animal park
with former TV game show host Monty Hall's mother?
Its theme song was "From the Zoo of Monty Hall's Ma."

4507   Did you hear about the small zoo that housed
a lion and a monkey in the same cage?
          A visitor asked, "How do they get along?"
          "Pretty well for the most part," replied the zookeeper. "Sometimes
they have a disagreement, though, and we have to get a new monkey."

4508   Two drunks meandered into a zoo, and, as they were passing
the lion's cage, the beast bellowed a raucous roar. "Let's get out of
here," shouted one drunk.
          "Not me," said the other. "I'm staying for the movie."

4509 What do you call the feeling that you've visited this menagerie before?
Déjà zoo.

As Porky Pig might put it:

That's all the jokes, Folks.

INDEX

For convenience, the index is divided into *animal* and *subject* lists.

Animals

Animals listed here are the 317 that appear in Part One, Animals A-Z (with bull, cow, salamander, and stallion added). Numbers in bold indicate jokes in each of the 317 particular sections. Other numbers indicate appearances in other sections.

Subjects

To include all subjects referenced would produce an index of several thousand entries, many of which are incidental to jokes. (*Mortgage*, for example, appears once, but the joke turns on *loan*.) The subject index is, therefore selective. It is hoped that it does direct the reader to most likely sought after jokes. Numbers in bold indicate the jokes contained in the eleven sections of Part Two. Items in the Classrooms, Contrasts, Crosses, Daffynitions, and Knock-Knocks sections are generally alphabetical, which may aid searches.